To Vicki

Best Wishes

Jonathan Livingston

# RELEARNING | EXPERIENCE

# RELEARNING EXPERIENCE
## to Resolve Emotional Problems

A new theory and practice

JONATHAN LIVINGSTONE

LEMNISCATE
BOOKS

## Relearning Experience: to Resolve Emotional Problems
### *A new theory and practice*

First published 2019 by Lemniscate Books
43 Clarendon Street, Leamington Spa CV32 4PN, UK
info@lemniscatebooks.co.uk

© Jonathan Livingstone 2019

ISBN 978-0-9563179-2-6

British Library Cataloguing-in-Publication Data
A catalogue record for this book is available from the British Library

**NOTE**

This book is intended to promote extraordinary healing and happiness,
but its ideas may not be applicable for all people in all circumstances.
The author and publisher accept full responsibility for all successes arising
from its use, but disclaim responsibility for any negative consequences.

Cover design by Lance Buckley
www.lancebuckley.com

To Charlotte & Abigail

You're always free to change your mind and choose
a different future, or a different past

Richard Bach

# Contents

## PART II NEW FOUNDATIONS

## PART III RELEARNING THERAPY

# Preface

What is a therapeutic problem? How is a therapeutic problem created? Can a therapeutic problem be finally and fully resolved? If full resolution is possible, how is it achieved?

The scholarship in the field of clinical psychology and psychotherapy is vast, and many of the practitioners and theorists highly learned. But they don't supply answers to these questions, and many would regard the questions themselves as invalid or impertinent. Even brief therapies, such as cognitive therapy, generally are looking for ways for a person to achieve goals *despite* her problems; they do not attempt to help the person to resolve the problem itself. And yet, isn't this why people present for therapy? Everyone has 'issues', described variously as psychological, emotional, therapeutic, or 'mental' issues, that affect performance and happiness, and wants them resolved; or would want them resolved if resolution was known to be possible and achievable.

A reader for a major publisher who saw an early draft of this work declared that its thesis – that permanent resolution of a therapeutic problem is achieved through identifying and resolving a problem at its origins – is the holy grail of psychotherapy, but is unachievable because, the reader insisted, the task is quite impossible. But consistent success has shown that the task is absolutely achievable for virtually any therapeutic problem, and is not even especially difficult, using the methods described here.

This book has been written for professionals in clinical practice or in training, to help them to be more effective practitioners. It is also intended for formal students of psychology and clinical psychology, and informal students (that is to say, lay persons), who want to understand the aetiology of a therapeutic problem: what a therapeutic problem is; how it is created; and why it manifests at a particular time. The aim of the book is to offer a comprehensive theory of the development and resolution of therapeutic problems. The reader will decide to what extent this is achieved.

If you are primarily interested in praxis, it's possible to skip to the chapters that explain how to do the therapy. You don't need to understand the theory to perform the therapeutic work effectively. However, knowledge of the theory provides an understanding of the work and why it is so effective.

The book is an exposition of the following ideas.

(1) A therapeutic problem is created when, in response to a difficult experience, a person develops behaviour that serves to ameliorate the threat to her personal dignity (emotional wellbeing).

(2) This behaviour, developed as a solution in a moment of crisis, sets an unconscious and involuntary precedent for future behaviour in circumstances perceived to be similar.

(3) Activated automatically by feelings, this behaviour becomes a therapeutic problem if it interferes with what the person wants.

(4) The difficult experience that occurred at the genesis of the therapeutic problem is discoverable via the feelings associated with the problem behaviour.

(5) An intervention at the origins of the problem which, in imagination, reconfigures the original behaviour, enables the person to choose her behaviour freely in the present, and resolves the therapeutic problem completely and permanently.

I am very grateful to all the people whose professional work and personal lives have contributed to the ideas presented here. All examples are from real experiences. All mistakes are my own.

# PART I

## NEW CONCEPTIONS

# 1

# To overcome a problem

**Mentor** I wasn't sure whether to expect you, because you seemed a bit unsure that you wanted to have this discussion. I sensed you were a little sceptical. I'm very glad you decided to come.

**Enquirer** It was an intriguing proposition. You're right, I am sceptical. I've been disappointed many times in the past by therapists, writers, theorists who claimed to have found the answer. But you were quite convincing when we met the other day . . .

**Mentor** I'm happy to see you again. I enjoyed talking to you – even though only briefly. You were very attentive. I hope I've found a way of looking at things that you will find helpful.

When you said that you're interested in the nature of psychotherapeutic problems, where they come from, and how best to resolve them, and in the philosophy of psychopathology, I thought you'd be interested in some of my ideas. I'm very keen to tell you about the work I'm doing, the discoveries I've made, and the theories I've developed.

From talking to you earlier, I understand that you are rigorous and meticulous, and I think you'll make sure that I express my ideas coherently – and that the ideas are coherent.

**Enquirer** I don't like poorly formed ideas and loose expression that sounds good but doesn't really make sense. The kind of talk that makes people nod, because it sounds like it should make sense, but leaves you feeling bewildered.

**Mentor** I trust you will hold me to account. But people usually come to see me because they have a problem to resolve, not because they want to understand how I work. They're not particularly interested in how we will work or the methodology behind it; their concern is that I help them to resolve their problem. In fact, people usually come to see me when they are desperate, because I am at the bottom of their list of resources.

**Enquirer** Why would you be at the bottom of the list?

**Mentor** I think it's because when a person goes to a therapist to resolve his issue, he knows he's going to have to change. Although people want to heal, they often don't want to change; or they think they don't want to change. They will try healing approaches that don't involve change. They have the apprehension that change will be painful or will take a long time. That is the story learned from traditional psychotherapy.

Or, very commonly, the person doesn't want to change because she can't see an appealing alternative to what she is presently doing. The options she has considered are less appealing than the present behaviour, even with the problems that come with that behaviour. However, when other approaches haven't been effective, or when the problem has become worse (as problems tend to do), the person becomes desperate enough to try anything – including change.

Isn't there something in you that needs changing, resolving?

**Enquirer** I'm pursuing an interest in personal development, and in therapeutic models and theories of personal transformation. It's just something I've always taken an interest in. I don't claim to have any specialist knowledge. If you're the *mentor* we could say that I'm an *enquirer*. Is that okay?

But I need to warn you: I'm a rational person. I'm not interested in angels or other irrational ideas. As you have noted, I'm looking for philosophic or scientific rigour. So let's see how it goes. I'm recording our conversation, as you suggested.

**Mentor** That's all good. I shall do my best to be rigorous and intelligible. And you will help shepherd my ideas.

You told me that you're interested in my method of resolving therapeutic problems. I'm very happy to talk about that. I'm also very happy at any point to help you to resolve an issue.

**Enquirer** No, I've already told you. That's not why I'm here. You wouldn't believe how many therapists I've been to see. I don't need to see anyone else. I'm tired of therapy and therapists.

**Mentor** You're sceptical. I like that. But I'm sorry you haven't had good experiences in the past.

**Enquirer** I'm not going to put myself in such a vulnerable position again.

**Mentor** Oh, it has been very bad.

**Enquirer** Therapists too often don't understand the power they have. I've felt so powerless and abused. I've had my hopes raised and dashed. My inquiry has now become a purely theoretical one.

You said that you can explain the therapeutic process, and how 'therapeutic problems', to use your words, are developed, and how they can be resolved. That's what I want to know. I've asked other people too – quite a few, in fact – to explain how psychological problems develop and how they can be resolved. You're not the first.

**Mentor** I can see this is important to you. What have they – the others who you've asked before – said to you?

**Enquirer** They have often claimed to have an answer, and then promised to reveal it. But, if they've given me an answer at all, it has been the usual shibboleths and completely inadequate. People considered eminent in the field have also told me that psychological problems, by their nature, are too complicated to explain.

**Mentor** But you're still willing to explore?

**Enquirer** I'm convinced that there must be an answer – or many answers. At least, better ones than those I've found so far. Like a child looking for hidden treasure, part of me is still ridiculously hopeful of finding it. On a rational level I don't feel confident that I'll find what I'm looking for; but on an emotional level I have a need to search and I'm still optimistic. I'm hoping you will have some answers; that you'll lead me to an understanding of the nature of what are generally called psychological problems or mental problems – which I've heard you refer to as 'emotional problems' or 'therapeutic problems'.

**Mentor** I understand your scepticism. I'm glad you haven't given up all hope. I accept your challenge and I'll do my best. I often give brief explanations about what I do, of course, but I've never explained it in great detail before. I hope that I can do this in a way that makes sense to you. I'll certainly try.

It's a great opportunity for me, and I'm excited about it. I've been wanting to do this for some time and I've been thinking about how I might do it. I'm grateful to you for giving me this opportunity. It won't be quick. There are certain established concepts that I need to challenge, and new ideas that I need to introduce. I hope you have the time. It might be quite intense. Some of the ideas you may not be ready for, but I want to be rigorous.

**Enquirer** I have put aside some time. I'm definitely ready – and won't mind at all if you need to challenge traditional ways of thinking. Whatever I think of your ideas, and however great my scepticism, I am grateful to you for spending the time and for revealing your secrets – especially since, you say, this is the first time you are doing so. I very much look forward to hearing what you have to say.

**Mentor** As I think I said to you earlier, I'm finally ready to share my discoveries. I believe that I now understand them well enough. So I'll explain to you my method to resolve therapeutic – or emotional, or psychotherapeutic (but not 'mental') – problems.

**Enquirer** Do you have a name for your method?

**Mentor** What shall I call it . . . ? Let's call it Relearning Experience Psychotherapy; or, maybe better, Relearning Experience Process – REP for short.

**Enquirer** Why Relearning Experience Psychotherapy or Process?

**Mentor** I have reservations about this, but I think that I want to situate the methodology within the field of psychotherapy and do my best to pre-empt any attempts to sideline it as marginal or 'alternative'. In short, the method identifies the experience in the past that has created a problem in the present and resolves it by 'relearning' it.

I'd like this to be a dialogue rather than a monologue – so that you can get out of it exactly what is most helpful to you, and make sure that my meaning is clear.

You asked a question when we met earlier.

**Enquirer** Yes. The question was: *What is the best way to overcome a psychological (or emotional, or therapeutic) problem?* You replied that it would be best not to have developed the problem in the first place. I was indignant. You can't overcome a problem by not having it in the first place, I said.

**Mentor** And you're right. I should rather answer like this. The best way to overcome a psychotherapeutic problem is to identify where the problem originated and find a resolution there, at its origins – a resolution that would have prevented it from becoming a problem in the first place. When a problem is resolved in this way it can't be triggered again in the future; it's as if it never developed. Without a foundation, the problem ceases to exist.

**Enquirer**  What do you mean when you say that resolving a problem at its origins prevents it from operating again in the future?

**Mentor**  If the problem is resolved at its source, the problem's not there any longer, so it no longer exists in the present and it can't recur in the future.

**Enquirer**  That's rather confusing. I'm very sceptical about your claim that it's possible to heal a problem completely. You don't make your claim more convincing by suggesting that you resolve the problem at its source. How can you resolve a problem at its source when you can't go back in time? What you're saying seems nonsensical.

**Mentor**  It certainly is possible to heal a problem completely; I believe I can demonstrate this to you to your satisfaction. However, healing a problem completely is only possible if it is healed at its origins. We do go back in time to do this – but of course only in imagination.

If the present manifestation of a problem could be healed, without healing the problem at its origins – if this were possible, and I'm not sure it is – then the problem would still be able to manifest in the future, either in a similar or dissimilar guise. In fact, not only would the problem be able to manifest in the future, it almost certainly would do so.

**Enquirer**  Do psychological problems necessarily have an origin in a person's past? And is it really possible to find out where a problem originated? I'd like to believe you, but I'm very sceptical. I understood it wasn't possible. Isn't the psyche too complex for you to be able to find discrete causes of psychological problems? Are there not too many psychical strands to a psychological problem? Scholars have said as much.

**Mentor**  I'll explain what a therapeutic problem is, and how it develops. When you understand how therapeutic problems originate you'll see how the origins of a problem can be identified so readily. – But you're still regarding me sceptically.

**Enquirer** I want to make sure I understand you correctly. You're saying that there are sources of psychological problems that are identifiable in a person's biography – in the person's past – and that these sources do not just exist theoretically but you can find them and identify them.

**Mentor** Yes. Exactly. And they can be resolved, thereby resolving the therapeutic problem.

**Enquirer** What is the nature of these 'sources' of psychological problems? Can you prove what you're saying?

**Mentor** The sources are events in the person's past that created the problem the person has in the present.

I'm confident you'll find my explanation convincing. But it will take a while for it to unfold. And you may need to change some of your ways of thinking, and I'm not sure you're ready for that.

**Enquirer** Try me. I'm interested. I may be sceptical, but I said that I'm prepared to be open minded, and I am. As I told you, I really want to find some meaningful and convincing answers.

**Mentor** Okay. I believe you! I'm really excited to do this.

## Key points

Emotional, psychological or therapeutic problems have their origins in a person's past experience.

The origins are discoverable and, through an intervention at the origins, the problem can be comprehensively and permanently resolved.

# 2

# Describing a therapeutic problem

**Enquirer** Can we start with a definition? What is a psychological or psychotherapeutic problem? You usually call it a 'therapeutic problem', don't you? And you don't like the word 'disorder', you were telling me when we met. Nor do you want to call them 'mental' or 'psychiatric' disorders. The term 'disorder' is pejorative, do you think? You also said that they are not 'mental' problems, because they are not of the mind. Please explain all of this.

**Mentor** The term 'disorder' is stigmatizing. I don't want a disorder. Do you? But to have an emotional or therapeutic problem or issue is ordinary and acceptable.

**Enquirer** It's something all of us can have. Who doesn't at least sometimes have emotional problems?

Anyone who claims not to have them is in denial, or very disturbed indeed.

Why do you think they're called 'disorders' rather than problems? In everyday life they're called problems. To describe a problem as a disorder is to medicalize it. It pathologizes what affects people every day.

**Mentor** Yes. A disorder is a condition. Recovering from a 'condition' is particularly difficult. A condition is something to be managed rather than healed. A psychotherapeutic (or therapeutic) 'problem', on the other hand, requires – demands, implies – a solution.

**Enquirer** Psychiatrists prescribe drugs, not solutions. What, then, is a psychotherapeutic problem?

**Mentor** This is how I often describe it. A psychotherapeutic – or therapeutic – problem is indicated when you behave in a way you don't like but can't change through conscious effort. It entails doing something you don't want to do or not doing something you want to do.

This is an important feature of a therapeutic problem: it is, by definition, resolvable. If it's not resolvable – resolvable by this method, that is – it's not a therapeutic problem.

**Enquirer** You're saying that a psychotherapeutic problem is to do with behaviour that is unwanted or problematic.

**Mentor** Unwanted behaviour is central to any therapeutic problem. A solution to a therapeutic problem involves a change in behaviour.

**Enquirer** Yes, I can see that many, perhaps most, therapeutic problems involve a behaviour that is problematic in some way – eating 'disorders', addictions, obsessive behaviour. But it seems to me that not all therapeutic problems relate to behaviour. For example, anxiety is a therapeutic problem, but anxiety relates to feelings rather than behaviour. A person with anxiety is concerned about the feeling, not about behaviour.

**Mentor** You're right that anxiety is very obviously a problem relating to feelings. In fact, any and all therapeutic problems involve uncomfortable feelings. Feelings, like behaviour, are central to all therapeutic problems.

**Enquirer**  Really? Both feelings and behaviour are involved in all therapeutic problems?

**Mentor**  Yes. All therapeutic problems have a behavioural component at their heart, including anxiety. The anxiety results from the desire to behave in a particular way – or not to behave in a particular way. If there wasn't an action or behaviour that the anxious person wanted to perform (or refrain from), he would not have the feeling of anxiety. The anxiety may relate to being liked and approved of and avoiding disapproval. This is why people who suffer social anxiety are often paralysed in their behaviour: they don't know what behaviour will bring approval or disapproval and so dare not do anything. Or the anxiety may relate to performing well in an upcoming test or challenge.

Any therapeutic problem necessarily also involves an uncomfortable feeling – although there is not always conscious awareness of this feeling. For some therapeutic problems, such as anxiety or fear, the uncomfortable feeling seems the most salient aspect of the problem. For other therapeutic problems, such as addiction or eating problems, the behaviour appears to be the most salient aspect.

**Enquirer**  Okay. Feelings and behaviour are both central to any psychotherapeutic problem.

**Mentor**  When an uncomfortable feeling is the most salient aspect of a therapeutic problem, it is either inhibiting desired behaviour or instigating undesired behaviour.

When unwanted behaviour (or inability to perform the desired behaviour) is the most salient aspect of a therapeutic problem, the agency driving the unwanted behaviour (or inhibiting the desired behaviour) is a feeling.

**Enquirer**  I'm not sure I've understood what you're saying.

**Mentor**  A therapeutic problem is about behaving in a way that you don't like, but can't seem to change. The undesired behaviour might be doing something you would rather not be doing, such as smoking, overeating, behaving aggressively. Or it might be not doing what you want to do, such as seeming unable to attract a suitable partner; not behaving assertively; being unable to deliver presentations with confidence; being unable to make decisions.

The distinction between doing something you don't want to do and not doing something you want to do is really about point of view and emphasis.

**Enquirer** If you're doing something you don't want to do, it means you're not doing something you want to do, and vice versa.

Both feelings and behaviour are central to any therapeutic problem. Sometimes people are more aware of the behaviour; and sometimes people are more aware of an uncomfortable feeling, such as anxiety, fear, guilt or anger.

**Mentor** Even when people are only aware of uncomfortable feelings, the uncomfortable feelings will either be inhibiting desired behaviour or driving undesired behaviour. And even when people are only aware of the undesirable behaviour, there are nevertheless underlying uncomfortable feelings.

So therapeutic problems are essentially about problematic behaviour that the person can't control. The problem behaviour – doing something or not doing something – is driven by feelings. That is why both these two aspects – feelings and behaviour – are central to a therapeutic problem.

**Enquirer** What characterizes behaviour as a problem?

**Mentor** Behaviour is identified as a problem for the person when his behaviour gets in the way of achieving something that he wants; that is, a goal. So another way of describing a therapeutic problem is that the person with a therapeutic problem has a practical goal that he seems unable to achieve because his behaviour is inconsistent with that goal.

**Enquirer** Stated briefly: a therapeutic problem exists when a person's behaviour is inconsistent with his goals.

**Mentor** Yes, that's correct. The person's behaviour that is interfering with his goal is the problem behaviour. Underlying and driving the problem behaviour are uncomfortable feelings.

**Enquirer** I suppose if behind the problem behaviour was just a thought, as cognitive behaviourists seem to believe, you could just change the thought.

What if the uncomfortable feeling is appropriate? And what if the goal is not appropriate? I have in mind, for example, a person who is feeling grief, and this grief is interfering with the person's new relationship. But the grief, though it's very uncomfortable, is entirely appropriate. Or someone might have the goal of having great confidence in a situation where the person lacks competence.

**Mentor** The feeling and behaviour have to be inappropriate for there to be a therapeutic problem. If the behaviour or feeling is appropriate in the present context, there is not a therapeutic problem. Appropriate feelings and behaviour are not therapeutic problems – however much one doesn't like them. Lack of confidence where there is lack of competence would be entirely appropriate and therefore not a therapeutic problem.

**Enquirer** Let me suggest a few more examples of where the emotions are appropriate and there is therefore not a therapeutic problem. If you're unable to concentrate or get on with work because you've recently lost someone close to you, your behaviour is appropriate and not a therapeutic problem. If you feel lonely because you don't have a partner, your feelings are appropriate and therefore not a therapeutic problem. If you're anxious about an exam because you haven't done enough study, the feeling is appropriate and not a therapeutic problem.

**Mentor** Yes. However, there may be a therapeutic issue underlying a situation where the emotional response is appropriate.

**Enquirer** Give me a few examples of therapeutic issues where the emotional response is appropriate.

**Mentor** There may be a therapeutic problem inhibiting the person's motivation for study. There may be a therapeutic problem stopping the person from attracting a partner.

The therapeutic problem is then not the feeling of anxiety, or the feeling of loneliness, since these were appropriate feelings in the circumstances. The therapeutic problem is the lack of motivation to study, or the problem attracting a partner.

**Enquirer** Feeling bad is not a therapeutic problem in itself. It may be entirely appropriate to feel sad, lonely, angry and so on. It's healthy to allow oneself to feel these things.

**Mentor** Definitely.

**Enquirer** But it's interesting to me to hear that anxiety can be appropriate. I assumed that anxiety was never okay and was always a therapeutic problem. But you're saying that anxiety can be appropriate.

**Mentor** Like all other emotions, anxiety is very useful when it is appropriate.

**Enquirer** When is anxiety appropriate?

**Mentor** Anxiety is there to tell you that you haven't attended properly to something, that you need a plan of action. For example, if you are not studying rigorously enough for an important exam, anxiety is your body's communication that you need to take action and make a plan. If you're encountering financial difficulties, the accompanying anxiety is telling you to work out how you're going to manage the difficulties.

**Enquirer** The purpose of anxiety, when appropriate (rather than pathological), is to tell you to make a plan. That's an important message, not a therapeutic problem.

**Mentor** Yes. Devise a plan and the anxiety, providing it is appropriate, will no longer be there. For there to be a therapeutic, psychotherapeutic, emotional or psychological problem – however you want to describe it (but it shouldn't be described as a 'mental' problem, which erroneously locates the problem in the mind) – for there to be a therapeutic problem, the behaviour or feeling must be inappropriate in the present moment. That's not the same at all as the feeling being unpleasant and unwelcome.

**Enquirer** Emotions that are uncomfortable can still be appropriate because they provide useful information, even if that information is not very welcome.

**Mentor** That's very important. Anxiety can convey a useful message. Other appropriate emotions are simply responding to circumstances. For example, sadness as a result of losing someone is about feeling that loss.

**Enquirer** I'm feeling confused now. Is anxiety appropriate or inappropriate?

**Mentor** It's appropriate if you haven't got a plan and need one.

**Enquirer** So when is an emotion not appropriate?

**Mentor** There's always a good reason for an emotion. An emotion is inappropriate when it is in response to something from the past rather than the present. If you've made a plan and you're still feeling anxious the anxiety is inappropriate. An inappropriate emotion is one that is not relevant to the present circumstances or its intensity is completely out of proportion to the present circumstances. Either way, the inappropriate emotional response is a relic from the past.

You often know when your feelings are inappropriate, because the inappropriate feelings make you behave in a way that you don't want or prevent you from behaving in a way that you do want.

**Enquirer** Unless the desired behaviour is at fault and it is the goal that is inappropriate.

**Mentor** Where the desired behaviour is inappropriate, the feelings inhibiting that behaviour are likely to be perfectly legitimate.

**Enquirer** In that case the person has appropriate feelings but inappropriate goals.

**Mentor** Precisely. People sometimes need the guidance of a therapist to know whether or not feelings are appropriate. People often need the guidance of the therapist to choose appropriate and appealing goals.

**Enquirer** I'm still struggling with the idea of what makes a goal legitimate or an emotion inappropriate. You say that a therapeutic problem relates to inappropriate behaviour or an inappropriate feeling, and this is something the therapist helps the person to determine. What determines whether the behaviour or feeling is inappropriate? This is surely a subjective evaluation.

**Mentor** The person with – or without – the problem decides whether the behaviour or feeling is inappropriate. No one else can decide for the person. If you think you haven't got a problem, as far as you are concerned, you don't have one.

A person cannot be helped to overcome a problem that she doesn't believe she has. If I'm not getting what I want, I'm alerted to a problem. If I can acknowledge that there is something in me stopping me from getting what I want, I've taken the first step to resolving it.

The first step is, always, acknowledging that you have a problem. If you can 'successfully' rationalize your feelings and behaviour so that you believe that it's everyone else's problem, not yours (there are not only individuals but also groups, organizations and nations that do this), then you can't be helped.

You'll rationalize your problem behaviour even more successfully if you manage to persuade others to collude with you – perhaps by threatening them or bullying them (physically or intellectually, overtly or covertly) so that they are too frightened to challenge you. This is a common tactic of people who doggedly maintain that the problem is not theirs.

Others might have a problem with you, but you don't have a problem – until you decide that you do.

**Enquirer** Until your strategy to circumvent the problem doesn't work any more.

**Mentor** A client once told me his girlfriend insisted he had a problem because he wiped the taps at home after he used them. He wanted to know whether I thought he had a problem. I asked whether it was a problem for him. He said no. It wasn't a problem for him. But that doesn't mean it didn't affect his relationship.

**Enquirer** In the interests of harmony he could decide to stop wiping the taps. Or maybe she was the one with a problem. I can think of a few things that aren't my problem but everyone else's. Sanity isn't statistical.

**Mentor** One way to think about it might be, *Are my beliefs and behaviour working for me; are they helping me?* This might well be a more helpful way to look at things than, *Am I right to think and behave as I do?*

**Enquirer** It's not always a question of right and wrong. So I decide whether I have a problem?

**Mentor** You decide for you. I decide for me.

**Enquirer** So if someone doesn't think they have a problem they don't have a problem?

**Mentor** If someone doesn't think they have a problem they don't think they have a problem. You can't be helped to overcome a problem if you don't believe you have a problem.

**Enquirer** Acknowledgement must come first.

**Mentor** That's right: acknowledgement must come first.

A problem is implicitly related to a goal. The therapist needs to determine what it is that the person wants. The person's behaviour is then interrogated to ascertain whether her behaviour is congruent with her goal.

If there is a disparity between behaviour and goal – if a person's behaviour is making her goal more difficult to achieve – then she should modify her behaviour so that it is more aligned with her goal. That is a logical step. The person needs to know what behaviour will make her goal achievable, and then behave accordingly.

If the person is readily able to change her behaviour so that it is consistent with her goals, she does not have a psychotherapeutic problem – she simply had a tactical problem (namely: *What do I need to do to get what I want?*) But if, despite her efforts, she is unable to modify her behaviour in the way desired, or cannot do so consistently, she has the opportunity to recognize that she has a therapeutic problem.

A therapeutic problem is, by definition (we have noted), resolvable: it is a matter of changing behaviour so that it is aligned with the goal; and this requires changing the feelings that drive the unwanted behaviour.

## Key points

Calling a problem a 'disorder' is stigmatizing. Emotional problems are normal and resolvable.

A feeling is inappropriate when it occurs in response to something from the past rather than the present.

A therapeutic problem involves inappropriate, uncomfortable feelings, and behaviour that, regardless of the efforts of the person, is inconsistent with what the person wants to achieve.

# 3

## Willingness to change

**Mentor** As well as acknowledging you have a problem, you'll also need to want to change. The resolution of a therapeutic problem requires the person to change. So a willingness to change is paramount.

**Enquirer** Can someone acknowledge she has a problem and be unwilling to change?

**Mentor** Certainly. It's extremely common.

**Enquirer** How can that be?

**Mentor** Acknowledgement of a problem is not in itself sufficient reason to want to overcome the problem. The problem may seem much more appealing than the alternatives.

For example, a smoker may acknowledge that tobacco is extremely harmful to health as well as very expensive, inconvenient and antisocial. Smoking is acknowledged by the smoker to be a huge problem. But without cigarettes the smoker thinks that life would be even more stressful, and he would be without his treat, his reward, his stress reliever, his break, his relaxation, his diversionary tactic, his sociality facilitator, his solace. Without an appealing alternative the smoker does not want to stop smoking. He acknowledges the problem but does not wish to change.

**Enquirer** Or he may only want to give up between cigarettes.

**Mentor** So acknowledgement of a problem is not sufficient motivation to change. The motivation to change requires that the alternative to the current behaviour is more appealing than the current behaviour.

It is stating the obvious to say that without the will to change, change will not occur. Unless the change is more appealing than the problem, the person with the problem will not have the will to change and therefore will not change.

These are the two preconditions for change: acknowledgement of the problem and the will to change. Without both of these, therapeutic help is of not avail and change will not occur.

**Enquirer** I had a conversation with the head of a rehab a little while ago. He admitted that many of the young people at the rehab had been unwillingly sent there by their parents. I queried whether, if they were there unwillingly, they would be open to change. He was quite defensive on that point. But it was in his interests to admit them; he would have had many fewer clients if he only accepted those who expressly wanted to be there.

**Mentor** Was the rehab successful in breaking the habits of the young people?

**Enquirer** No. Most relapsed within a short period of returning home.

**Mentor** I suppose it's possible that the young person might begin to see things differently by being exposed to the viewpoint the rehab pressed on him. But, unless he decides for himself that he wants to change, he won't. Rehabs often have a specific agenda

(the Twelve Steps programme) that they impose on their clients.
The institution determines the goals for its clients and attempts
to persuade – or even coerce – the client to adopt them. This is
the wrong way round. It would be much, much better if, instead,
the person herself were to determine her goals and was helped to
achieve them.

**Enquirer** I agree. That's the basis of Motivational Interviewing.
Who wants to do what someone else wants them to do? Most of us
react against this. And we should react against it. A person should
create his own agenda and live according to it.

**Mentor** Yes. Living according to the ideas of others (parents,
church, peer group, clinic) is a recipe for unhappiness; the cause
of a great many therapeutic problems; and an abandonment of
self-responsibility – the first principle of emotional health and
wellbeing.

**Enquirer** The resolution of a therapeutic problem requires the
person to change. If you're going to submit yourself to change,
you're going to have to want to change. Even if a person acknowledges a problem and wants it to disappear, she may be unwilling
to change.

**Mentor** Yes. The willingness to change depends on the goal or
outcome being more appealing to the person than the problem.
And the problem always has an appeal to the person.

The same is very often true, by the way, of people who have serious
physical illnesses. Without change, the illness will not heal; or, if
effective medical intervention has facilitated physical healing, the
illness is liable to recur because its conditions remain. Even after
the body is healed on a physical level, if the emotional issues that
contributed to the formation of the physical problem haven't been
resolved, the illness is liable to recur.

**Enquirer** That's why it's called remission. Forgiveness of sins
does not necessarily mean an end to sinning. Accepting the need

to change is vital. I understand that. But wanting to change – submitting yourself to change – isn't easy. The desire to change doesn't naturally or inevitably follow from the desire to be healthy.

**Mentor**  A desire is a wish. Change requires action: a change of behaviour. This requires will.

**Enquirer**  Willingness to change also admits a failing. You've got it wrong up to now. But the question is, how do you persuade yourself that you want to change and commit yourself to action? How does a person do this when changing seems so difficult?

**Mentor**  That's a really important question. It's why people can get entrenched in a difficult place, not knowing how to change or whether they even want to.

What is it that motivates change? Willingness to change – unless motivated by absolute desperation for things to be other than how they are now – requires a knowledge of what you want the change to be. At the very least, it requires a trust that the change, whatever it is, will be for the better. To be inspired to change, you need to know how you want to be instead. If you don't know the nature of the change, it's very hard to be sure that you really want to make the change. You need to know what you want the change to be, and this change has to be more appealing to you than how you are now.

If the alternatives you envisage are unattractive to you, or no more attractive than the current situation, you'll almost certainly prefer to stay as you are. Why would you want to change if your current behaviour is probably preferable? You won't change simply because others want you to, even if you love them and want to please them – that isn't motivation enough.

If you just want to be rid of the bad feeling or troublesome symptom and keep the (problem) behaviour and problem beliefs (as many people do), you'll be disappointed. For example, if you feel anxious and want to feel okay but are unwilling to change your behaviour or beliefs in any way, it's not going to work. Or if you want to stop smoking but don't want to address the emotional issue sustaining it, you'll find it very difficult indeed.

**Enquirer** The distress will remain, and you'll need to take medication to dull the feelings.

**Mentor** That's true. If people don't want the bad feelings but don't want to change, they need to take drugs or use some other kind of anaesthetic or analgesic. Lots of people do that. That's why people smoke, drink, gamble, take drugs, or are involved in other unhealthy occupations – to avoid feeling the discomforting emotions.

**Enquirer** The bad feelings aren't going to go away just because you want them to.

**Mentor** That's right. In fact, they are likely to get worse. The bad feelings are there to tell you that something is wrong. They don't disappear because you don't like them.

People are able to find many ways of living with discomfort. But none of them, from the therapist's vantage point, is satisfactory. Change is the only solution. Change is the only way to overcome the discomfort. Anything else is just a way of coping with it. However, to be motivated to change, you need an alternative to how you are in the present; and that alternative has to be more appealing to you than what you are doing in the present.

**Enquirer** People live with discomfort because it seems preferable to change.

**Mentor** So the alternative goal is of paramount importance. A goal must be at least as appealing as the current behaviour for there to be the possibility of change. But at this point people with problem behaviour often run into an apparently insurmountable difficulty.

**Enquirer** What is that?

**Mentor** People very often can't identify an attractive alternative to their current behaviour. This prevents them from seeking help. They've thought of an alternative (or possibly more than one) and decided they don't like it (or them) at all. Why would they seek help from a therapist to adopt behaviour that they reject as unappealing? Why would they even consider changing their behaviour if what they're doing now seems to be the best of the available alternatives?

The person acknowledges that her present behaviour is not okay. But, after considering the alternatives, she decides that she would rather stay as she is. She may not say this to her partner, friends or parents, because she knows it will not be acceptable to them. She may agree to their plans for her and go through the motions of visiting a therapist or clinic. She may not even explicitly admit to herself her opposition to the well-meaning plans of others. Nevertheless, she has chosen to remain as she is and nothing external to her can alter this as long as it remains her choice.

**Enquirer** There might however be other possibilities that would be appealing to her, but she just hasn't considered them.

**Mentor** Yes. Absolutely. People have often not thought through the possibilities at all. In fact, they may have considered only a single alternative – usually the complete opposite of what the person is currently doing. People seem to consider the polar opposite as the only alternative to the present situation, when there may well be an entire landscape of alternative options.

**Enquirer** The tendency to swing from one extreme to the other seems to be a universal human tendency. I'm thinking of Hegel's model of history: thesis; antithesis; synthesis. There is a tendency to go from one extreme, or polarity, to the other; and then, hopefully, find a middle ground.

**Mentor** I'm reminded of a young man –

**Enquirer** Call him Jayden.

**Mentor** Jayden was sent to rehab by his parents. In therapy he admitted that, as a student, not only did he enjoy being a wild party animal but he also really enjoyed the prestige he got from dealing drugs to his fellow students. Jayden was out of control but at least he was interesting and had some status. His life was full of drama and high emotion. He was in intimate contact with other wild creatures who, he believed, thought that he was wonderful.

What was the alternative to this wild and esteemed persona, in Jayden's perception? The only alternative he could see was a person characterized by austere sobriety who (he was sure) would be boring, sedate, conservative, alone, passionless, undesired, unloved and without status. If this was the alternative, what was he going to choose?

**Enquirer** He would definitely prefer to stay as he was, despite the consequences of his behaviour. Anyone would.

**Mentor** Most of the time he probably won't consider the consequences of his behaviour.

**Enquirer** Easier not to.

**Mentor** A very important role of the Relearning Experience therapist is to help the person identify appealing alternatives. In fact, the problem behaviour – as we shall see later – provides a solution to a problem. This is why it is appealing to the person – or once was. This is why the behaviour developed.

**Enquirer** Changing requires conscious will, as you say. The will is motivated by something appealing.

**Mentor** If you don't consciously want to make the change, quite obviously you're not going to make the change. You have to want to change, and you have to have a good reason to make the change.

This is a critical point that you may well think is obvious, but can't be overstated. The body will help you to achieve what you want to achieve, providing that you want it explicitly on a conscious level. Clearly, it won't help you to achieve anything you don't want.

The body takes its cue from the conscious mind. What the conscious mind wants – what you consciously want – the body does its best to help you to have. The body is obviously not going to help you to make a change that you don't consciously want. This is true even if the body is not happy with what you are currently doing (though the body will signal its objection through uncomfortable feelings); and even if what you are currently doing is detrimental to the body or to your happiness.

**Enquirer** So the 'body', as you call it, won't help a person to change even if it's not happy with what the person is doing?

**Mentor** The body's job is to support the person's pursuit of what she wants. However, if a person is doing something that is harmful to herself the body will express its discomfort. If a person wants to work too hard, not sleep enough, not eat properly, the body won't stop her from doing this. It will cope the best it can in support of her chosen lifestyle. But negative repercussions will be experienced in the body. The body may protest and issue distress warnings, but it will still be at the service of conscious intention.

**Enquirer** The body strives for what the person consciously wants – even if what the person wants is contrary to the person's health and wellbeing. But it issues warnings.

**Mentor** That's right. The body is ally to the conscious mind. Unhealthy behaviour will always have symptoms expressed by the body, but the body will only directly intervene in a person's behaviour in a way that is contrary to the conscious will in a crisis situation. Direct intervention by the unconscious is psychosis. In short, the body is not going to help someone to change if on a conscious level he doesn't want to change. However, if the behaviour is detrimental to the person, the body will continue to register discomfort – and the person will, no doubt, attempt to suppress and deny this discomfort.

## Key points

Two preconditions of change are: (1) the acknowledgement of a problem; and (2) the will to change.

A vital role of the therapist is to help the person to identify an appealing goal.

The goal must be more appealing to the person than the present behaviour, or change will not occur.

# 4

# The unconscious body

**Enquirer** I don't understand why you're using the word *body* in this context. Don't you mean the unconscious mind? There is the conscious mind and the unconscious mind. Isn't this the case? I'm confused by your use of the word 'body'.

**Mentor** You have expressed what is the common view. It's true that the collocation unconscious mind is ubiquitous; and that people with psychological problems are considered to have mental problems. However, the unconscious isn't a mind. The concept of unconscious mind is erroneous and, I believe, nonsensical. The unconscious is body. That's why I refer to the unconscious body. But I don't want to explain this now because I fear we'll get distracted from our purpose.

**Enquirer** You don't want to get distracted. But I am distracted. I'm wondering what you mean about the unconscious being a body. It is generally accepted that psychology is about the mind. People suffer from mental illness. This isn't just the medical view; New Age literature proclaims the power of the subconscious mind.

**Mentor** It's such a common misconception, such an accepted part of everyday thinking, you may not want to change your view.

**Enquirer** I'm searching for what's true, what makes sense to me. Because a view is traditional or established does not in itself give it more authority in my mind. So explain why the unconscious is 'body'.

**Mentor** You're right that psychology is considered – apparently by almost everyone – to be about the mind. *Psyche* comes from a Greek word and has the association of life and breath: it relates to a person's whole being, rather than just mind.

**Enquirer** I've just looked up *psyche* in Wikipedia. The entry states that the psyche is 'the totality of the human *mind*, conscious and unconscious' [emphasis added]. Sigmund Freud, the father of modern psychology, explicitly conceived of the unconscious as mind.

**Mentor** It's probably Freud's influence that has made the concept of unconscious mind so entrenched. You can see why Freud thought of the unconscious as mind. His method was analysis – an activity of the conscious mind. Fritz Perls disparagingly called psychoanalysis 'mind fucking'.

**Enquirer** In Freud's conception of the unconscious, the id is a maelstrom of conflicting instinctual drives, and what is called the 'latent content', or real meaning, of a dream can never be finally discovered; analysis is interminable, and psychological problems are ultimately unfathomable.

**Mentor** Freud regarded the unconscious as a 'mind' and represented the conscious mind as a smaller component of a greater entity of 'mind', most of which in his representation is unconscious.

**Enquirer** I find it very hard to conceive of psychological problems as not being mental or of the mind.

**Mentor** I intend to demonstrate to you that psychological problems relate primarily to feelings, which are the body's way of communicating with the conscious mind. These feelings are located in the torso (abdomen and thorax) and are obviously not a creation of the mind. Regarding psychological problems as aspects of mind makes them unfathomable and interminable.

The idea of the unconscious as mind doesn't actually make sense. Think about it philosophically for a moment. What is the substance or 'material' of the mind? It's *thoughts*, isn't it? The mind engages in thinking; thoughts are its material. Thoughts are equated with consciousness: *cogito, ergo sum*.

The conscious mind doesn't only think, though. It also perceives.

**Enquirer**  Our sense organs perceive, not the mind.

**Mentor**  That's true. I'll put it more carefully. Sense impressions – the impressions of our sense organs – are presented directly to the mind. My mind consists of thoughts and of impressions from my senses.

**Enquirer**  All right. Consciousness consists of thoughts and sense impressions. René Descartes, in his *Discourse on Method*, argued that thoughts are the central feature of identity. He said that he could be mistaken (or tricked) about the objects of the senses. But even if a demon was tricking him, and his sense impressions did not accurately represent the reality of an external world, or if there were no external world at all, he would still be having thoughts. Because he has thoughts, he argued, he must exist. Even if he was wrong about everything else, he was still having thoughts, and this meant that he existed.

**Mentor**  There's another aspect of consciousness. Something else that is apprehended by the mind that is distinct from thoughts and sense impressions. It's interesting that in *Discourse on Method* Descartes makes no mention of this aspect of consciousness. He ignores it completely.

**Enquirer**  What is this other aspect of consciousness?

**Mentor**  Emotions – a third element of consciousness, apprehendable in the mind alongside thoughts and sense impressions.

**Enquirer**  You're saying that emotions are distinct from thoughts and sense impressions, but they are an aspect of consciousness.

**Mentor**  Yes. Sense impressions are not like thoughts. Thoughts are a voluntary product of consciousness: they arise in me and I am their author. Sense impressions are involuntary and impress themselves on me from outside. Whether sense impressions are accurate representations of reality or not, they are involuntary. In consciousness I am aware of them, but I don't create them. Emotions are different from thoughts and from sense impressions since they are neither voluntary nor external to me.

Thoughts and sense impressions without emotions would be barren. I'm not even sure consciousness would be possible without feelings, the counterpart of emotions. Thoughts are present only to the thinker. No one else has direct access to them. But without feelings, thoughts would have no purchase; it would be hard to credit them as belonging to the self. But by being associated with feelings and emotions, thoughts become attached to an identity.

**Enquirer**  You're saying that feelings are evidence of being – even more than thoughts are. They somehow guarantee existence.

**Mentor**  This will make more sense when we discuss emotions in greater depth in a few minutes. A particular understanding of emotion is central to our purpose. But, first, let's finish our conversation about the unconscious body.

You said that you find it very hard to conceive of psychological problems as not being of the mind. Look at it in this way. Thinking is a product of the brain on a non-physical level. The brain produces thoughts – or, if you want to say that the mind produces thoughts, then the mind is a product of the physical brain. The brain is physical, but thoughts aren't physical. Thoughts don't occupy physical space. The brain process relating to a thought occupies physical space, but the thought itself doesn't. If you think of a tree in your mind, this 'tree', or the concept of it, has no physical location. If you open up the brain you won't find this concept of a tree anywhere. There's nothing resembling a miniature tree anywhere in the brain. Mental events are produced by physical events, but mental events differ in quality from physical events.

**Enquirer** I understand. Mental ideas are different to the physical brain processes that produce them.

**Mentor** Thoughts are entirely subjective. Nobody can ever have direct access to your thoughts, apart from you. Thoughts are conscious. You have them. They're private and exclusive to you.

**Enquirer** Yes.

**Mentor** Thoughts are a product of the brain but on another level. An activity of the brain produces a thought, but is not the thought. We know thoughts exist because we think them. But being entirely subjective, you only have my word for it that I have thoughts. You have no direct access to my thoughts. You could, I suppose, have direct access to my brain activity and other activities in my body when I think, but you can have no direct access to the thoughts themselves.

**Enquirer** That's true.

**Mentor** Now imagine thoughts that have no thinker and no author . . . What would produce unconscious thoughts? Where would they reside? What would give them existence as thoughts (rather than simply brain processes)? Conscious thoughts occur in consciousness; the thought itself doesn't occur as a physical activity in the brain (even though a corresponding physical activity does occur in the brain). An 'unconscious mind' would have thoughts that occur nowhere in space, that no one is aware of, and that have no author.

**Enquirer** Unconscious 'thoughts' would indeed be extremely rarefied things.

**Mentor** Not easy to imagine or explain. The concept of unconscious mind implies the existence of unconscious thoughts.

Conscious thoughts occur in the conscious mind; the person is the author of conscious thoughts. But unconscious thoughts wouldn't have a thinker. Unconscious thoughts would be invisible and inaudible and have no author.

**Enquirer** It is an extraordinary idea! An unhelpful metaphor. So, for you, the unconscious is an element of the body and the material of the unconscious body is not thoughts. If not thoughts, what is the material of the 'unconscious body'?

**Mentor** That's not an intelligible question. It's like saying, *what's the material of the physical body?*

**Enquirer** Right. The unconscious is a set of processes occurring in the body.

**Mentor** That's a nice way of looking at it.

**Enquirer** Yet hypnosis is supposed to be about harnessing the power of the subconscious or unconscious mind . . .

**Mentor** Yes. People talk about it in those terms.

**Enquirer** But they're wrong . . . ?

What do you think is the difference between the subconscious and unconscious, incidentally?

**Mentor** I prefer to use the term unconscious. For me the distinction is important. It makes sense to use 'unconscious' with reference to the unconscious body. To talk about a subconscious body wouldn't make sense, would it?

But even when the unconscious is regarded as mind, there is a significant difference in connotation. Subconscious mind implies a mind subordinate to and dependent on the conscious mind. An unconscious mind would not have to be subordinate. In Freud's reckoning, the unconscious is the dominant agency and the conscious mind is subject to the dominant unconscious.

Some people might possibly use the word subconscious to mean what Freud called the preconscious: that which is capable of becoming conscious but isn't conscious at a given time – but that would be an unofficial usage.

## Key points

The concept of unconscious mind implies the existence of thoughts that occur nowhere in space, that no one is aware of, and have no author.

The unconscious is a set of processes occurring in the body and is better conceived as the 'unconscious body'.

# 5
## Neither mind nor body

**Enquirer** Is psychology about the body, rather than about the mind, in your view? Is that what you're saying?

**Mentor** Remember that I'm specifically talking about therapeutic issues, which is my area of expertise.

**Enquirer** All right. You're saying that therapeutic problems are about the body, not about the mind. Is that right?

**Mentor** Kind of.

**Enquirer** Now you're being enigmatic. What's the qualification? If therapeutic problems are not about the mind, they must be about the body – mustn't they?

**Mentor** There's a distinction between mind and body, isn't there?

**Enquirer** What do you mean?

**Mentor** I'm not trying to catch you out. When a person thinks, when you think, the thoughts are in your mind, aren't they? Your mind is doing the thinking?

**Enquirer** Yes. We have already agreed that.

**Mentor** But when you stub your toe the pain is in your toe, isn't it? It's not in your mind.

**Enquirer** That's right. The pain is in my toe.

**Mentor** And you digest food in your body, not in your mind.

**Enquirer** That's right. I see your point: the awareness is in the mind, but the pain and digestion are not themselves in the mind.

**Mentor** So, thoughts take place in the mind, and physical feelings and physical processes take place in the body – even though you have an awareness of them in your mind.

It's the same with perceptions. The objects of perception are not in the mind, but the mind, though the senses, perceives them.

**Enquirer** Okay. But none of that sounds particularly controversial. You need to explain how therapeutic problems don't relate to body. You've said they don't relate to mind; surely they must therefore relate to body. There are only those two possibilities. Is that not the case?

**Mentor** This is where emotions come in. There are three pillars of consciousness: thought, perception and emotion.

**Enquirer** Now I'm getting confused. I really don't think you're being clear. Don't emotions relate to mind? But you describe the unconscious as body. It's confusing.

**Mentor** Be patient. It will become clear. This is the interesting thing. Are emotions in the mind or the body? Are they mental or physical?

**Enquirer** You mean do I experience them in the mind or body? I haven't really thought about it. They're generally considered to be mental, aren't they? Are you suggesting that they're not? I thought you said that they were. I'm now very confused.

**Mentor** Remember that perceptions are an interplay of external things and internal representations. Emotions are similar.

What do you think? Are emotions mental? Are they like thoughts? Do they occur in your mind?

**Enquirer** I'm not sure. I'm beginning to doubt myself. They are often considered to be in the mind . . .

**Mentor** It is true that they are generally associated with mind. Can you think an emotion?

**Enquirer** I'm not sure what you mean . . . I can think about an emotion. I can think about love or sadness . . .

**Mentor** Is thinking about an emotion the same as having an emotion?

**Enquirer** No. The two are different. I can think about an emotion without having the emotion; and I can have an emotion and not be thinking about that emotion.

Emotions are therefore not the same as thoughts. In fact, they're totally different. I can think whatever thoughts I like, but I don't have an emotion just by thinking it.

**Mentor** Yes. That's an important distinction. Thoughts are voluntary. If we are to maintain that human beings have free will we have to say that thoughts are voluntary. Emotions, on the other hand, are involuntary. That's a major difference between thoughts and emotions.

If emotions are not something you think, but something you have, where do you have them? Thoughts occur in the mind. Physical feelings occur in the body. Where do emotions occur?

**Enquirer** I don't know . . .

**Mentor** Do they occur in the mind?

**Enquirer** No, I don't think so. Emotions are not like thoughts. Emotions are involuntary and I do not create them in my mind as I create thoughts. But I'm aware of emotions.

**Mentor** Yes, you apprehend emotions in the same way that you apprehend a pain in your toe. Isn't that right?

**Enquirer** I suppose so.

**Mentor** I'm aware in consciousness of my perceptions, though the objects of perception exist externally to my mind and may also be external to my body. In my consciousness I'm aware of a tree, even though the tree is external to my mind and my body. A pain in my toe is not in my mind; it's in my toe. But I'm aware of the pain in consciousness, which is to say in my mind. In this regard emotion is similar to perceptions: I have awareness of an emotion in consciousness even though my consciousness hasn't created the emotion.

**Enquirer** Yes.

**Mentor** With regard to your senses, you can choose what to apply your attention to: you can choose, with your conscious mind, what sense organ to prioritize and even what particular sensory matter you want to give your attention to. For example, I can choose to focus my attention on the feeling in my toe, or on the television in the room, or on the birds outside. I could instead focus my attention on the weight of my body on the chair, or features of the painting on the wall, or the sound of the traffic. I can choose what to focus my attention on, but whether or not I have conscious awareness of any particular element, it is still there in the world.

I have the same choice with regard to emotions. I can choose to attend to a feeling; or I can choose to ignore it. Just as I don't create the objects of perception, I don't create emotions through a conscious act.

**Enquirer** But you can make yourself feel particular emotions, can't you? For example, I can easily make myself feel sad.

**Mentor** How do you do that? What would you do to make yourself feel sad?

**Enquirer**  I'd do it by thinking of something that makes me sad.

**Mentor**  You can make yourself feel sad by thinking about something sad. You didn't directly create the feeling of sadness. You didn't think the feeling. You created the feeling only indirectly – by thinking about something which produced sadness in you. Emotions aren't thoughts; you can't think them. The thought (which has sadness accompanying it) was voluntary; the feeling was involuntary, but followed from the thought.

**Enquirer**  Yes, I see that. We should pay more attention to what we think about. Dwelling on sad things will make you feel sad. I imagine actors think about specific experiences they have had to convey emotion in a role.

**Mentor**  We agree that emotions don't exist in the mind.

**Enquirer**  Yes. They're apprehended by the mind but they are not generated in or by the mind.

**Mentor**  So emotions are not of the mind. Are emotions of the body, rather; do they occur in the body?

**Enquirer**  They must occur in the body, if they're not of the mind.

**Mentor**  Are you sure?

**Enquirer**  I can't think of an alternative.

**Mentor**  Can you find an emotion anywhere in your body?

**Enquirer**  An emotion is not in my body like a pain is in my toe or an ache is in my stomach.

**Mentor**  If emotions are not in your body, is there anything that is similar to an emotion that is in your body? For example, what happens to you, what do you experience, when you get anxious, or scared, or excited, or sad?

**Enquirer**  I get a feeling in my body – a tightness in my chest, a churning in my stomach. Those are familiar feelings to me when

I'm nervous or anxious. But those are physical feelings; they're not exactly emotions.

**Mentor**  That's interesting, isn't it?

**Enquirer**  I hope you're going to help me out of this confusion. Emotions are not mental; but they're not physical – although something is going on in the body. That is confounding. Where do emotions come from, then? And what have they got to do with the unconscious?

**Mentor**  Those are certainly pertinent questions. And I intend to answer them.

**Enquirer**  I'm keen to hear your answers. You've suggested that therapeutic issues are not about the mind, but I don't think you have established what they do relate to.

**Mentor**  You're quite right. I still need to do that. Therapeutic issues relate to feelings and emotions. I will explain how feelings and emotions are central in the development of therapeutic problems and their resolution.

**Enquirer**  This is still hard for me to accept. Just as anatomy is about the body, psychology is about the mind – so therapeutic issues (which are psychological) are about the mind. Surely this is the case.

**Mentor**  Let me explain.

**Enquirer**  But wait a moment. We need to finish our present conversation first. I am in suspense! If emotions are not mental or physical, what are they?

## Key points

Emotions are apprehended by the mind through consciousness; but, like perceptions, they are not created by the mind.

Thoughts are voluntary; emotions are involuntary, but can be ignored.

Thinking about an emotion is not the same as having an emotion.

Feelings are physical and exist in the body, but emotions are not physical.

# 6

## Distinguishing emotions and feelings

**Mentor** We often talk about emotions and feelings as if they're the same, don't we? I *feel* lonely. The *emotion* of anger. The *feeling* of guilt. Are they exactly the same, do you think, emotions and feelings?

**Enquirer** Yes, I think they are. We talk about loneliness, anger or guilt as feelings and as emotions. The terms are both interchangeable, aren't they?

**Mentor** You feel these in the body, don't you? When you are angry, for example, you feel it in your body?

**Enquirer** Yes. That's definitely true. Anger is a feeling in the body. The physical feeling of anger can be overwhelming. The same is true of other emotions such as grief and fear. Emotions affect the physiology – posture and facial expression are affected by feelings. Emotion is felt in the body.

This means that emotions are in the body. Emotions are physical. Intensely physical, in fact.

**Mentor** Feelings are held in the body. Emotions are not.

**Enquirer** I don't understand.

**Mentor** Feelings and emotions are different. They are absolutely connected. But they are substantively different. If we are to understand these terms properly – and this understanding is crucial to our explication of REP – we need to understand the difference between them.

The feeling is the physical manifestation – the physical counterpart – of the emotion. And you're right, of course: feelings are felt in the body; the body manifests them, embodies them. The stronger the emotion, the more pronounced its manifestation in the body. The somatic feeling is how the emotion is experienced in the body.

**Enquirer** I don't think I've come across this distinction before. I've always thought that feeling and emotion are exactly the same.

**Mentor** Generally, the two terms are used interchangeably. I use them interchangeably myself very often. I will do so – and probably have already done so – during our discourse. But if we speak more technically, more precisely, the feeling is the physical counterpart or somatic aspect of the emotion. The emotion exists as a phenomenon distinct from the feeling. The feeling is physical; the emotion is something else. Just as a thought is not a physical object but has a physical counterpart in the brain, so emotion is not a physical phenomenon but has a physical counterpart in the body. Brain process and thought; physical feeling and emotion – these are connected events but occurring at different levels.

**Enquirer** However, if we have free will the mind is autonomous and has agency over thoughts; whereas the mind has no control over feelings.

**Mentor** Yes. The conscious mind is responsible for thoughts; whereas the body is responsible for feelings.

**Enquirer** Do all emotions have a counterpart in the body?

**Mentor** Yes, they do. Just as all thoughts have a corresponding brain activity.

**Enquirer** I'm still not clear. You say that emotions aren't physical, but have a physical counterpart; and that emotions aren't of the mind or of the body. But you haven't said what they are.

**Mentor** Emotions are immensely special, I think, and defy classification as mind or body. They are not constructed by or in the mind as thoughts are. And they are not perceptions arising from any of the five senses. There is no traditional sense organ, like ears or eyes, that perceives them. Emotions are real; they are not a figment of the imagination. But they're not out there in the world. They have an expression in the body – a counterpart in the body – but the emotion itself is distinct from the physical feeling. The emotion is not the physical feeling; it is something else.

**Enquirer** Perhaps the faculty to 'perceive' emotion is the elusive sixth sense – although apparently we have twenty or thirty senses.

**Mentor** Yes, it really is like a sixth sense, because emotions are the means of communication from the connective unconscious to the (disconnected) conscious mind.

**Enquirer** The unconscious is connective in what sense? It's connected to the external world?

**Mentor** Yes. The unconscious, as a physical entity in the physical universe, is connected inseparably to everything else, but the conscious mind is disconnected from and separate to the external world. That is an essential quality of subjective consciousness: it is discrete. My consciousness belongs to me; no one else has access to it. Through consciousness I distinguish myself from everything else. Consciousness separates me from everything else. The body, on the other hand, is part of the world. The unconscious, as body, is a shared part of the world; it's connected to everything else. Consciousness is connected to the world through the body.

Emotions are internal to the person, yet they are not a product of the mind, and they're not physical.

**Enquirer** They are ineffable, in that case.

**Mentor** They are ineffable. But – and this is crucial – they are dependent on consciousness. Emotions are experienced in and through consciousness. They have no other existence. Human beings are the only species with consciousness, and *ipso facto* are the only species capable of experiencing emotion.

What are emotions? For me, being neither physical nor mental, they are the quality unique to and essential to humanity. They are the essence of humanity; the part of the human being formed in the image of God. God defined as infinite consciousness. Human consciousness, bound within a discrete subjectivity, ironically reaches beyond physical and mental towards transcendence, spirit.

**Enquirer** Hold on a minute. Come on, now. You've lost me with this transcendental God stuff. Let's go back a step. You promised to be rigorous and scientific.

**Mentor** I don't think I said 'scientific'.

**Enquirer** That's right. You didn't. What do you mean human beings are the only species that are conscious? Aren't animals conscious too? Don't animals have feelings? Aren't they awake?

**Mentor** Animals clearly have feelings, because feelings occur in the body, and they're definitely awake much of the time. But animals don't have emotions because animals are not conscious. But do we need to have this discussion? We're in danger of travelling too far from our purpose.

**Enquirer** Right now, I've forgotten what our purpose is, and I'm more interested in the question of consciousness.

## Key points

Emotion has a somatic expression in the body.

The unconscious body is intimately connected with the world; the conscious mind is disconnected.

Emotions are internal to the person, but they are not a product of the mind, and they're not physical – so they are ineffable.

Emotions can be experienced only through human consciousness and have no other existence.

# 7

# Consciousness

**Mentor** I think consciousness is really interesting. But virtually impossible to explain.

Obviously, I don't mean that human beings are the only species who are awake. It's true that the term 'conscious' is also used to mean awake. But I'm not talking about being awake or asleep; I'm talking about the difference between being aware and having no awareness. It is this awareness, unique in humans, which I'm referring to as consciousness. It is this awareness that allows me to know that I'm me and can be no one else: my subjectivity. Without consciousness, I wouldn't be me; there would be no me.

**Enquirer** This is a hard concept to grasp, because I can't conceive of not being conscious. I sort of know what it means to be asleep, but I can't conceive of not having consciousness.

**Mentor** You're right. It's impossible to imagine not being conscious, because imagination necessarily involves consciousness. In fact, all understanding requires consciousness. Me-ness, like consciousness, is impossible to explain, because it is synonymous with consciousness. The state of an animal, being awake and unconscious, is not something we can apprehend through consciousness. It is something we can appreciate rationally, but not imagine.

**Enquirer** If animals aren't conscious, why do they matter to us? Why do we have pets? Why should we be kind to them?

**Mentor** Even human beings don't start out with a conscious mind; the conscious mind develops gradually through childhood and adolescence, starting around the age of eight. So we've all 'experienced' being awake and not being conscious when we were very young – but that doesn't really help; it's still impossible to imagine.

I suppose a daydream is fairly close to being awake and unconscious. Being in hypnotic trance is being awake (hypnotized people are not sleeping) but – at least in certain types of trance – not conscious. We perform habitual acts unconsciously. You may not remember locking the car door, for example, and need to go back and check. Consciousness is limited: we are not aware of everything in our perceptual range. Anything that has been learned is mostly done unconsciously. If we had to be conscious of every action and movement, movement would be impossible, and Parmenides would be right. The unconscious body, the autopilot, takes care of most things.

There are degrees of consciousness. My experience as an adolescent was of becoming more and more conscious as each year passed. Perhaps we never achieve full human consciousness. Advancing age should bring greater consciousness, but doesn't necessarily do so – depending on how much we close off from experience. Our prejudices and blind spots represent inhibitions of consciousness. Perhaps full human consciousness, though impossible, is a state to aspire to – assuming it's even comprehensible. Continuing to develop consciousness should be an aspiration.

**Enquirer** Entry into language – into the symbolic realm, as Jacques Lacan calls it – is a precondition of consciousness, because without language there is no medium of reflection or expression. I don't think consciousness without language would be possible.

**Mentor** That makes sense. But at the same time language is a robber of consciousness, because language imposes versions of consciousness, precluding other versions. Awareness is limited – boundaried, delimited – by language and culture. Human consciousness is compromised from the very beginning.

Consciousness is not either on or off; in human beings there are levels of consciousness. Just as adolescents have a developing level of consciousness, in waking life we can be more or less conscious. The hypnagogic and hypnopompic states are states of low or semi-consciousness.

**Enquirer** You're saying that unconsciousness is the natural state of animals. Are dreams a low level of consciousness? Is death ultimate unconsciousness?

**Mentor** When we are fully asleep we are unconscious. Unconsciousness implies the possibility of consciousness; death denies that possibility.

**Enquirer** I've heard it argued in philosophy that you can never be sure that you are awake because when you're asleep you might believe you are awake.

**Mentor** That argument makes the assumption that when you are asleep you are conscious; but that's not the case. When you wake up you may remember your dream; but when you were asleep you were not conscious. Let me give you an analogy to help you understand unconsciousness.

**Enquirer** Oh, yes?

**Mentor** Unconsciousness is equivalent to things that happen to you, or are within your perceptual field, but you do not notice.

**Enquirer** I don't follow that.

**Mentor** Consciousness is what you notice; unconsciousness is what you don't notice. For example, there are things your eyes can see but you're not aware of. You're probably aware of my face and voice right now, but you may not be aware of the colour of my eyes, the wind in the trees behind me, the singing of birds, traffic in the distance. These are available to your senses, and will have been apprehended by your unconscious body, but you hadn't – till now, possibly – placed the focus of consciousness on them, so they remained unconscious.

**Enquirer** The unconscious body can apprehend something without the conscious mind being aware of it.

**Mentor** Yes. And you can do something without being consciously aware of it. You put something down somewhere but don't know where (and your body helps you to locate it later); you lock the car automatically (but don't trust yourself and need to check); you steer the car on the motorway while your mind is on something else; you're hurt while playing sport or during some other activity that was holding your attention, and didn't notice the pain till later.

The awareness of the conscious mind is very limited. Consciously, you can't attend to very many things at the same time – somewhere between three and seven, I think we're told. When you learn something, it's your unconscious that has learned it, and you no longer need to think consciously about how to do it. The conscious mind is very limited; the unconscious seems to have no such limits. Many things occur outside of consciousness but are available to perception and therefore to the unconscious body. The body gets on with so much that, if it was all conscious, would be overwhelming and unmanageable.

**Enquirer** I understand that some people on the autistic spectrum are unable to filter out the peripheral information from their senses and so are overwhelmed by the mass of data their conscious mind apprehends. You and I are able to filter out much – maybe most

– of the information from our senses. But in new environments this is difficult, because we don't know what to select, and so new environments are very tiring. But in familiar environments much of what's going on we just don't consciously take in.

**Mentor** Yes, that's true. Most of us are not conscious of all the information available to our senses and, in fact, are cognizant only of a small proportion of that information. Now imagine shrinking the conscious focus, so that the conscious mind has cognizance of fewer and fewer of the elements of perception. Even thoughts disappear. Imagine shrinking this focus down further, and eventually to nothing, so that your area of consciousness is zero. That's what it's like to be awake and not be conscious.

**Enquirer** I still can't imagine it, but I can conceive it.

**Mentor** Consciousness develops as understanding increases. As we get older, if we remain open (and many people don't), there should be greater consciousness, as we understand more.

Consciousness is what makes humans special and different from animals. People often think it's intelligence that marks out human beings. But intelligence is a faculty shared with animals; human beings have much greater intelligence than most animals, but animals have a degree of intelligence too. Animals have some intelligence; but they have no consciousness at all.

Consciousness seems so natural to human beings that, like gravity, we take it for granted, and the absence of it is unimaginable. But it's a truly amazing faculty, unique to our species.

## Key points

Consciousness relates to what you notice; unconsciousness to what is unnoticed.

Consciousness, not intelligence, makes human beings unique.

# 8

# Apprehending and identifying emotions

**Mentor** Without consciousness, of course, emotions cannot be experienced. The apprehension of emotion requires consciousness. Without consciousness emotion has no existence. Physical feeling (the counterpart of emotion), does not require consciousness.

A physical feeling in itself carries no additional information to consciousness. The feeling is, however, expressed in the physiology and, unless there is consciously directed intervention, it unconsciously drives behaviour. All animals have physical feelings which are expressed in the physiology. Unlike humans, animals have no consciousness to mediate their behaviour.

Feelings of anger, sadness, guilt and so on are very recognizable in many mammals. Animals certainly have feelings, but they don't have emotions. Emotions are uniquely experienced by human beings because the apprehension of an emotion depends on the agency of consciousness, which is unique to human beings. Animals are not conscious and so have no sense of self – indeed, they have no self, because without consciousness there is no self.

**Enquirer** A lot of people won't agree with you about that. Many dog owners will want to believe that their dog has consciousness and emotions. But I understand what you're trying to say – animals look like they're having emotions but, because they are not conscious, they only have feelings.

**Mentor**  To an observer, there is no distinction between feelings and emotions: we can observe feelings expressed in physiology; we cannot observe emotions because they are subjectively experienced. For this reason, to an observer an animal's feelings can look very similar to those of humans.

**Enquirer**  What is the feeling of anger if it is different to the emotion of anger? I'm still not clear what an emotion is, if it is distinct from a feeling.

**Mentor**  A feeling is felt in the body. An emotion is experienced in consciousness. A feeling carries to consciousness no information in itself; it is either pleasant or unpleasant, comfortable or uncomfortable. The feeling has to be interpreted. An unpleasant or uncomfortable feeling is a communication that something needs to be attended to. In response to such a feeling, the conscious mind might analyse the situation to determine what the problem is and how to remedy it.

An emotion, on the other hand, carries meaning as an inherent part of it. The meaning is not a communication in language but is rather a quality that is conveyed to consciousness. The emotion communicated can be subtle and may not be reducible to a single-word descriptor such as anger, fear, anxiety. These words are however usually effective in conveying the meaning in shorthand form.

**Enquirer**  Emotions are abstruse, then. And language doesn't quite describe them.

**Mentor**  Language gives an approximation only.

**Enquirer**  Unlike a physical feeling, an emotion can be overlooked and ignored.

**Mentor** Yes. In fact, because emotions require awareness for their apprehension, ignoring them is very easy. Ignoring physical feelings, on the other hand, requires effort. The feelings are there whether they are attended to or not. Ignoring a feeling – especially a powerful one – requires an active effort. But there are many ways to avoid feelings, including use of anaesthesia, analgesia, a more powerful sensation, or focusing attention elsewhere.

**Enquirer** Avoiding feelings requires an exercise of will; apprehending emotions requires an exercise of will. Ignoring a physical feeling requires action; ignoring an emotion requires no effort whatever. Freedom of choice gives human beings the option to ignore emotions. It's an easy option: it requires doing nothing.

**Mentor** To experience emotions you have to opt in.

**Enquirer** What is the effect of refusing to acknowledge emotions? Is it possible to do this without repercussions?

**Mentor** Depression is the result of refusal to acknowledge emotions, of continually opting out of experiencing emotions.

**Enquirer** Depression is the suppression of emotions – although it is more omission than active suppression.

**Mentor** The refusal to acknowledge emotions, coupled with the suppression of the unwelcome physical feelings, is what causes depression. The counter to depression is the acknowledgement of emotions, and also the acknowledgement of the accompanying physical feelings. If emotions are acknowledged, depression is not possible.

**Enquirer** But depression also feels bad. Feeling can't be avoided. Suicide is the ultimate opt out from feeling.

**Mentor** That's true. We can't not feel.

**Enquirer** The solution to depression is for the person to allow herself to feel bad?

**Mentor** That's right. The therapist can help by finding out what the person doesn't want to feel and helping her to feel it. If there is a belief that certain emotions need to be avoided – because they are shameful, for example – the belief needs to be appreciated, and transformed.

**Enquirer** If you acknowledge emotions, you won't get depressed. But how do you acknowledge emotions? It's not self-evident.

**Mentor** That's true. I will explain.

**Enquirer** You've said that the apprehension of emotion requires consciousness and suggested that, if you're not aware of an emotion, you're not having one. The somatic feeling is there, regardless of whether or not it is acknowledged; but the emotion requires acknowledgement for its very existence.

**Mentor** Yes. Feelings occur in the body involuntarily and occur whether or not awareness is drawn to them. Unless there is something demanding your attention with greater urgency, you'll know for sure – at least, when the intensity rises above a certain threshold – that you're having a feeling.

The experience of an emotion depends on the specific direction of conscious awareness. Emotions don't exist without an effort of consciousness.

**Enquirer** Are there many feelings too subtle to notice?

**Mentor** You have feelings at every moment that are subtle and barely noticeable. There are lots of demands competing for attention when you're awake, and the conscious mind cannot focus on more than a few things at the same time. To register the feeling, it needs to be palpable enough, or other demands on your attention need to be less pressing. If the feeling is very habitual you may cease to notice it.

**Enquirer** The same is true of other types of physical sensation, such as a sore or a bruise. Physical feelings of all kinds vary in strength, and the stronger the feeling, the harder it is to ignore.

**Mentor** That's right. And people use many different strategies to ignore and deny unwelcome physical feelings.

**Enquirer** If you've carried around your feelings of anger, resentment or guilt for so long, you can cease to be aware of them – just as you cease to notice a persistent sound.

**Mentor** Yes. But even if you are no longer aware of the feeling, you still respond to it, though unconsciously. A feeling that is ignored and unacknowledged will still drive behaviour. It's significant that feelings drive behaviour even when – actually, especially when – those feelings are not acknowledged.

All attempts to silence and suppress the body will end in failure. The attempt to silence the body has a cost, often a significant cost. The feelings of the body – whether emotional feelings or strictly physical feelings – are important messages. You can use drugs, food, addictions, distractions of all sorts to try to stifle or overcome the body's messages, but none of these efforts will succeed. What generally happens when you try to ignore a feeling?

**Enquirer** I'm not sure.

**Mentor** The messages get stronger. The symptoms become more pronounced. If you still refuse to attend to the body's messages, they may translate into physical disease as the expression of the feeling persists and intensifies.

**Enquirer** So the response to unwelcome feelings isn't to try to subdue and subjugate the body. In fact, doing so is impossible.

**Mentor** The body isn't the enemy. Its communications are very important; they're for the benefit of the person. You need to attend to them.

**Enquirer** Don't shoot the messenger. But it's very tempting to avoid the symptom, or try to quell it, because it's unwelcome.

**Mentor** Yes. It's because it is unwelcome that we try to quell it and, if it persists, begin to regard it, or the body, as an enemy.

**Enquirer** The marketing of pharmaceuticals, and perhaps medical practice generally, tends to encourage this attitude. If you feel bad you need to feel better quickly. If you don't want medication there are the old-fashioned methods, such as alcohol, cigarettes, pornography, recreational drugs. And there are new methods, such as social media, computer games and the internet.

**Mentor** This takes us to a very common difficulty.

**Enquirer** What's that?

**Mentor** People get their emotions wrong.

**Enquirer** They do what?

**Mentor** They misidentify what they're feeling. It's very common for a person to mistake the feeling he's having. He may think he's angry when actually he's sad; that he's disappointed when really he's feeling guilty; and so on. Misidentifying an emotion occurs when a person intellectually interprets the feeling rather than experiences the emotion.

**Enquirer** That seems remarkable. How do people do that?

**Mentor** I'll explain. What is an emotion?

**Enquirer** We've already talked about that. It's an ineffable something that is neither of the mind nor of the body.

**Mentor** That's right. How do you know what you're feeling? Let's say you know you're having an emotional reaction to something. How might you decide what emotion you're having?

**Enquirer** Well, I'd probably think about it . . .

**Mentor** You'd think about it.

**Enquirer** Yes. I'd probably think about what's happened.

**Mentor** Give me an example of how you would come up with your emotion.

**Enquirer** Say something happens to me and I don't like it. I know that I'm feeling something about it because I can feel it in my body.

**Mentor** Your hand is over your chest as you speak.

**Enquirer** Yes, I get a feeling here sometimes while I'm talking to you.

I know I'm feeling something in my body. Then I consider what I might be feeling, and decide on the emotion that I'm having.

**Mentor** The process is a bit like this. You feel something in your body and you wonder what you could be feeling. Something has happened. You consider what it is you should feel or would expect to feel in response to this occurrence. You decide that you'd expect to be feeling anger, sadness, or some other emotion. Therefore, you conclude, that emotion is what you must be feeling.

**Enquirer** Yes. Something like that.

**Mentor** Thinking and feeling are different realms, though, don't you think?

**Enquirer** That's true. I was deciding what emotion I'm feeling through a process of reasoning. But emotions are not thoughts. So I might be wrong.

**Mentor** Exactly. Reasoning is a cerebral activity; thinking is something you do in your head. Emotions are not in the head: they relate to feelings which take place in the body. Thinking is the wrong way to determine what you're feeling.

**Enquirer** How do you determine what emotion you're having? If not by thinking, how do you do it?

**Mentor** Through an act of consciousness. Through bringing awareness to the body.

**Enquirer** I don't really understand what you mean.

**Mentor** I'm going to explain. Every emotion has a somatic counterpart – a physical feeling – in the torso. Specifically, in the stomach or chest – the abdomen or thorax.

**Enquirer** Every emotion has a corresponding physical feeling – in the stomach or chest. Why not in the back, the legs, or the head? I sometimes get feelings in my head and my back which I'm sure are emotion related.

**Mentor** Emotions have direct physical expression only in the abdomen or thorax, or both. You may have feelings in your back or head or legs, and they may have a relationship with the emotion (or the emotional problem) you are having, but these feelings are physical symptoms of an ailment, they are not direct physical expressions of the emotion itself. The direct physical expression of the emotion is always in the abdomen or thorax.

**Enquirer** And what about the throat? I often have feelings in the throat.

**Mentor** That's a need to express yourself or, even more commonly, the (suppressed) need to cry. The feeling in the throat may be the most intense feeling, but it won't be the only one. There'll also be something going on in the abdomen or chest.

**Enquirer** Right. Like butterflies in the stomach when you're nervous. Or tightness in the chest when you're anxious.

**Mentor** The abdomen and chest are where the physical expression of the emotion is felt. 'Butterflies' in the stomach is one example. Although people no doubt experience the bodily feelings in different ways, there're a few adjectives that seem to account for all of the somatic feelings.

**Enquirer** What are those?

**Mentor** One of the following will describe pretty much any of the somatic expressions of emotion: heavy, pulling, tight, and (if in the abdomen) churning.

**Enquirer** All right. There's a physical feeling in the abdomen or thorax corresponding with the emotion. You don't determine the emotion by thinking. How do you determine what the emotion is?

**Mentor** This is how to do it. Tune in to the physical feeling in your stomach or chest which corresponds with the emotion. That is, focus your attention, your consciousness, inward, on the physical feeling in your body – without thinking about it. Resist any temptation to think about what the feeling is and where it comes from; just focus on the physical feeling itself. Connected with that physical feeling is the emotion . . .

**Enquirer** Really?

**Mentor** Why not try it now? Give this your full attention.

Think of something that gives you an emotional response. It could be something that's happened to you; something you're going to do; how you feel about someone or something. Allow yourself to have the emotional response . . .

Bring awareness to your body.

Actually, stand up, if you would. Sitting down is not a very good position for accessing emotions. It's easier to do this either standing up or lying down on your back. If the person I'm working with is having trouble accessing his emotions I ask him to stand up.

**Enquirer** I'm not having difficulty accessing my emotions.

**Mentor** Sure. It's just that sitting is not ideal. Now relax. Breathe. Bring awareness to your body. You need to relax and breathe. You may need to stay with it for a few moments to really get in touch with the feeling and the corresponding emotion.

**Enquirer** It's important to be relaxed?

**Mentor** Yes, it's very important. If you're tense you cease to be aware of your feelings. That's why we tense up – to avoid feeling. People do this a lot. It's as if you are bracing yourself for a physical attack. Any kind of stress – the frustrated fight-or-flight response, or other kinds of emotional and physical stress – creates tension in the body. Emotional stress could be from anxiety and fear, and the suppression of anger or of other emotions. Physical stress could be from cold, pollutants or unhealthy food, for example. Tension inhibits the apprehension of feeling.

**Enquirer** What do you mean by saying 'frustrated' fight-or-flight response? Why 'frustrated'?

**Mentor** When the body senses that it is in danger, the natural response is to run – flee – or, if cornered, fight. The physiological response in fleeing or fighting is similar. Sensory awareness is heightened; digestion stops, and there may be a purging; the thinking parts of the brain relinquish blood, which flows to the major muscles to facilitate action (legs, for flight; arms, for fight).

That's why it's impossible to think when the body is in fight or flight: blood has vacated the thinking parts of the brain. When you're in danger, questioning whether to be or not to be is mis-timed: you need to act. The body takes over.

**Enquirer** Yes. I understand all of that. But why 'frustrated'?

**Mentor** If the body was doing what it's primed to do – that is, to fight or flee – there would be no stress; or, at least, not so much. The stress comes because the body wants to flee (or fight), but the conscious mind is preventing it. The body wants to behave in one way and the conscious mind is overruling it, creating a conflict. Stress is about conflict.

**Enquirer** Like a rope pulled forcibly from both ends.

**Mentor** You're giving an important presentation, say. Your body perceives the situation as perilous and responds with the fight-or-flight mode. But the conscious mind insists that the body neither flees nor fights. You will remain where you are and give your presentation. But you're now unable to think because the blood is being channelled to the muscles for fight or flight.

**Enquirer** I see. It's frustrated because the body's natural impulses are being thwarted by the conscious will.

**Mentor** The result is stress and tension. Many people are in a quasi state of fight or flight much of the time.

**Enquirer** I'm standing and relaxing my body.

**Mentor** That's good. Relax and breathe – but breathe normally. Focusing on breathing begins to bring your focus to your body.

**Enquirer** I'm focusing on my breathing.

**Mentor** That's good. Now that you are relaxed and focusing on your internal sensations, tune in to the physical feeling associated with the emotion.

Tuning in is about bringing your consciousness to that physical expression of emotion in the body.

No – don't think about what the emotion might be. Just be with the physical feeling.

**Enquirer** How did you know I was thinking just then?

**Mentor** You were looking up. That indicates you were thinking. If you're accessing your emotions you'll look down – well, if you're accessing sombre emotions (which they're sure to be if the feelings are troublesome) you'll look down.

**Enquirer** So if you're accessing excitement I guess you'll look up. I wonder if depressed people could be helped by some kind of eyepiece that inhibits looking down.

**Mentor** Be with that emotional experience. Take a moment. Be in your body . . . Tune in to it. Be aware of the physical feeling in your body. Focus on it and be with it . . . That's better. I can see that you're now accessing feelings, not thinking.

Show me where the feeling is in your body. I ask people to show me where in the body they have the feeling and describe it. This encourages them to tune in and allows me to calibrate this. You've put your hand over your chest: the feeling is in your chest.

**Enquirer** Should I give the feeling a colour or a name? I've done that kind of thing before.

**Mentor** No. I don't want you to metaphorize the feeling by describing it in other terms. That would take you into your head and away from the feeling itself. I'm just asking for a simple description of the physical feeling.

The point is to check that the person really is tuning in to the feeling. (To an extent, of course, any description of a feeling is going to be metaphorical, since feelings don't exist anywhere externally in the world.)

I also give suggestions to make the feeling easier to describe. Is it a heaviness, a tightness, a pulling, or – if the feeling is in the abdomen – a churning?

**Enquirer** It's a heaviness, and a tightness.

**Mentor** You are tuning in to the physical feeling so that you can become aware of the associated emotion . . . As you tune in to the feeling, what emotion comes up? . . .

**Enquirer** Yes. I've got the emotion. And the physical feeling has calmed, which I didn't expect. Fritz Perls noted that focusing on feelings will bring a person back to the present and reduce anxiety about the future.

**Mentor** I should have asked you to say in advance what you thought the emotion was, and then you could have compared both descriptions and noted whether or not you were right.

**Enquirer** Well, I can tell you. In relation to the memory that came up, before tuning in to it, I thought the feeling was anger. But when I tuned in to the feeling, I got the emotions of sadness, desolateness, and the sense of having to manage by myself. Very different from anger!

So now I know what I am really feeling – which is very interesting. But how does it help me? Does it really make a difference to know I'm feeling sad and desolate rather than angry?

**Mentor**  It's good to know, isn't it?

**Enquirer**  Yes. It has to be useful for my self-understanding.

**Mentor**  It's something you can do any time for yourself. I hope that when you are assessing your emotional response to something you'll do less thinking and more tuning in.

Knowledge of an emotion is important in the Relearning Experience Process to help the person access the origins of a therapeutic problem. But this knowledge is helpful in another very important respect: it enables a person to act through consciousness rather than submitting his behaviour to the mercy of his feelings.

## Key points

Emotion carries communication from the unconscious.

Depression results from suppressed feelings and denied emotions.

Repercussions follow attempts to suppress the messages of the body.

People often use intellect to decide what emotion they're feeling.

Experiencing an emotion requires an active effort and direction of consciousness.

The communication of an emotion is received by relaxing, breathing, and tuning in to the physical feeling.

# 9

# Emotions and morality

**Enquirer** Sometimes I think human beings would be better off without emotions. They cause all the trouble.

**Mentor** For Descartes, thinking is the most essential element of human existence. But thoughts might not necessarily require consciousness. I think that the most important element is therefore consciousness – which encompasses thought but also, perhaps even more importantly, the capacity to experience emotion. It's feelings which connect consciousness with the physical world. Without feelings human beings really would be ghosts in machines. Feelings enable you to attribute your thoughts to your body and therefore to your self. Is consciousness even possible without a sense of self? Without feelings you would have no self. And human beings would be indistinguishable from robots.

**Enquirer** You'd pinch yourself and nothing would happen – like in a dream.

That's the mistake those AI people make when they suggest robots and humans could (at some time in the future, when technology has significantly advanced) be indistinguishable. They disregard feelings and consciousness.

**Mentor** Yes. Feelings connect you to yourself. Consciousness itself, in the absence of feelings, would not be enough to differentiate oneself from others or from the world. Similarly, feelings alone do not give a sense of self (animals have feelings but no consciousness and therefore no sense of self).

**Enquirer** You're saying that both consciousness and feelings are required for a true sense of self.

**Mentor** Yes. And emotions, which render feelings meaningful, and elevate *Homo sapiens* from material beings with consciousness to the realm of humanity with sensibilities and a connection with ethereality, able to experience love and joy.

**Enquirer** But also able to experience hate, resentment, spite, jealousy and rage.

**Mentor** That's true. You can't have the pleasant emotions in the absence of the unpleasant ones. Like light and dark, or any polarities, they depend on each other.

All emotions, including the ones that feel most uncomfortable, are indispensable, because they give valuable information – as well as enabling the polar emotion to have meaning.

Emotion is the quality that gives life meaning and value. Take away emotion and nothing valuable or meaningful is left. Remember that emotions are not only the strong feelings that impose themselves on consciousness; all experience is imbued with emotion. There is no thought or action that doesn't carry emotions with it.

**Enquirer** Yes, emotion brings colour and life. But without conscious recognition of an emotion the emotion has no existence, you said. So experience can't be imbued with emotion unless there is conscious recognition of the emotion. But wouldn't there be an awareness that there is an emotional response, even if the nature of the emotion is unclear?

**Mentor** I'm gratified that you are attending so carefully. Let me rather say that feelings accompany all thoughts, and all feelings carry the potential for emotion. Even though I'm identifying self with consciousness, the living being very much encompasses the unconscious too; and all unconscious potentialities are always tantalizingly close. Emotions provide a foundation for consciousness. They also provide the basis for morality.

**Enquirer** Surely morality is based on reason, not emotion.

**Mentor** Shouldn't we avoid that discussion – which risks being too abstract . . . But, yes, morality is founded on emotion. You know what's right and wrong on the level of feeling.

**Enquirer** It's a bit late to try to avoid abstraction! Are you really trying to say that morality is 'emotional'; that what's right and wrong is determined at the level of 'feeling'? And do you mean feeling, or do you mean emotion?

**Mentor** Feeling and emotion are different manifestations of the same thing.

**Enquirer** Okay. Sometimes you use one term or the other when you are not intending to differentiate between them.

**Mentor** To distinguish between them constantly would be tiring and unnecessary. My argument here is simple. Morality has to be based on emotion. Reason can take you anywhere and is not to be trusted. It can lead to the justification of war, slavery, tyranny, holocaust. All types of wrongdoing have been justified by reasoned arguments. Anything can be rationalized. Just look at what is argued by politicians and ecclesiastics.

**Enquirer** You're right. Let's not go there . . . I can see that reason is not to be trusted. But feelings can also take you anywhere. You have envious feelings and you act maliciously; you feel angry and behave rudely. So feelings can't be a good guide to what's right and wrong.

**Mentor** You're right that, when unacknowledged, feelings are not a good guide to right and wrong. But when, for example, envy or anger is acknowledged, and proper responsibility is taken, the person is hardly able to act maliciously, despite the feeling. He can choose to act maliciously but, when he acknowledges that his emotion is his own responsibility, he cannot blame the other for his own behaviour, and therefore acts with full moral consciousness. People are unwilling to accept responsibility for behaving wickedly and so must rationalize the behaviour as not wicked or disclaim responsibility for their actions. Acknowledging emotions is central to personal emotional health and emotional intelligence – and to good behaviour.

Unacknowledged feelings can lead directly to immoral and heinous behaviour. After the fact – after the act; that is, after the unprincipled and unreasonable behaviour – the behaviour is then justified through the faculty of reason. The feelings in themselves are not to blame for the behaviour or for the false 'reasons'; nor are the feelings in themselves moral or immoral – only actions can be judged morally. Freed from the interference of those justifications and rationalizations, human beings know what's right and wrong by attending to their emotions – their feelings – not their thoughts, not 'reason'.

**Enquirer** You're contradicting yourself. Behaviour is driven by feelings, you say, and feelings are not to be blamed for action.

**Mentor** A person must always retain moral responsibility for her behaviour. The refusal to acknowledge emotions does not excuse a person's behaviour or save her from moral censure. But with consciousness of her emotions, a person is able to remain captain of her behaviour and can behave according to her principles rather than be the captive of her feelings.

**Enquirer** I've always thought that reason, rationality – not emotion – is the highest quality of human beings. It is true that love is often said to be the most valuable human capacity, and love is an emotion. But I've never met anyone who actually loves her enemy or even her neighbour as herself (not platonically, anyway). So I've considered the injunction to love as just a fanciful ideal.

But I understand why you're saying that emotions are so valuable. If we couldn't feel anything life would be sterile: it wouldn't be life.

According to your argument, if a person is unaware of her emotions it means that she's not having emotions (even if she's still having physical feelings). However, people generally aren't tuned in to their feelings and so don't experience their emotions, and misidentify them, deny them, or suppress them. If emotions are so important, but so many people are unaware of them so much of the time, doesn't that mean that most people are living a seriously impoverished existence as human beings?

What exactly is the value or status of a physical feeling without the ethereal emotional experience?

**Mentor**  Those questions are worth thinking about.

**Enquirer**  Have you noticed what a beautiful day it is today? It's worthy of our appreciation. Shall we just walk for a few minutes and experience and appreciate it?

## Key points

Consciousness is the most essential element of human existence.

Feelings connect consciousness to the self.

All emotions are indispensable and give life its colour and value.

Anything can be argued with the faculty of reason; emotion is the basis of morality.

Unacknowledged feelings lead to problematic behaviour. When feelings are properly acknowledged, responsible behaviour follows.

# 10

## Motivation to act

**Mentor** I wanted to put this thesis to you. You may think it's radical. I may have already mentioned it, but I'd like you to consider it because it's central to our methodology. It's this: *feelings motivate action.* The power of the motivation is equal to the strength of the feeling.

**Enquirer** I think I have heard you say that before and I have to say that I'm not convinced. Actions are surely driven by thoughts, or by the will. Doesn't a person first think, and then act, according to her will?

**Mentor** Thoughts are not so powerful that they naturally motivate action. People very often act without any thought at all; just as people may have a thousand unheeded intentions. In fact, many routine actions don't require thought. And just thinking something won't make it happen. Thoughts are sedentary. Wanting to do something or intending to do something won't mean you'll actually do it. Thoughts are even weaker than desires and intentions in precipitating action. Feelings are required to motivate action. Everything you do is motivated by feelings. No feeling: no action.

**Enquirer** What about the role of the will? Isn't it the will that is the force underlying action?

**Mentor** I think of will as conscious effort. The more muted the feeling motivating action, the more effort is required to act; the stronger the feeling motivating an action, the less will is required. In other words, actions that are in line with the aims of the body are easy to carry out; those which are at variance are more difficult. Restraining behaviour through the will – refraining from doing something – is very difficult if your feelings are impelling you to do it. Willing yourself to some behaviour, when your feelings aren't supporting that behaviour, or are opposing that behaviour, is equally laborious and may seem impossible.

Conscious will is however very important, since it is the conscious will that informs the unconscious body what it is that you want. But, in itself, conscious will does not mandate action.

The feelings that motivate you aren't necessarily 'positive' – in the sense of attracting you to something. You may be 'negatively' motivated – motivated to get away from something or avoid something. Some people get out of bed in the morning because they look forward to going to work. That's positive motivation. Others would rather stay in bed, except for consideration of the consequences of not turning up for work. That's negative motivation.

**Enquirer** Better, generally, to be positively motivated: motivated by desire for what you want, rather than fear of what you want to avoid.

**Mentor** Yes. Fear pushes you away from what you want to avoid – but in any direction.

**Enquirer** Out of the frying pan, but possibly into the fire. Better to be motivated by love of your work than by fear of penury. But some things are worth getting away from.

**Mentor** That's true. The strength of negative motivation can be very useful.

**Enquirer** I'm still not sure I'm totally convinced that feelings are the motivation for action. Can't I just decide to do something and do it? Such as put up my hand now (to give an example that the philosopher John Searle likes to give).

**Mentor** You're not going to do anything that's random. And you're not going to do anything that isn't motivated. Without feelings there is no motivation. Putting up your hand requires very little effort, and so very little motivation is required. The action was motivated by the idea that preceded it. You were proving a point. Raising your arm was very easy. You wouldn't run a marathon to prove the same point.

You decide to do things because you're emotionally invested in them – or because your fear of what will happen, or won't happen, if you don't do them is greater than your desire to do something else.

**Enquirer** It doesn't sound so radical when you put it like that.

What's the relationship between feelings and thoughts?

**Mentor** The mind, the realm of thoughts, is an autonomous realm. I believe this because if it were not true it would mean that free will is an illusion. Without free will nothing makes sense. But thoughts don't occur in a vacuum. Naturally, thoughts are influenced by context, including sense perceptions, your associations of those perceptions and the feelings accompanying those perceptions.

To exercise the greatest freedom, your behaviour should be congruent with your feelings. This is only possible if you are in tune with your feelings.

**Enquirer** I'm not sure what you mean.

**Mentor** If your feelings are impelling you to behave in one way, and your will is pulling in another direction, you are at war with yourself.

**Enquirer** I agree congruence of mind and body gives peace and comfort because of the absence of conflict. I'm not sure it gives freedom. The idea that freedom means conforming with your nature sounds paradoxical.

**Mentor** The body is not telling you what to do; it's telling you what you need and what is good for you. Your behaviour always remains your choice. I would argue that we have greater choice if we know what's good for us – and we know what's good for us if we pay attention to the messages of the body. By being in tune with the body, you are making a free choice, but an informed choice. Ignorant choices are not free choices. Ignoring the needs of the body does not make the choice more free.

When a person denies, or refuses to recognize, the messages his feelings are trying to communicate, not only is he denying himself valuable information about his own needs, but the feelings will operate outside of awareness to motivate behaviour that he hasn't consciously chosen. That is certainly a curtailing of freedom.

The denial of feelings leads to problem behaviour as the feelings find opportunities to express themselves, despite the person's will or intentions. Let me put that in a different way: if a person denies his feelings those feelings will look for opportunities to express themselves in behaviour that he may well not like or approve. The person is subject to this behaviour; he is not author of it. He will then seek to explain his behaviour, to himself and others, with rationalizations. The idea of rationalization is important and we'll talk more about it a bit later.

**Enquirer** So, behaviour isn't actually driven directly by feelings, but by the interpretations the conscious mind makes of those feelings. Which isn't really the same thing.

**Mentor** Interpretation is only possible when a person consciously acknowledges the feelings. If he does acknowledge his feelings, he is able to interpret his feelings and can be in control of his actions.

If he doesn't acknowledge his feelings, his feelings are in control of him – of his behaviour, that is.

Behaviour is driven by feelings; but, with the interpretation and mediation of the conscious mind, through emotional consciousness, the person is not at the mercy of his feelings and can be the author of his behaviour. With consciousness, the meaning of the emotions associated with the feelings become accessible. Once feelings have meaning, good behaviour becomes possible.

**Enquirer** Bad behaviour is still possible, even with acknowledgement of the emotion. I'm angry with you. You made me angry. I want to punish you.

**Mentor** Taking responsibility for one's own anger, and holding a person accountable for her behaviour, is very different from the punitive impulse that derives from blame – don't you think?

**Enquirer** What about envy?

**Mentor** Envious feelings without consciousness of the emotion can lead to meanness towards someone; with consciousness, the same feelings can provide motivation to pursue the attributes the person so desires.

**Enquirer** Or to a re-evaluation of the person's values.

**Mentor** Absolutely. And, as a result of the re-evaluation, the envious feelings may cease to exist. For example, you feel envious because of your neighbour's greater wealth. You acknowledge this, and realize that the love you have from family and friends is far more important to you than the yacht or expensive car your neighbour possesses. You can then readily let go of the envious feelings and even feel compassion for your neighbour, whose economic success is not matched by success in personal relationships.

**Enquirer** When feelings are denied are you saying that the actions of the person are completely unconscious?

**Mentor** Behaviour is usually consciously enacted. It's the motivations that are unconscious. Behaviour is not considered, according to any psychological account, to be fully explainable as the corollary of conscious, rational decision making. When a person has no awareness of the emotion, he reacts crudely to the feeling; or, as long as he has the resources to do so, he suppresses the feeling or constrains his behaviour – a struggle requiring effort and vigilance which will not always be successful.

We are always responsible for our actions. It's only in extreme circumstances of danger that the body takes over completely – making you throw yourself out of the way of that bus; or making you tumble in a way that's least damaging to your body; or sending you into madness (complete loss of conscious control), when no conscious solution seems available.

When feelings are denied, a person's actions are conscious, but his motivations are unconscious. When a person's motivations are unconscious there is a very strong tendency to justify and rationalize the behaviour. This, of course, entrenches the problematic behaviour and makes change more threatening to the ego.

I hope that now you're beginning to see the importance of feelings and emotions in behaviour generally and in therapeutic problems in particular. The study of pathological behaviour and therapeutic problems is fundamentally not about the conscious mind.

**Enquirer** That's the reason that cognitive therapy fundamentally misses the point.

According to your argument, emotions are engendered by feelings occurring in the body. That means that the body gives rise to emotions; emotions don't create the feelings in the body. Emotions are therefore just expressions of the body, experienced in the realm of consciousness.

**Mentor** That sounds like a good way of putting it.

**Enquirer** I'm not sure I like that idea. It's like the philosophical view that consciousness is just an epiphenomenon of the physical brain, and the mind has no power or efficacy but is just a shadow.

**Mentor** Like you, I don't like that idea. I want to believe that the conscious mind has efficacy. But you're right that emotions are epiphenomena of the somatic feelings of the body, if you want to look at it that way.

**Enquirer** Couldn't emotions be the cause of the corresponding physical feelings, rather than the other way around?

**Mentor** No. If the body isn't producing the emotions, what is producing them? They're not created by consciousness. We've demonstrated that, haven't we? Emotions are not creations of the conscious mind. They can't be willed into being. You can think about something that makes you sad, but it is the memory of that event that makes you sad, not your will.

It's important to understand that this is how the body communicates with the conscious mind. The message is communicated via the physical feeling; but the message is carried in the emotion, not by the physical feeling itself. The physical feeling is the vehicle; the emotion is the message. A tight feeling in the chest is not in itself a communication. The emotion accompanying the physical feeling is the communication.

Remember that we're not conceiving the body in a nineteenth century way, as something rank, base, frail and tawdry. That may be why emotions are equated with mind, because traditionally the body, 'flesh', has been denigrated and the mind elevated. There is nothing base about the unconscious body.

Physical feelings are the means by which the body communicates its remarkable connective knowledge to the conscious mind.

Perhaps you're not yet totally convinced.

**Enquirer** I wouldn't say that. But I'd like to challenge you on something that occurs to me. The condition where a person has compulsive thoughts. This is a therapeutic problem, isn't it? Compulsive thoughts are to do with the mind, not the body. Isn't this true?

**Mentor** That would seem to be the case, because the symptom of the problem, compulsive thoughts, indeed occurs in the mind. But, in fact, compulsive thoughts are driven by feelings. When a person presents with compulsive thoughts, the therapeutic task is the same as it always is: to find the feelings that underlie the thoughts and resolve the experiences that have created those feelings. With those feelings resolved, the compulsion ceases.

**Enquirer** But then our thoughts are not entirely voluntary.

**Mentor** Compulsive thoughts are indeed involuntary; that's why they're a problem.

**Enquirer** What would you say is the relationship between emotions and intuition?

**Mentor** I think you may now be able to answer that yourself.

**Enquirer** Let me try. The unconscious body knows what's good for you and wants to help you to have it. It knows what your needs are and whether they are getting met. Information coming to the conscious mind must be filtered or it will be overwhelming. The unconscious, on the other hand, doesn't need to limit input and circumscribe interpretation, but is able to absorb information holistically with multiple possible potential interpretations. It therefore has a much better apprehension of what's going on than the conscious mind. This is the connection you speak about – the 'connective unconscious'. Intuition is when the conscious mind tunes in to the messages the body gives via the emotions and thereby gains access to some of this unconscious knowledge.

**Mentor** Would you say this conception of the unconscious is different from Freud's notion of the id?

**Enquirer** Yes, it's very different. The id is a place of chaos, of uncontrollable desire and turbulence, where the superego is necessarily in conflict with the id's demands, and where the conscious mind must suppress or sublimate the id's insatiable desires. Your idea of the unconscious body is more like an inner god.

**Mentor** As you say, intuition involves a special tuning in to the body. It is an awareness in consciousness of what the unconscious body knows and has communicated. If everything is fine, and your feelings are in harmony with your thoughts and you're at one with yourself, then your emotions are an appropriate response in the present to what's going on in your life. But if things are not going well, and you're behaving in a way that is inconsistent with achieving your goals, your body will tell you by giving you uncomfortable feelings. It's then your choice – and often a difficult one to make – whether to tune in to the messages and heed them.

**Enquirer** So, if you have uncomfortable feelings that are inappropriate it's very often an indication that you're doing something wrong, or that something's wrong in your life.

**Mentor** Yes. An uncomfortable emotional feeling is the body indicating that there's a problem – just as physical discomfort, or pain, is an indication of a problem. If the emotional feeling is inappropriate, there's a problem in you; if the emotional feeling is appropriate, there may be a problem externally.

**Enquirer** Okay. I understand that if I'm about to do something emotionally or physically dangerous my body is warning me of the peril. But what if I'm suffering from irrational anxiety or debilitating fear?

**Mentor** For example?

**Enquirer** For example: anxiety or fear about entering into a relationship, public speaking, asserting opinions.

**Mentor** It's doing the same thing. It's still giving you a warning of what experience has taught you is perilous. Rationally, you might think you know that the feared behaviour is not perilous; or you might consider it necessary to do (what your body interprets as) a perilous act. Whatever you believe on a conscious level, according to your experience the behaviour is perilous, and the body needs to communicate this to you in a way that is beyond your conscious control.

**Enquirer** But the behaviour might not be perilous.

**Mentor** The body knows it to be so. If the feeling is inappropriate in present circumstances, it comes from the past. The perception of peril is there because of something that happened in the past. Your body has learned from a past experience that this circumstance is perilous and, through feelings, is warning you.

**Enquirer** But the circumstances aren't perilous. I need to be able to do this thing without fear and anxiety preventing me!

**Mentor** If the fear and anxiety are inappropriate now, they were appropriate at some time in the past. The experiences in the past that created this apprehension of peril can be identified by tracking back to the origins of these feelings. The resolution work will enable you to relearn the experience and remove the apprehension of danger.

**Enquirer** So, the aim of the therapy is not to quell the uncomfortable physical feeling so that you can feel better.

**Mentor** Therapy should never have that intention. The body is your ally. The feelings are there for a reason. You can't make them go away. They won't – thank goodness. People try, of course, through many means.

**Enquirer** Some therapists try too! I agree: it doesn't work. The body will not be defeated! The feelings are likely just to get stronger.

**Mentor** Shall we honour the body and have a break?

## Key points

Feelings, rather than thoughts, provide the motivation for action.

Freedom is experienced where a person's behaviour is congruent with her feelings.

Problematic behaviour is subsequently justified and rationalized.

Where feelings are acknowledged, free choice is possible and behaviour has potential to be rational.

The body learns about perils from experience and communicates warnings through feelings.

# 11

## Judging emotions and behaviour

**Mentor** You should never deny your feelings. But it's easy to do so and many – perhaps all – of us do so frequently. You can pretend to yourself that you don't have these feelings that you'd rather not feel. Or you can find ways to ignore them. If they are chronic, eventually, you will become inured to them. They don't go away but become normalized.

To avoid feelings, you can simply direct your attention elsewhere until they pass. If you focus strongly enough on something else, you may not even notice the physical feelings, because the conscious mind is limited in the number of things it can focus on.

**Enquirer** What strategies do people use to ignore unwanted feelings? Dissociation is the ultimate avoidance – apart from death, that is.

**Mentor** Anything that diverts and distracts. Addictive substances; food, television and radio; computer, mobile phone or other digital devices; the gym and physical activities; ultra-sociality; being overly busy; finding activities so as never to be still. Mobile phones provide the perfect contemporary distraction.

**Enquirer** Mobiles do what cigarettes used to do. Nature is the perfect antidote to bring you back to your feelings and connection.

**Mentor** Avoiding feelings may require dedication: physical feelings can be insistent. They become more and more difficult to ignore. So you may be tempted to take increasingly drastic measures to try to avoid them. Measures that can be self-destructive.

**Enquirer** Such as taking drugs, smoking, alcohol. Addictions of any kind.

**Mentor** Yes.

**Enquirer** I've heard it argued that addiction to sex, pornography or gambling aren't really addictions, because they don't involve ingesting a substance and developing physical dependence.

**Mentor** Physical dependence is the least important aspect of an addiction. Anyone can manage physical withdrawal with a little help. Addictions of all kinds – and I would certainly include compulsions for sex and gambling, and other activities such as eating 'disorders' – are motivated not by physical dependence but because these activities camouflage the uncomfortable feelings in the body of the person.

**Enquirer** Who wants to feel bad?

**Mentor** Avoidance of bad feelings can become a slavery. You may want to avoid the feelings because they feel bad. You may also want to avoid them because you disapprove of what they're telling you. If you disapprove of them, clearly they feel bad, but it may not be the discomfort itself that you want to avoid but the admission that you have them.

Take the example of envy. You may disapprove of feeling envious, because you have the belief that envy is not a good thing. If you're religious you might even believe it's a 'deadly sin' to feel envy. So you try to banish the feeling from consciousness. You pretend to yourself that you don't feel it. The same may apply to anger or hate or any other emotion that you disapprove of. If you believe you should not feel a particular way, you may pretend to yourself and even try to prove to yourself that you don't feel that way.

You might also deny an emotion, such as anger, because you fear it – usually as a result of childhood family experiences.

**Enquirer** But the emotion of envy isn't a good thing, is it? A person shouldn't be envious.

**Mentor** Such a belief – that envy, or any other emotion, isn't good – can easily lead to the emotion being denied and banished. What else can you do with an emotion you disapprove of?

When you deny something in yourself, you project it on to others. This is the basis of racism in Christian cultures. Those characteristics that were regarded as sinful and not acceptable in oneself (characteristics associated with blackness) were projected on to other peoples, especially those with dark skin. If those unacceptable characteristics are outside of you, you can hate them with much greater freedom than if they are within you – although you need to keep the hatred up, because the unacceptable forces within will keep wanting to emerge. Of course, projection is not only realized in racism; anyone's characteristics can be the victim of a person's projections.

**Enquirer** Disapproving of an emotion leads to personal and social disorders.

**Mentor** Emotions are involuntary and all emotions have an important purpose as a communication from the unconscious. It is really important to remember that we should subject *behaviour* to moral judgement, not emotions. No emotions are bad in themselves. You might hear people refer to 'negative' emotions, but no emotions are negative. Clearly, there are beliefs that are very unhelpful and there is behaviour that is reprehensible, but all emotions are good because they give valuable information.

**Enquirer** I don't see how envy can possibly be good.

**Mentor** Feeling envious is an important reminder that there's something in your life that you don't have and that you want. You may need to put more energy into getting this thing that you want. There's nothing wrong with feeling envy. Unacknowledged, of course, envy can lead to resentful behaviour; but if the feeling is acknowledged, a person can still behave well. In fact, when the feeling is acknowledged, behaving badly becomes very difficult, because you know the fault is in yourself.

This is vital to emotional health and worth repeating: don't judge your emotions; judge your behaviour. Your emotions are involuntary; your behaviour is voluntary. Similarly, don't judge other people's emotions; judge their behaviour. People are entitled not to like you or your opinions. They're not entitled to be rude to you because they don't like you or your opinions. Don't judge people according to what you think their intentions are; and certainly do not judge someone's behaviour on the basis of your emotional response to someone's behaviour. Nobody else is responsible for how you feel. They are responsible for their behaviour; as you are responsible for yours.

**Enquirer** We can never know someone else's intentions – unless they tell us. We hardly truly know our own.

**Mentor** That's right. The claim to know someone else's intentions is an attempt at 'mind reading'. This is a naive but very common mistake in human relationships. We may think we know someone's motivation or intentions, but we can never know for sure. The best way to find out is to ask.

**Enquirer** But a person can easily lie about her motivations and intentions.

**Mentor** That's true – which is why we should generally judge behaviour rather than intention.

**Enquirer** Perhaps. But sometimes we can't do that. The law certainly considers intention.

**Mentor** You're right. There are accidents and people make mistakes.

**Enquirer** You're suggesting that coveting your neighbour's possessions, or even your neighbour's partner, is not bad in itself – if it doesn't lead to action. That's contrary to Christian teaching, which considers intention as paramount.

**Mentor** Well, intention is very different from desire. Intention is precursor to action. Desire doesn't have to become intention, and so doesn't imply action. You may desire what you cannot afford to buy, for example; this doesn't mean you are at risk of stealing. Similarly, desire for a person who is not your partner certainly does not have to lead to infidelity.

**Enquirer** Desire isn't necessarily bad in itself, but dwelling on it might be.

The church makes a great fuss about the risks of sexual 'coveting' no doubt because insistence on non-sexual imperatives would upset the political authorities. As long as the church focuses on sex it's not going to tread on the toes of the state – but it's going to be regarded as irrelevant if fewer and fewer people share its values.

So envy can be a good thing. Is anger also a good thing? Lots of people – including some authorities in the field of emotional health – seem to think it's not. But it must be, you would say.

**Mentor** People are afraid of anger because it can have great destructive power. But the emotion of anger needs to be differentiated from bad behaviour that can result from anger. Like all emotions, anger can be a very positive emotion. Anger gives courage and strength to confront and stand one's ground. It gives power and energy if you are threatened or hurt by another. It gives you motivation to confront wrongs against you personally, and against others you care about, or to fight for your principles. You need to be able to defend yourself, your principles, and the people you care about. Anger provides this power.

**Enquirer** Yes, it does. And love can also lead to bad behaviour.

**Mentor** That's right. Any emotion can lead to bad behaviour. Feeling angry doesn't mean you have to behave badly – just as feeling love doesn't mean a person behaves lovingly. People often behave badly when they're angry, of course. And behaving well when you're very angry requires restraint – which comes from conscious acknowledgement of the feeling itself and the acceptance of responsibility as author of the feeling (rather than blaming someone else for your feeling).

Young men have often yet to develop this restraint. The same is true of many older men too – and women – especially when the anger is inappropriate because it comes from elsewhere. Unassertive people will use anger as a way to give them the strength to assert their feelings – often to the great surprise of those suddenly subject to it.

It's the inappropriate expression of anger that is treacherous – not the emotion itself. Inappropriate expression results from denial. When people deny an emotion it builds up inside them and continues to build up until it is uncontainable and needs to find expression and temporary release.

**Enquirer** Is the release only ever temporary? Can a release of anger ever lead to a depletion or termination of the anger, so the anger is gone for good? Does bashing the hell out of a cushion help? Some psychotherapists encourage cushion bashing. In fact, I've done some cushion bashing myself.

**Mentor** Did it help you?

**Enquirer** It made me feel better – for a while. It didn't take the anger away. But it felt good to express it.

**Mentor** Right. It helped temporarily. By getting the anger out, you felt better for a while. It provided a release. It's certainly better than damaging the crockery or hitting someone. But expressing the anger, whether through organized cushion bashing or in a manner spontaneous and uncontrolled, doesn't resolve the anger. The source of the anger is still there. The pressure will gradually increase again. It will have to blow its top, probably inappropriately, some time – without some more timely cushion bashing.

Any expression of anger provides a temporary release, but is not a solution to the anger. For permanent resolution, the specific cause of the anger needs to be identified and resolved. The same is true of any denied emotion. Any suppressed or, I think I'd rather say, denied emotion requires release and will find expression somehow; but the release is only temporary and the energy of the denied emotion will build again until it again finds (temporary) release. Resolution of the origins of the inappropriate emotion is the only permanent solution.

**Enquirer** You need to explain how it is possible to resolve the emotional issue permanently.

**Mentor** Yes. I'm going to explain it all. But even if you have not resolved the problem permanently you can still be in control of your behaviour by acknowledging the emotion and taking responsibility for it.

**Enquirer** What about hatred? Are you also going to insist that it's okay to feel hatred?

**Mentor** Hatred is anger plus powerlessness. If you feel powerless in the face of wrongdoing you are likely to feel hate. If you acknowledge the hate (as your responsibility, not created in you by the other), you are likely to behave well in your attempt to challenge the wrongdoing, and the hate will subside.

The larger part of anger is usually self-anger; and the larger part of hate is usually self-hate. Chronic self-hate is probably the introjection of a parent's projections.

**Enquirer** All right. People avoid or deny their emotions because the emotion is uncomfortable or because they disapprove of the emotion and want to pretend they don't have it.

**Mentor** That's right. A person may have been taught that certain emotions are unacceptable, and therefore doesn't allow himself to acknowledge them. For example, a man might feel that being vulnerable or upset is unacceptable and incompatible with manliness; or a woman might feel that being angry is unacceptable and incompatible with femininity. And so the person denies these feelings. Or a person might have the belief that grief is too painful to be borne, and so suppresses the feelings of grief.

## Key points

People use a variety of strategies to avoid feelings, including addiction to substances or activities.

Behaviour should be subject to critical scrutiny; emotions should not be judged. Disapproving of an emotion can lead to its suppression.

Denial or suppression of emotions leads to bad behaviour; acknowledgement facilitates appropriate behaviour.

Expressions of emotion provide temporary release, but only resolving the problem at its origins brings permanent resolution.

# 12

## Distorting reality

**Enquirer** You can see why it's tempting to deny your emotions. There's a presumption that, if you deny them, somehow they cease to exist. But it's much better to acknowledge what you feel, even if it feels really bad, or even if you don't like it or don't approve of it.

**Mentor** Your denied feelings will sooner or later emerge in the form of behaviour and, possibly, physical ill health. Pushing feelings down just makes them go underground and operate insidiously, without your knowledge or conscious control. Suppressing feelings is therefore counterproductive. It also distorts the way you express yourself in the world.

**Enquirer** How does suppressing emotion distort the way you express yourself in the world?

**Mentor** Your feelings direct your behaviour. But that doesn't mean you don't have freedom of choice. When you properly acknowledge your feelings and pay attention to the emotion, you retain authorship of your behaviour. But if you deny your feelings, you lose that freedom of choice, because those feelings need to find expression, and will do so in a way other than that of your choosing. They'll express themselves when your defences are low; when resources are low; when conscious control is inhibited.

Now, when a person behaves badly, he wants to justify his behaviour so as to uphold his human or personal dignity. To justify his behaviour he has to construct a version of reality according to which his behaviour seems okay.

**Enquirer** Right. To do bad things and make yourself the good guy, you need to stretch reality to fit. People don't knowingly do bad things: either they rationalize them into something that isn't bad; or they reason that the bad thing is justifiable.

**Mentor** Here's an example. We were talking about envy a few minutes ago and how it's a useful feeling because it is a reminder about what you want. A fellow, call him Jake, is envious of his acquaintance, called Vincent. Maybe he considers that Vincent is more attractive than he is, or more financially successful. Jake wishes he had Vincent's attractiveness and financial success. Jake believes that those are markers of esteem and prestige, so Vincent is a continual reminder to Jake of what he thinks he's not, and Jake feels inadequate around him. If Jake denies his feelings of inadequacy and his envy (and you can see why he'd want to), how is Jake likely to behave?

**Enquirer** He'll secretly hate him. Jake might say undermining things to put Vincent down. He might tell stories to others about Vincent that put him in a bad light. He might make 'jokes' that undermine Vincent and say, 'Can't you take a joke?' He might even verbally attack him.

**Mentor** Yes, he might do any or all of those. He's not going to like how he feels when he's around Vincent and may attempt to feel better about himself by attacking Vincent and putting him down. He can only do this if the story he tells himself is that his attacks are justified by Vincent's faults rather than motivated by his own feelings of inadequacy.

**Enquirer** That's true. If Jake acknowledged that the problem is in himself, attacks on someone else would be madness. But blaming Vincent is seriously delusional! It's very common, though, and I guess we all do it to a greater or lesser extent.

**Mentor** If a person doesn't like what's inside him, but can't admit to it, he might well claim that the problem is in the other person. Denial (of one's own inadequacy) leads to a projection (that the other is at fault). And that's a distortion of reality – which needs to be continually justified and maintained. Jake's envy, once denied, becomes (in Jake's mind) Vincent's arrogance, or Vincent's insecurity. He's distorted reality in an attempt to rescue himself from admission of his inadequacy.

**Enquirer** Does envy derive from feelings of inadequacy?

**Mentor** If you acknowledge your envy you are able to recognize there's something you want that you need to strive for so that you can get it. That's a healthy response to envy, and it doesn't imply inadequacy. But if you tell yourself that you can't achieve it, then you're assuming an inadequacy in yourself. Wanting something that you believe you can't get easily leads to jealousy, resentment and blame.

For some people, the feeling of inadequacy does not relate to achievements. However much success they have, they still carry the belief that they are not successful and not capable of success. Many apparently very successful people do not consider themselves so; just as many perfectly attractive people regard themselves as unattractive. Such people feel envious of others not because of what others have that they don't have, but because of their pathological feelings about themselves. No achievements in the real world will banish the bad feeling.

**Enquirer** Much better to be motivated by desire than by a lack.

**Mentor** In therapy, the discovery of an internal difficulty indicates a therapeutic problem. Envy for another person's achievements is not a therapeutic problem. The belief that you can't do something (if the action is perfectly possible on a practical level) is a therapeutic problem. You can't directly help someone to be successful, but you can directly help someone to remove the belief that he is a failure and to remove internal obstacles to success.

**Enquirer** Would you say that therapy is about helping change a person's belief systems?

**Mentor** Therapy, according to the conception advocated here, is primarily about changing behaviour rather than beliefs. You might think of the undesired behaviour as relating to certain kinds of unconscious beliefs. However, in the model I'm presenting to you, belief would not be an appropriate word to describe unconscious learning. A belief is a phenomenon of the mind, it seems to me, and is therefore something conscious. If behaviour is directed by something unconscious, I'd rather not describe it in terms associated with the conscious mind.

I intend later to explain how unwanted behaviour originally developed as a response to make more bearable a difficult situation in the past. Pathological behaviour is learned; but I wouldn't describe the learning as a belief, since the learning remains unconscious. REP therapy is therefore not about changing a person's intellectual or conscious beliefs but about changing learnings that have developed through experience and have become unhelpful.

Having said that, if a person consciously adheres to a belief that underlies or contributes to her therapeutic problem, changing this belief may be a precondition for resolution of the problem.

**Enquirer** How does a person know she needs therapy – how does she know if she has a therapeutic problem? You don't want therapy to be a waste of money and time. You want to be more attractive, let's say, but you're not pretty and nothing is going to change that. You want to become rich, but you just don't have the skills. Such people don't need therapy; they need a new face or different genes.

**Mentor** There may be practical ways of achieving goals like those. If you want to be more attractive, you set yourself this goal and take action to achieve it – not with plastic surgery, one would hope, but by paying greater attention to your health or enhancing your appearance by good grooming and flattering clothes. Maybe it's your behaviour, not your looks, that is turning people off. If you want greater wealth, you put more energy into improving your financial circumstances. Or you decide your work is your vocation, despite not being so well paid; or you learn to have a full appreciation for the non-material things in life.

But if you're already doing this and still feel unattractive; or if you try to improve your circumstances but it's not working; or if you achieve success but still feel unsuccessful – then it's likely that you have a therapeutic issue.

It's very important to have appropriate goals. It is by pursuing appropriate goals that you discover internal obstacles interfering with your goals, which can be overcome by the appropriate therapeutic work. Unless you have goals, and pursue them, you don't know whether the problem is in you or in the world. Actually, you don't even know that you have a problem. By formulating explicit goals and working to achieve them, the internal obstacles are revealed – providing the opportunity for healing.

When goals are vague and unformulated, you experience unhappiness, but you don't have a clear idea of why you're unhappy.

**Enquirer** People who have created a distorted reality to justify their behaviour – or have inhibited their consciousness to shut down legitimate hopes and desires – will never apprehend this healing opportunity and are doomed in their unhappiness. It seems to me that human beings are destined to a journey of personal development. In this journey, you're saying, internal obstacles are therapeutic opportunities.

**Mentor** Yes. And opportunities for personal development. Relearning Experience will enable you to resolve the internal obstacles so that you can achieve your goals – or, at least, so that you experience no internal obstacles while pursuing your goals.

**Enquirer** Explicitly formulating goals requires you to question and interrogate what you really want. You may realize that you don't really want those things you thought you wanted.

**Mentor**  That's true. You may realize that a desire you professed for wealth and beauty is not really your desire at all. You may realize that desires you believed were yours are based not on your values but values you have mistaken for your own. Rather than pursue beauty and wealth you might want to challenge and assess the values you are professing. They may be your parents' values or society's values. You may discover that you have skills and knowledge that make a significant contribution, despite having more humble financial means. You may discover that you have personal qualities that make you beautiful to others, even if you're not exquisitely beautiful according to cultural norms.

You can learn to feel good about yourself through valuing your qualities and what you have to offer, rather than feeling bad about yourself because of an unquestioning acceptance of values that aren't actually your own – and how can they be your own if they are against your true interests?

**Enquirer**  Uncomfortable feelings are an opportunity for personal development, if they are acknowledged. But this opportunity involves an openness to not being perfect, and to letting go of the need to protect the ego that wants to claim rectitude.

**Mentor**  If a person is able to do this, she'll have the readiness to change.

## Key points

Rationalizing inappropriate behaviour leads to distortions of reality and inhibits personal development.

Setting and pursuing goals brings opportunities to identify and overcome therapeutic problems and to challenge associated distortions of reality.

# 13

## Conscious and unconscious

**Enquirer** Your theory, you say, is based on the premise that we learn from experience.

**Mentor** Yes. The learning is primarily unconscious. We can't usually articulate what we have learned even when we know that we have had a significant learning. It's not so much a cognitive as a behavioural learning. We learn from experience which situations to repeat and which to avoid; or how to behave in certain situations that will lead to a pleasant experience rather than an unpleasant one.

Sometimes, however, this learning seems to be unhelpful. The body is trying to avoid something that the person consciously wants – and that's the basis of a therapeutic problem.

**Enquirer** But how can a learning from the past help a person in the future, when all situations are different? You never encounter exactly the same situation.

**Mentor** That's true. In fact, we wouldn't be able to learn from experience if the learning only applied to exactly the same experience, since it's impossible for events occurring at different times to be exactly the same. The body compares an upcoming or potential event with previous experiences that are comparable and generalizes from the previous experiences to evaluate the upcoming event. The body is the conscientious librarian of all experiences.

**Enquirer** Like Freud's analogy of the mystic writing pad.

**Mentor** Remind me about that . . .

**Enquirer** Freud believed that everything that has ever happened to a person is recorded by the unconscious, even those things that the conscious mind has no recollection of, and he gives the analogy of the child's mystic writing pad. The child scribbles on the pad and, when she wants a fresh surface to scribble on, peels open the plastic page. The writing on the page disappears, but the scribbles remain permanently on the pad underneath. The conscious mind is represented by the visible scribbles on the plastic page; the unconscious is represented by the pad underneath, where all the marks ever made are recorded indelibly.

**Mentor** The unconscious records everything. It doesn't matter how much time passes: the recording is as clear as ever. There is no time in the unconscious.

**Enquirer** The body evaluates potential events in the light of what has happened in the past, even if there is no conscious recollection of the past experience.

**Mentor** Yes. The person receives this evaluation on a conscious level directly through feelings. Good feelings communicate something beneficial, to be sought after; uncomfortable feelings communicate something detrimental, to be avoided.

The more conscious a person is about his behaviour the more he is in a position of choice. Much behaviour is unconscious. A hypnotherapist will tell you that all the hypnotic phenomena (such as amnesia, analgesia, catalepsy) are common in everyday waking life. The unconscious is operating all the time. We learn how to do things so they can be done unconsciously and automatically. But we have the ability to choose our behaviour consciously.

In extreme circumstances, the unconscious body takes over and completely dictates the body's response. You might have experienced this yourself if you've had some kind of accident. Your body, in the instant, knows exactly how to conduct itself to give you maximum protection from harm.

**Enquirer** The body goes into shock.

**Mentor** Yes. Shock is the state of not being fully conscious, because the unconscious body takes charge. That is why memory for what happened during a traumatic event can often be faulty, incomplete, or absent. The body took over control, and the person was not conscious, or consciousness was substantially usurped, during that time. Compromised consciousness will compromise memory. In the absence of consciousness, the person may have no memory of the event.

**Enquirer** Is anything like that happening when a person has a psychotic episode? It's as if the person loses her conscious mind.

**Mentor** Psychosis is an extreme countermeasure by the unconscious to take control of the person who is unable to function effectively on a conscious level. A gambler came to see me who had lost control of much of the functioning of his conscious mind. It was an extreme but very effective measure to divert the person from his highly destructive pursuit. Not being in his right mind, he couldn't think straight enough to gamble.

**Enquirer** Right.

**Mentor** The unconscious body communicates to the conscious mind what is beneficial and harmful through feelings. The person will want to pursue activities that produce pleasant feelings and avoid activities that produce uncomfortable feelings.

**Enquirer** Indeed. This much we have already established.

**Mentor** However, at the same time, the body is at the service of the conscious mind. It is trying to help the person to do what she consciously intends. The imperatives of the unconscious body can come into conflict with the desires of the conscious mind. The body can't not produce symptoms of discomfort in response to something the body interprets as detrimental – even if the person doesn't want to feel the discomfort because she is pursuing that very thing. The harder the conscious mind tries to quell the symptoms of discomfort, the more insistent they are likely to become.

This is why the body is so insistent: it is an imperative of the body to communicate its discomfort. Feelings have to be more powerful than the will. Despite the indefatigable insistence of feelings, people will nevertheless go to every effort to try to overrule them.

**Enquirer** There's an NLP 'presupposition' that every action or every symptom has or once had a positive intention. Is this what the NLP principle is referring to?

**Mentor** That is another way of looking at it. The 'positive intention' of the body (in responding to a situation that carries uncomfortable feelings) is to flag a situation that it interprets as dangerous. Such feelings can't be overcome through an act of will. Nor can they be overcome by denial or other means: they will find a way of expressing themselves.

**Enquirer** But I'm not entirely convinced. It doesn't seem like there is anything positive going on when a person is driven to behave in ways that are destructive to herself or others.

**Mentor** I think the body always functions to protect the person and never has the intention of being destructive.

**Enquirer** Except in the case of suicide.

**Mentor** Even there, though the result is destruction, the intention isn't to be destructive but to avoid pain where no other option seems possible. The job of the body is to survive and be healthy, avoid danger, keep safe. Human beings also, uniquely, have a conscious mind. The body, the unconscious, works best when it's cooperating with the conscious mind. This means the two agencies need to be in communication. In other words, for a person to be comfortable in her own skin, mind and body need to work together.

**Enquirer** That's congruence.

**Mentor** Yes. Congruence means working together. It isn't the submission of the conscious mind, or of the unconscious body, but the alignment of conscious and unconscious.

But congruence is only ever temporary. The aim is for the conscious mind and unconscious body to align frequently, not to attempt impossibly to share a path. Curiosity, ambition and desire will – and should – always ensure that discomfort is a frequent and familiar accompaniment.

**Enquirer** The body seems to be trying to hold the person back.

**Mentor** Not really. The body has two roles. First, it is at the service of the conscious mind and wants to help the person get what he wants on a conscious level. For this reason it's vital for the person to clearly delineate his goals. If the person is unclear about what he wants, the body can't help him to get it. This is self-evident. It's why fortune favours the bold. Second, it has the duty to look after the health and wellbeing of the person; that is, to champion the person's emotional needs and secure his personal dignity. This second role involves the dual tasks of protecting the person from harm (the need for safety and refuge), and satisfying emotional needs that require social interaction (the need for adventure).

With these parameters, it is easy to see the inevitable potential for discord and contradiction, since the tasks and roles are invariably in conflict.

**Enquirer** Conflict arises when the person wants to do something that the body recognizes as harmful.

**Mentor** The body, with the benefit of all of the person's experience, including that which is not accessible to the conscious mind, has its own notion of what is good for the person and what is harmful, and attempts to communicate this to the conscious mind through feelings (on the level of behaviour), and through emotions (on the level of consciousness). The conscious mind may have other ideas, of course.

I'd like to talk more about the concept of personal dignity and how the body learns from experience a little later, because these ideas are central to the methodology of Relearning Experience.

**Enquirer** The unconscious communicates with the conscious mind through emotions. How does the conscious mind communicate with the body?

**Mentor** The conscious mind doesn't have to make any effort to communicate with the body. Thoughts may be the material of the mind, but they are nevertheless a process of the body. The mind is intimate to the body. Put crudely, the body knows what the mind is thinking. Hence the importance of clarity about what you want.

But the converse is obviously not the case: the mind doesn't have direct access to the information held by the unconscious body. The conscious mind is a wonderful agency but extremely limited in comparison.

**Enquirer** The body communicates, you have said, with the conscious mind through feelings and emotions. The communication is quite discreet, then?

**Mentor** The feeling isn't necessarily discreet. But the meaning of the feeling can be very discreet. You wouldn't want the unconscious talking to you, would you? You might think that you were going crazy! You don't have to do what the body dictates. This freedom is possible because of consciousness.

**Enquirer** You have free will not to go along with the wishes of the body.

**Mentor** Yes – through the agency of consciousness. The more developed the faculty of consciousness, the greater the freedom.

**Enquirer** The communication itself is subtle, since it's not the physical feelings themselves that provide the content of communication but the emotions associated with them.

**Mentor** That's right. Physical feelings are just physical feelings – though they may be pleasant or unpleasant. The content of the communication requires the attention of the conscious mind.

**Enquirer** But the feelings don't go away just because you don't pay attention to them – just as someone doesn't stop shouting just because you have your hands over your ears.

**Mentor** In fact, they will probably shout louder. Ignoring feelings is a major undertaking. It requires, as we have noted, determination, persistence and effort.

**Enquirer** But many people are up to the task. Is it always wrong?

**Mentor** Yes. Aren't you yet convinced? What happens to people who ignore their feelings?

**Enquirer** They typically make poor decisions.

**Mentor** Yes. That's the risk. And what happens to people who consistently suppress or deny their feelings?

**Enquirer** I don't know. I suppose if you really want to ignore persistent feelings, you will need to suppress or deny them.

**Mentor** If you suppress or deny your feelings consistently, you get depressed. If you don't do that, and if you keep acknowledging them – even though you don't like them – you will have to do something about them, and you won't get depressed.

**Enquirer** How do you work with someone who's depressed?

**Mentor** The depressed person will still have the uncomfortable feelings, even though she is denying and ignoring them. The feelings still persist in the body, in reach of consciousness (providing they are not obscured by medication). The healing or resolution process is the same as for anything else. The REP therapist helps the person to identify the feelings she doesn't want to feel; finds out what makes these feelings so difficult to acknowledge; finds where this difficulty comes from; and resolves the issue at its origins. There is then no longer any reason to suppress the feelings: the feelings can be acknowledged, and the depression lifts.

## Key points

The body evaluates potential events in the light of past experience and communicates to the conscious mind through feelings.

In extreme circumstances the body takes over consciousness, which may compromise conscious recollection of an event.

Congruence, which necessarily occurs only temporarily, is alignment of conscious and unconscious, without domination by either.

The body aims to achieve the desires of the conscious mind – which is why goals should be clearly formulated.

Unconscious communications, transmitted via emotions, are subtle and do not interfere with conscious reckoning.

# 14

## Vulnerability to feelings

**Enquirer** You said that feelings drive behaviour, and you're also suggesting that rationality gives people the freedom to choose their behaviour. Isn't that a contradiction?

**Mentor** Behaviour, as I've argued, is driven by feelings. Without the intervention of consciousness, envious behaviour follows from feelings of envy, guilty behaviour follows from guilty feelings, and so on. Animals, which don't have the agency of a conscious mind with a potential to mediate between feelings and behaviour, express in behaviour exactly what they feel – or, where there is a conflict of feelings, act on the strongest feeling.

**Enquirer** That would explain why behaviourism is a good way to explain animal behaviour.

**Mentor** Human beings, however, can mediate their behaviour according to conscious will – that is, through consciousness. We have this amazing faculty, reason or rationality, a product of consciousness, which potentially enables free choice of action.

However, if feelings are denied, the feelings need to find expression in behaviour. This occurs outside of conscious awareness.

Freedom – conscious freedom to act, that is – is therefore compromised when feelings are not acknowledged. When feelings are acknowledged, a person can choose how to respond to them.

Think of the example we considered previously – feeling envious about someone's attractiveness or financial success. If you deny the feeling, it will find a way to express itself when your defences are lowered, and may well express itself in an insidious and pernicious way. If you acknowledge the feeling, you can choose to act in a positive way that will serve your true interests.

**Enquirer** Okay, I understand. If you deny your feelings you are likely to behave badly and you'll explain and justify your behaviour through the potentially faulty and dishonest faculty of reason. But how does awareness of your emotions give you control over your behaviour?

**Mentor** If you don't want to admit you feel envy (for example), and ignore the messages from your body, which come in the form of a physical feeling and accompanying emotion, your body will find a way to express the emotion you're trying to deny. This is a good thing. The body needs to assert its feelings. You need your body to use this principle in its operations, even if you don't like the feelings or behaviour in a particular circumstance.

If you deny your feeling, you create a conflict between what you want on a conscious level (you want not to have this horrible or immoral envious feeling), and what your body wants to express (that the other person has something you want and haven't got).

**Enquirer** If you deny the feeling of envy, you're battling against yourself, because your body wants you to know that you also want what the other person has.

**Mentor** Your body will naturally express your needs. Behaving well while denying your feelings requires you to keep your guard up to prevent the suppressed need from expressing itself. But there are times you won't manage to maintain your guard.

**Enquirer** That is why being a 'good person' – in a sort of nine-teenth century, Christian way – is so difficult. The good person has to deny that she harbours what she would consider to be 'immoral' impulses – since thoughts (and not just behaviour) are subject to moral judgement and censor, and so thoughts considered wrong must be banished. Constraining the expression of the suppressed feelings will require remarkable effort. It's a battleground where the enemy – sin – is always and inevitably more powerful. This explains the church's view that we are all sinners and – providing it can persuade enough people to adopt its view that sin inheres in thoughts as truly as in actions – keeps it in business.

**Mentor** The church is the only winner in the battleground of morality.

It takes a lot of energy to divorce yourself from your feelings. The feelings are always there, lurking, ready to pounce. There will be times when your guard is down, when you're less vigilant. This is when you are most 'vulnerable'.

**Enquirer** The repressed returns when you're tired, intoxicated, or under stress. That's when the true feelings come out.

**Mentor** The conscious mind has loosed its overarching control.

**Enquirer** That's why drunk people sometimes behave inexplicably badly and in a way that seems out of character. The inhibitions are lowered and the body is finally able to express itself. Perhaps people even have a need to get drunk so the body can express itself. I've noticed sometimes people seem to try to repeat traumatic experiences when they're drunk – which seems to the observer a crazy thing to do. Maybe it's the body trying to understand and thereby recover from the traumatic experience.

**Mentor** When a person is drunk (or tired, or stressed) the body is no longer attempting to communicate through feelings.

**Enquirer** That's right. It tried that and got nowhere. Now the body is acting out!

**Mentor** The conscious mind has lost its power to mediate and censor unwelcome behaviour, and feelings translate directly into action.

**Enquirer** When drunk, the angry man doesn't just feel angry, he swears at people, or he hits someone. A woman can become bitchy and impossible. People also act out their sadness, exuberance, amorousness, neediness, and everything else that was constrained by what Freud called the superego – but I don't suppose the superego figures in your scheme.

**Mentor** I think Freud's descriptions were intended to be metaphorical and provisional. It's only through the conception of both conscious and unconscious as *mind* that, for Freud, the ego and superego could span both entities. The conception of unconscious mind has led to all sorts of muddled thinking in psychology.

When the conscious mind is compromised because of stress, drugs, tiredness, or some other factor, it loses its power to inhibit actions the person considers unacceptable, and feelings gain sway. The constraints of the conscious mind are useful. Spontaneity can also be great, especially in the expression of happy feelings. But the expression of feelings generally requires conscious direction. Without conscious direction, behaviour is under the sway of feelings.

**Enquirer** So what Freud believed to be instinctual drives of the chaotic id is simply the body trying to express suppressed feelings when the guard of consciousness is inhibited. Your position and that of Freud sound fairly similar to me.

The development from infant to adult is about gradually developing this conscious guard. Children are told all the time to constrain or inhibit their behaviour. Maturity is about learning to behave yourself despite what you feel. This is the ego containing the id.

**Mentor** During teenage years, the child needs to develop principles to guide behaviour, while consciousness brings awareness of what her feelings mean. Principles, allied with consciousness, create moral responsibility.

**Enquirer** Moral responsibility requires conscious acknowledgement of feelings.

**Mentor** If the person denies her feelings, the body still needs to find a way to express itself. But if the person acknowledges her feelings, the body's communications have been successful. It's then up to the conscious mind to determine how to behave in response to this feeling. This special consciousness results in moral behaviour.

**Enquirer** But the feeling of envy, hate, or whatever, is still there.

**Mentor** The intensity of the feeling is bound to reduce if the conscious mind properly acknowledges the needs of the body. The acknowledgement will reduce the urgency of the message: the message has been received, so it is no longer so pressing. But the person still needs to take action.

**Enquirer** One way to put it is that the body needs to express what the mind denies. If the conscious mind acknowledges the problem, action is pretty sure to follow and the body won't need to express it.

Isn't physical illness also an expression of what the mind denies?

**Mentor** Yes, I'm sure very often that is the case.

**Enquirer** Is the acknowledgement of emotions really so difficult? The penalties for ignoring them seem so onerous and the advantages of acknowledging them seem so great.

**Mentor** People very often judge their emotions negatively, and so want to deny them. Even more significantly, acknowledgement will require action. How can you acknowledge that something is wrong and not want to do something about it? Yet much easier to do nothing. If you deny what you feel, you can avoid the need to take action: the message has been denied, disavowed.

**Enquirer** Acknowledging the emotion requires you to do something about it – or what kind of fool are you?

**Mentor** If you acknowledge the message, it has got through and you have to do something about it. The message has achieved its purpose.

## Key points

When feelings are acknowledged, behaviour can be directed consciously and rationally.

Denying feelings creates a conflict within the person between conscious mind and unconscious body.

When the conscious mind is unable to function strongly, the body is likely to express suppressed feelings in problematic behaviour.

# 15

## Acceptable emotions

**Enquirer** You said that the body is doing its best to do what's good for you. But feelings can drive people to all sorts of abominable behaviour.

I understand the idea that envy or anger are not bad in themselves because this is how the body tells you that you're not content with your present circumstances, or something else that you need to know.

But what about other bad behaviour – motivated, according to your argument, by feelings, by the body? For example, the mischief people get up to in relation to their addiction. The violence that can accompany anger. The feelings that lead to a terrible choice of partner.

**Mentor** The person's behaviour is not the fault of the emotion. It never is. If you deny the emotion it has to find insidious expression. But if you acknowledge the emotion you can choose how to behave.

**Enquirer** All right. But the feeling drives the behaviour so, according to your methodology, the feeling must be responsible.

**Mentor** Even if the feeling drives the behaviour, the person is nevertheless always responsible for her behaviour. Human beings are responsible for their feelings, even though feelings are involuntary. It's in a person's interests, and perhaps it's her civic duty, to acknowledge how she feels. By acknowledging her feelings a person is in a position to use consciousness to direct behaviour.

**Enquirer** What about anger? You can acknowledge that you're angry – it's hard not to – and still express your anger in an aggressive way.

**Mentor** You're right. It's not so easy to disavow anger. And it's easy to declare that your anger is someone else's fault. Blame is native to anger. Anger readily points externally to hold another responsible. So anger is often easier to admit to.

Other emotions more readily point inwards and are often more difficult to admit to. Guilt and fear, for example. Guilt implies you're to blame; and fear can suggest weakness.

**Enquirer** Men can admit anger because they can be angry and still be right.

**Mentor** If you don't take responsibility for your emotions, blaming someone else lets you off the hook. He made you angry and he's responsible for your angry reaction. Absurd, yes; but a very common stance.

Acknowledging the emotion also entails taking responsibility for it. Blaming others for one's anger is not taking responsibility for the emotion. You are accountable for your behaviour, not what you feel; and you can hold others to account for their behaviour, not for your feelings. Nobody else is responsible for your feelings.

However, people often deny their anger, because they disapprove of it. They may be frightened by anger, or they may be embarrassed to admit to being angry.

In fact, anger, especially anger that lingers some time after the event, is very often self-anger, projected – externalized – on to someone else. This is not always the case, of course: sometimes a person blames herself rather than the perpetrator. This is commonly true of children who were abused. But very often, when a person blames someone else, she's really most angry with herself, and needs to forgive herself.

**Enquirer** You said something similar earlier. Can it really be true that anger is often redirected self-anger?

**Mentor** Yes. Check it out next time you're angry; or think about something you're still angry about and feel you should have got over by now. The greatest part of your anger is probably with yourself for your part in what went wrong. But it's much more convenient, more comfortable, to blame someone else. You don't want it to be you who's done wrong.

**Enquirer** People want to be right. Admitting to being wrong, getting it wrong, is so difficult. But anger, like any other emotion, is fine if it's appropriate.

**Mentor** That's right. If it's really yourself who you're angry with, aggression towards another person is displacing the anger. If you blame someone else for your anger you are not taking responsibility for your emotions. Anger with yourself can certainly be appropriate – providing you are able to move along from it fairly quickly.

**Enquirer** Taking responsibility for your emotions, rather than blaming someone else for them, is the heart of emotional intelligence. If you are able to recognize that you are actually most angry with yourself, how do you overcome your self-anger? Is it difficult?

**Mentor** You can overcome your self-anger by identifying and accepting the learning that you need to take from the experience. If you consciously learn from the experience, then you'll usually be able to forgive yourself quite readily. If you forgive yourself, you'll no longer feel angry.

**Enquirer** How important is forgiveness in healing? You hear about how important it is to forgive. Does someone have to forgive the perpetrator in order to get over her anger?

**Mentor** People do say that. In fact, you don't need to forgive your perpetrator to get over a problem. But if you are cross with yourself, you do need to forgive yourself.

**Enquirer** Forgiveness is a good thing, though, isn't it?

**Mentor** Maybe from a theological perspective. As a therapist, I'm not concerned with the issue of forgiveness, except with regards to healing. Self-forgiveness is important for healing. Forgiveness is also important in couples therapy or family therapy because of ongoing relationships. In other circumstances, forgiving or not forgiving another person is usually pretty academic. The third-party wrongdoer is probably long gone and doesn't know and almost certainly doesn't care in the least if he is forgiven. It would be different if the wrongdoer has apologized and feels a deep need for forgiveness; or, as I say, if the person has an ongoing relationship with the wrongdoer.

You certainly don't need to forgive the wrongdoer in order to heal. Why would you want to forgive someone who is not sorry for what he has done? I can't see any benefit in doing that. But you do need to let go of the anger; and, if there's any self-blame, you do need to forgive yourself.

**Enquirer** Then I'll let go of trying to forgive my transgressors. But there's still the challenge of feeling angry and behaving well.

**Mentor** If you acknowledge the emotion, and take responsibility for it, it's not a problem to behave well. Behaving well, which means behaving respectfully but not unassertively, involves the appropriate expression of your anger.

**Enquirer** Saying 'you made me angry' is not taking responsibility for your anger.

**Mentor** That's right. You're not taking responsibility, and you're giving another person power over your emotions – which is in itself a reason to be angry (with yourself). When you take responsibility for your emotions, you can't blame others for what you feel. But you can – from a position of authority that comes from speaking with emotional maturity – hold them to account for their actions. By taking responsibility for what you feel, you can judge the person's behaviour without blaming the other for how you feel.

It's a simple principle but people often find it very hard to understand – probably because the failure to differentiate one's own emotions from those of others is the basis of co-dependency.

**Enquirer** I do understand. I'm not responsible for other people's feelings and they're not responsible for mine. It's such a stress trying to second guess another's feelings in an effort to avoid hurting or offending someone. By paying attention to my behaviour instead I can avoid all the stress. A person's emotional response may of course have nothing to do with my behaviour. If the person's emotional response is misplaced, or too intense, then the feeling is inappropriate – and not my concern.

**Mentor** Yes. And you can always be sensitive to the feelings of others – providing you're not inappropriately shielding them from alternative viewpoints that would be useful for them to encounter.

Any emotion not appropriate in the present must come from the past. This could be any time in the past, including the recent past or very early childhood.

**Enquirer** If the emotion is not an appropriate response to the present circumstance, it must come from somewhere else.

**Mentor** That is the key to the creation and the resolution of a therapeutic problem. If an emotion is unhelpful and inappropriate in the present circumstance, it comes from a past experience.

**Enquirer** That could be one reason why a person might want to deny his emotions – because they are inappropriate in the present circumstances. It's ridiculous for me to be angry, resentful, guilty, or whatever it is; the circumstances don't warrant it: so I'll pretend I don't feel it.

**Mentor** Yes. The person sees that the emotion is not appropriate, and therefore regards it as unacceptable. Inappropriate or over-intense emotions are undesirable. What should you do with emotions that are considered unacceptable? They can be denied, suppressed or ignored.

**Enquirer** But of course it is vital that they are acknowledged.

## Key points

Anger is easier to acknowledge than some emotions because it suggests the responsibility lies with someone else.

You are accountable for your behaviour, not what you feel; others are accountable for their behaviour, not your emotions.

If an emotion isn't appropriate in the present, it derives from an unresolved experience in the past.

People often deny emotions that they disapprove of or regard as inappropriate or unacceptable.

Most anger is displaced self-anger. Self-anger can be forgiven if the learning is consciously extracted.

Forgiveness of the perpetrator is not necessary for healing to occur.

# 16
## Rationalization

**Mentor**  When somebody behaves badly because of denial of her feelings, how does she then account for her behaviour? For example, imagine that there's someone who is envious of you and so behaves badly towards you. Would she admit to herself that she's behaving badly?

**Enquirer**  She would probably justify and explain her behaviour in a way that is favourable to her and puts the other at fault.

**Mentor**  That's right. She would rationalize her behaviour by explaining it and giving reasons for it. She won't say, *I was mean because I felt envious* – though this is the truth behind her behaviour. She would say, rather, that the other person is stupid, or arrogant; and she would use half-truths and exaggerations – making her bad behaviour somehow the fault of the other person.

This way of attacking others is very common when a person denies the feelings that underlie her behaviour. She rationalizes her bad behaviour, and thereby distorts reality. She falsely attributes negative qualities to the other person so that she can hide from herself the characteristics she doesn't want to admit to having. She makes up reasons to justify her abuse of the other.

If a person feels envious towards you, she may construe you to be the inadequate, inferior one – although this is what she's feeling about herself. She feels inferior around you because you have qualities she desires, and she tells herself that you are considering yourself to be superior – when in fact she is feeling inferior.

This is the mechanism of projection, the externalization of a person's issues. Do you see how it works? She feels envious of you, but doesn't want to admit it. She feels inferior to you, but denies this feeling. So she claims that you are claiming to be, or behaving as if you are, superior to her. And if you challenge and resist that, as you may well, she accuses you (not necessarily to your face) of being envious of her! Projection of her motivations allows her to evade responsibility for her feelings: you are at fault; you are responsible.

We can avoid all these distortions of reality created by prejudice simply by acknowledging what we feel.

**Enquirer** You feel strongly about this.

**Mentor** It's the key to living an emotionally healthy life. It's the key to emotional intelligence and mutual respect.

**Enquirer** And world peace.

**Mentor** The tendency to rationalize is so ubiquitous, and so dangerous. Acknowledging feelings defends us from behaving badly.

**Enquirer** Please give me another example of the consequences of denying feelings, just to help me to be clear.

**Mentor** You're feeling irritable and snap at a colleague. You feel guilty but don't want to admit it to yourself. You can't bear to admit that you've done wrong. So, instead, you justify your behaviour by emphasizing the faults of your colleague. These criticisms are an effort to excuse your own behaviour.

**Enquirer** Admitting to yourself your irritable feelings would make you less likely to snap at your colleague.

**Mentor** You might snap at him because you're feeling irritable. You don't need to be perfect; everyone's entitled to be irritable. But you wouldn't justify your behaviour and criticize your colleague unfairly. You'd recognize that your behaviour derived from your feelings and wasn't the fault of your colleague. You may well admit your fault and apologize.

**Enquirer** You believe that behaviour has a positive purpose. This is similar to the NLP presupposition we mentioned earlier, that all behaviour has or once had a positive intention. But I struggle with this idea. Let me tell you what I have in mind.

A good friend of mine for partners chooses abusive men. Not a rare situation, I'm sure. When one abusive relationship ends, she finds another. I'm sure this choice isn't conscious: she wouldn't deliberately choose to hurt herself. But how is the 'body' doing its best to do what's good for her if it just finds people who will be abusive towards her?

**Mentor** You're concerned that your partner's behaviour is not positive. But the suggestion is not that the behaviour itself is positive or has a positive consequence but that the *intention* behind the behaviour is – or once was – positive.

This idea is actually a foundation of the resolution work of REP. We'll see later that what is identified as problem behaviour was, originally, the best way the person could find at the time to handle a difficult situation. In my view it's a helpful thing – it's a useful principle – for inappropriate feelings (such as the desire for a potentially abusive partner) to try to express themselves, because it provides an opportunity to identify a problem and to heal and change. Without these challenges, there'd be no motivation for personal development.

**Enquirer** And without opportunities for personal development life would lose its purpose. It would seem a high price to pay.

**Mentor** In the circumstances you describe, your friend would in all probability know very early on, and possibly right from the very start, that she's chosen an abusive partner, but she still sticks with him. Why would she do that? To an observer it would seem to be crazy behaviour. No doubt she'll have many rationalizations for choosing her partner and staying with him. But what's the real reason your friend stays, do you think?

**Enquirer** Well, her abusive partners are all just like her father. But why would she want to choose someone who is like her abusive father? Wouldn't you rather want to run away from such a person?

**Mentor** Isn't it because the body wants to resolve the childhood issue? That's how I see it. No doubt there is a bundle of psychological problems associated with her relationship with her father. She needs to work these out before she can choose a suitable partner and have a good relationship. She doesn't know how to have a good relationship, because her model of relationships is fundamentally flawed. By resolving the relationship with her father she will finally learn how to have loving and caring relationships.

The resolution to the problem need not involve her actual father at all. It's the historical relationship, which she's carrying around in her psyche, that needs resolution. She might have developed, in the present, a very good relationship with her father. It's very possible. The present relationship might not need healing; but the historical problems haven't yet been resolved. With the resolution of the historical problem relationship, she can begin to develop her own way of relating healthily in an intimate partnership.

**Enquirer** I can see why she needs to resolve her relationship with her father first. And she will keep choosing him – or someone very like him in a crucial aspect – until she works it out. But isn't resolving such a relationship extremely difficult?

**Mentor** Remember that we're resolving a historical relationship that no longer exists except in the body of the person with the problem. The problem is internal to the person and resolution of the problem does not involve the other party.

**Enquirer** So you don't need to resolve the relationship with the father in the present?

**Mentor** The person's current relationship with her father is irrelevant: it's the historical relationship that is preventing her from having a successful and fulfilling relationship in the present. Resolving the historical relationship might not benefit the person's current relationship with her father (who might be dead) – though it might well.

So, no, it is not difficult to resolve the relationship. You look sceptical. But this work is not long or arduous.

**Enquirer** Give me an example, then.

**Mentor** I'm thinking of a person who couldn't let go of her philandering boyfriend. They had been together for ten years.

**Enquirer** Martha.

**Mentor** The boyfriend had left Martha five times before. Always without warning – out of the blue. Of course, each time he had met and started a relationship with another woman. And each time, after between three and five months, when the relationship ended, he would insinuate himself back into Martha's life again. And she always took him back. She knew she shouldn't, but she couldn't seem to help herself.

When she came to see me he had recently left her again, and she was devastated. She couldn't go through this again. She needed help to let go of him. Why couldn't she let go of him? She had a number of rationalizations: she thought she'd be able to change him; she loved him; when things were good they got on so well. None of this explained why, despite her efforts, Martha still wanted him back, hoped he would make contact, and felt such unbearable guilt and sadness.

**Enquirer** So why couldn't she let go of him, and how were you able to help?

**Mentor** Many years earlier, when Martha was in her twenties her father had, without warning, left her mother for another woman. He was soon married and started another family. The separation of her parents had been dramatic, unexpected and very distressing. Martha was very angry and had not seen her father since. She didn't want to; she was still mad at him. Even though she had previously had a wonderful relationship with her dad, she shut him out completely from her life and had had no contact with him at all.

Repeatedly taking back her boyfriend was a displacement for Martha's real need, which was to have a relationship with her father. Once the traumatic past events were processed, Martha was able to open her heart again to her father. In doing so, it was much easier for her to let go of her (former) boyfriend – although more work was required before this became possible. She also, crucially, needed to make a deliberate, conscious decision to close any possibility of renewing the relationship; for the heart will only let go when the will makes this determination.

## Key points

Projection allows a person to evade responsibility for her feelings and behaviour.

Acknowledgement of feelings is the antidote to problematic behaviour and consequent rationalization and distortion of reality.

Problematic childhood relationships repeat in adult life, as opportunities are provided to heal the dysfunctional 'model' relationships of childhood.

The legacy of a dysfunctional childhood relationship inheres in the body of the affected person, and is healed independently of the other person.

# 17
## Addiction

**Enquirer** Is this a good moment to talk to you about addiction? What's behind addiction? How can addiction be tackled successfully therapeutically? What do you think of Twelve Steps? And how do you help people to stop smoking?

**Mentor** In REP the treatment of addiction is no different from the treatment of any other type of problem; but it can take longer. For the person with an addiction, the most important thing to understand is that the addiction provides a *solution*. Even if the addiction also constitutes a problem for the addicted person, the solution the addictive object provides is of greater value. That's very important.

**Enquirer** How is that possible, when addiction can wreak such havoc? Surely the addiction itself is the biggest problem?

**Mentor** Havoc may be the external perception of the situation, rather than necessarily the perception of the addicted person. For the person locked in addictive behaviour, the solution the addictive object provides is more significant.

**Enquirer** In what way is the addictive object a 'solution'?

**Mentor** What do you think the person with the addiction is trying to get away from?

**Enquirer** I don't know – from circumstances in his life.

**Mentor** Yes. But more directly.

**Enquirer** It could be many different things.

**Mentor** That's true. But there's something which all people with addictions are trying to get away from. It's their feelings. The person with an addiction has very uncomfortable feelings he wants to get away from. The addictive object provides an anaesthetic that dulls the uncomfortable feeling; or it provides a more powerful feeling that overwhelms the uncomfortable feeling.

The point about an addiction, which can make it more difficult to overcome than other therapeutic problems, is that it's a one-stop shop. It works for just about everything. It's therefore a very satisfactory solution for the addicted person. It doesn't matter what the problem is, the addiction provides a solution because it anaesthetizes the bad feelings or produces good feelings that eclipse the bad feelings.

Many addictions also involve an activity, often a ritual, which further serves to take the person away from the uncomfortable feelings or enhances the good feelings provided by the addictive object.

Addiction can look very complicated, but the solution provided by the addictive object is always the same: numb the bad feelings or generate stronger feelings that overwhelm the bad feelings. Addiction is a systematic way to do this.

**Enquirer** Some addictions create more powerful feelings, such as eating, gambling, pornography; some addictions, such as smoking and alcohol, numb the feelings. I believe the late Allen Carr, creator of the *Easy Way To Stop Smoking* books and workshops, would get his clients to smoke several cigarettes in a row so that they would become sick of smoking just before they stopped. Do you do anything like that when you help people to stop?

**Mentor** When I help someone to stop smoking I always ask the person to have his last cigarette at least an hour and a half before coming to the consultation. I want him to arrive at my office craving a cigarette.

**Enquirer** What's the advantage of that?

**Mentor** We need to access the feelings underlying the desire to smoke. If he's just had a cigarette he'll be numb and won't have much of a desire to smoke.

**Enquirer** Is the purpose of smoking really for smokers just to make themselves numb? Don't they also smoke for pleasure? And doesn't the physical addiction itself play an important part in keeping the person smoking?

**Mentor** Nobody would continue to smoke, knowing what everyone knows about the damage smoking does to the health of the body, if it was just a matter of a physical addiction. Nor would anyone smoke for the 'pleasure' – experienced only through the addiction (nobody gets pleasure from smoking until they become addicted) – which wouldn't be worth the financial cost, never mind the cost to health.

Addiction and pleasure – these are the rationalizations that people give for smoking; the reasons people give to explain why they smoke: they are not why people smoke.

**Enquirer** So why do they smoke?

**Mentor** People smoke for the same reason as any other addiction: to mask the uncomfortable feelings they carry inside them. The anaesthetic effect of smoking seems to work even between cigarettes, since smokers experience a generalized impairment of the capacity to feel. Smoking very effectively provides an ongoing anaesthetic for uncomfortable feelings, and it also gives a powerful momentary surge of feeling when the smoke is inhaled, overwhelming any uncomfortable feelings.

**Enquirer** Unfortunately for the smoker, he has no ability to target this effect specifically: both good and bad feelings are inhibited by smoking.

**Mentor** Yes. His general capacity to feel emotion is reduced. This is the purpose of the habit. Smoking damages health and finances, and it also damages the smoker's connection with his own body. Smoking, however, amplifies the physiological feelings of excitement as the poison makes the heart beat faster. Smokers can't feel happiness, and they're certainly unable to experience subtle feelings at all; but, with the help of a cigarette, they can at least feel excitement.

When a smoker is asked, *Where is the feeling in your body?*, he will often say that the feeling is in his head. Of course, that is not where you have feelings.

**Enquirer** Smokers get stuck in their heads. I used to be like that.

You said that you ask smokers not to smoke for an hour or two before they arrive for their quit-smoking appointment, because you want them to arrive wanting to have a cigarette.

**Mentor** That's right. The person's apparent desire for a cigarette is the basis for the therapeutic work. It's that feeling of discomfort, which the smoker interprets as wanting to smoke, that will provide the information to help him stop. This is the important point: the feeling that prompts the desire for a cigarette isn't actually a desire for a cigarette at all. The feeling has nothing to do with the physical addiction of smoking.

**Enquirer** You're saying that the desire for a cigarette isn't a desire for a cigarette?!

**Mentor** What is taken to be a desire to smoke is something quite different: an uncomfortable feeling coming from a past experience.

**Enquirer** How does a feeling that's got nothing to do with cigarettes become mistaken for a desire to smoke?

**Mentor** Through association. You'll be familiar with Ivan Pavlov's dog experiments. The dog would be fed every time a bell rung, and eventually it would salivate at the sound of the bell.

**Enquirer** Yes. It might have been a metronome rather than a bell. You're referring to the 'conditional' or conditioned reflex. In NLP this response is used deliberately to create an association, called anchoring, to associate (for example) a specific touch and a positive mood, so that the positive mood can be voluntarily triggered using the specific touch.

**Mentor** Like Pavlov's dog which salivated on hearing a bell, or whatever the instrument was, because it expected food, the smoker comes to associate a desire for a cigarette with a bad feeling. The association is formed in this way. You feel bad. You have a cigarette. The bad feeling disappears. Soon the bad feeling is associated with (and attributed to) the need or desire to smoke; and the disappearance of the bad feeling (facilitated by the drug) is associated with the action of smoking.

The therapist's task is to help the person to identify the feelings underlying the desire to smoke. This can involve some effort since, as we've noted, the smoker may initially be unable to recognize his feelings. Once he is able to get in touch with them, we find out where the feelings come from, through the REP process of *tracking*, and do the resolution work. After this, the feelings that were driving the smoking are gone. So the desire to smoke is no longer there. It was the bad feelings associated with the old experience, not the chemicals in the cigarette, that were behind the addiction. It's easy to test. The person arrived wanting a cigarette. After the work, the desire to smoke is no longer there. The uncomfortable feeling underlying that desire is no longer there.

**Enquirer** Is smoking, like other addictions, also a one-stop shop for all the smoker's problems?

**Mentor** Yes, it is. It is convenient, doesn't interfere with general performance, and it's legal. It used to be socially acceptable and permissible almost everywhere – but that's obviously fundamentally changed now.

Although, like any addiction, smoking is the solution for just about any emotional issue – because it takes away the uncomfortable feelings – I've found that helping people to stop smoking usually just requires the resolution of one specific issue. It seems generally to be primarily one issue that underlies the desire to smoke. Once that issue is resolved, the bad feeling associated with that issue disappears and the desire to smoke vanishes with it.

**Enquirer** Is the same true of most other addictions: that there's one primary issue that needs to be resolved; or is it the case that often there is a whole set of problems that must be resolved before the addiction can be overcome?

**Mentor** People with other addictions generally also smoke cigarettes, because smoking is such an effective and convenient anaesthetic. Smoking doesn't do the whole job for such people, but it helps. Other addiction-type issues, including drug addiction and what are called eating disorders, seem to relate to difficult childhoods, involving a range of problems that require healing before the addiction can be overcome.

However, although many addictions seem to be associated with a number of childhood issues, and require substantive therapeutic work, I suspect that there is a primary key (rather than a specific problem) underlying many types of addiction.

**Enquirer** What kind of key?

**Mentor** I suspect that there is an ongoing, unreconciled, and (to the person) apparently irreconcilable dilemma behind serious addictions: the person perceives himself to be in an untenable situation which he can't see any way out of – or the ways out look even worse that his present predicament.

Because he can't see any solution to his situation, he needs something to make the present situation more bearable. The addiction helps to do this by anaesthetizing the bad feelings or overwhelming them with more powerful feelings; and, very often, the addictive substance has the supplement of a symbolic ritual, or even a diversionary alternative lifestyle. If the real world is perceived to be the problem, then a surreal or subreal world to escape to provides an attractive supplement; if the person's physical body is perceived to be the problem, then obsessions about the physical body, such as eating obsessions, may seem to provide an expression.

**Enquirer** Give me an example or two of untenable and irreconcilable situations that a person might experience.

**Mentor** Here are three examples.

First. Imagine that you're up against a situation that demands resourcefulness. In fact, several areas of your life are not working very well and require resourcefulness: your work; your relationships with friends; and your relationship with your partner. The problem is that you have the belief that you're hopeless and unable to resolve problems all by yourself. That's an unreconcilable dilemma: you need resources and believe you haven't got them. You're in a mess, and you know no way to get out of it. You escape from your awful dilemma through the addiction.

Second. The only person who will ever love you (because you have the belief that you're essentially unlovable) is treating you badly, and you'd rather be treated badly than be on your own (and, anyway, being unlovable, you deserve no better). Again, impossible to resolve. Addiction provides frequent temporary escape.

Third. In the public eye you're successful, but in your eyes you're a fraud and don't deserve the acclaim (which you feel you desperately need) because you feel you're not good enough. Again, there's no way out of the dilemma, but the addiction allows you to escape from it or forget about it for a while. Even better if it allows you to enter an alternative world.

These dilemmas may only be glimpsed by the addicted person. Full apprehension would immediately indicate that the dilemma does not have to be hopeless. And this apprehension would be the first step towards resolution.

**Enquirer** I need to think about all that. Addiction isn't the only response to those dilemmas.

**Mentor** What other response might the person have? Resignation; acceptance?

**Enquirer** I see what you mean.

**Mentor** The point about the dilemma is that there is no apparent alternative that is desirable. The alternatives that are apparent – if any are – look even less appealing than the present situation. So change isn't possible, or desirable; only stuckness.

Healing starts with intention to change. As with any other type of emotional issue, the addicted person needs to acknowledge she has a problem; want to take action to remedy the problem; and know what action to take. For the person with an addiction, there is often no intention to change because no change the person envisages looks desirable. The activity of the addiction is therefore the only way out of the problem that she can see. That's why denial is so prevalent.

**Enquirer** For Twelve Steps 'recovery' is perpetual.

**Mentor** Twelve Steps shares the addicted person's perception. There is no way out of the addiction and no solution. The person must just accept that she is a lifelong addict. That's not helpful. There are always alternatives. The addicted person needs guidance about what alternatives are possible. But until those alternatives look more appealing than the present behaviour, the person will have no motivation to change, and no change will be possible.

**Enquirer** There's something else I often wonder about. People sabotage themselves, don't they? Don't people sometimes have a need to subvert their own interests? I'm thinking of Freud's death instinct, Thanatos. Isn't addiction an example of self-sabotage?

**Mentor**  No. I wouldn't look at it like that. I don't think that anyone intentionally sabotages herself. Even if that's the perceived effect of the behaviour, it's not the intention. The underlying, if unconscious, intention is always positive.

Addictions can be difficult to overcome because they differ from most therapeutic problems in a crucial respect. Most therapeutic problems involve a behaviour that was developed in the past to provide a solution to a problematic experience, but the behaviour is now experienced not as a solution but as an impediment – though there may be 'secondary' benefits. In contrast, addictions continue to provide, in the perception of the addicted person, an effective solution in the present. In other words, addictions provide a perceived benefit to the person in the present, whereas other types of therapeutic problem seem to be chiefly detrimental in the present.

## Key points

Addiction, which is primarily emotional rather than chemical, provides a one stop shop solution for the addicted person.

The addicted person often feels his situation has no solution.

The addictive object provides an anaesthetic and, sometimes, a diverting ritual or alternative lifestyle.

As with any emotional issue, healing requires (1) acknowledgement of a problem; (2) the will to change; and (3) a more appealing behaviour.

# 18

# Practical goals and therapeutic problems

**Enquirer** You've been clear that a psychotherapeutic problem is not a problem of the mind and so 'mental' health is a misnomer. Psychotherapeutic problems, or therapeutic problems, as you also call them, are about emotions, not about thinking.

**Mentor** Yes. You'll recall near the beginning of our discussion that I described a psychotherapeutic problem as occurring when you are doing something you don't want to do or not doing something you want to do, or feeling something you don't want to feel. I explained that it's not thoughts that make you behave in ways you don't like, but feelings – because if it were thoughts we could just change them; but feelings are involuntary; and feelings, not thoughts, drive behaviour. I might have added that feelings are more powerful than conscious will. So if there's a battle in a person between feelings and thoughts, or between feelings and will, to dictate his behaviour, feelings will ultimately win.

**Enquirer** Why do you say 'ultimately'?

**Mentor** I say 'ultimately' because, with a great effort of will, the person can have temporary victories over his feelings.

**Enquirer** Let's have an example.

**Mentor** For example, a person has a problem with eating more than allows him to keep slim (a lifelong struggle for many of us). He wants to be slim, and with great effort of will he can diet and lose a few pounds – even quite a few pounds. But what happens? Invariably, he puts them on again. The great effort of will is unsustainable and his feelings will prevail sooner or later.

**Enquirer** That's why diets don't work. You need to deal with the underlying issues.

**Mentor** It is a good thing in general that feelings win out over conscious intentions, because feelings are more reliable than thinking when it comes to self-preservation. If there's a bus bearing down on you, debating whether to be or not to be is mistimed. You need to get out of the way of that bus and consider the merits and demerits of being when the issue is less pressing. The body takes over – the feeling is so intense that evasive action is mandatory – and the person moves out of the way of the bus as fast and efficiently as is possible.

The body responds to threats to emotional wellbeing – or threats to *personal dignity* – with no less urgency. Shame and humiliation are as damaging to a person as physical injury. The fear of shame and humiliation is as palpable as the fear of physical danger.

**Enquirer** That all makes sense. I'm still not really clear what a psychotherapeutic problem is. How would you differentiate a psychotherapeutic problem from a practical problem? An athlete wants to perform better. A co-worker isn't getting the promotion he wants. Don't people look for therapeutic help for these problems? But they don't sound like therapeutic problems, do they?

**Mentor** The distinction between a practical problem and a therapeutic problem is very pertinent in REP. People who have a therapeutic problem very often don't know what the therapeutic problem is. And, actually, they don't care.

**Enquirer** What do you mean by saying that people don't care about their therapeutic problem?

**Mentor** They're not interested. In the perspective of REP, the therapeutic problem is of concern to the therapist, not to the client. The client is concerned about achieving a specific goal, changing her undesirable behaviour, eliminating an uncomfortable feeling; she is not concerned about overcoming a therapeutic problem – which is a task that would seem abstract and philosophical. This is why clients are not necessarily excited about overcoming a therapeutic problem. The REP client arrives with a therapeutic problem she has had for years, and leaves without it. What an achievement! But she is frequently underwhelmed.

**Enquirer** I'm not quite sure what you're saying.

**Mentor** A person identifies she has a problem when she's unable to achieve something she wants – let's call that a practical goal – and recognizes there's something in her (the therapeutic problem) that is preventing her from achieving what she wants. It's the practical achievement that the person is concerned about; it's not the therapeutic problem. The practical goal is tangible; the therapeutic problem is an abstract concept. When someone can't achieve a practical goal because of something going on inside her, she recognizes that she has what we're calling a therapeutic or psychotherapeutic problem, for which she requires therapeutic help. The therapeutic problem in itself is of no concern to her – except in as much as she recognizes that it interferes with her goal.

In short, the person presents for therapy generally because there's something specific – which we are calling a practical goal – that she wants but she's unable to achieve. She feels she should be able to achieve this goal, but can't. The obstacle, she recognizes, is internal, it's something in her.

An athlete, for example, is not going to seek therapeutic help to perform better if she feels she's reached the limit of her capacity, or if she knows what is required of her (such as more rigorous training) in order to perform better, but simply doesn't want to do it. She seeks therapeutic help because she feels she can improve her performance but senses that there's something in her that is preventing her from doing this. She may well not know what that something is; a person very often has no conscious idea what is stopping her behaving in a way consistent with achieving her practical goal. But she knows very clearly that the problem is internal; that the struggle is with an aspect of herself.

**Enquirer** I understand the distinction you're making. The practical goal is what the person wants to achieve; the therapeutic problem is the issue internal to the person stopping the person achieving this goal. Give me examples of a therapeutic problem that might stop an athlete from, say, running as fast as she believes she's capable.

**Mentor** It might be fear of success. It might be a desire not to achieve better than her sibling. It might be that there is a conflict in her between the desire to train and some other interest, and this is preventing her from training rigorously. This 'interest' could be a demanding boyfriend, for example. She wants to do the training, and considers this to be a high priority, but she submits to her boyfriend's demands to spend time with him instead. Or the therapeutic problem can be anything else, of course. Maybe it's just not so important to her and it's others who want her to achieve more. The therapist needs to determine what the therapeutic obstacle is: the thing that is in her that's stopping her from achieving her practical goal.

**Enquirer** If it's not her own goal but the goal of others, then the problem is external not internal, and the therapist can't help. If the practical goal is to be able to run faster, the therapeutic obstacle is the thing in her that's stopping her from running faster. But she probably doesn't know on a conscious level what that obstacle is.

Not knowing what the obstacle is might stop a person presenting for therapy – if she thinks the therapist won't know and won't be able to find out. Not having an appropriate goal may also prevent a person seeking therapy.

What if the person has failed to get a promotion? What might be the therapeutic problem for him?

**Mentor** The person who has failed to get promotion must believe there is an internal deficiency, an emotional block, interfering with his prospects.

**Enquirer** He believes that he has the necessary experience, qualifications and skills. If he didn't believe this, he would need to improve these; he wouldn't need therapy. If a person doesn't have the necessary experience, qualification or skills, the question is, how does he get the requisite experience, qualification or skills?

**Mentor** That's right. Therapy doesn't provide skills – unless the skill required is the very particular one of emotional intelligence, which a therapist may be the right person to teach. There may however be therapeutic obstacles which are interfering with him gaining the qualifications or skills.

**Enquirer** Yes. All that is true, no doubt. However, therapy is not necessarily going to change the opinion of his employers and make them see their error in not promoting him. Nor will they necessarily perceive the change in him and change their perception of him. Even if the problem is internal, therapy won't necessarily lead to promotion.

**Mentor** If he presents for therapy it's because he realizes that there's something in him that's stopping him from moving forward in his career. His goal is practical: he can't get the promotion he wants. But he realizes that what's preventing this from happening is something in him, not something external. An internal transformation may or may not be recognized by his employers; but it gives him a better chance.

**Enquirer** What kind of internal issues might he have?

**Mentor** There are many possibilities. It might be that promotion involves assuming authority and he has an issue with authority; or that he does not want the additional responsibility or burden of extra work that promotion will bring; or that promotion will mean managing people and he has a lack of assertiveness or boundaries. These are all therapeutic problems.

**Enquirer** Really? I would have thought these were matters of personality, rather than therapeutic issues. It's a therapeutic problem if a person doesn't want additional work?

**Mentor** It may be. But it may not be. Perhaps the person just needs to work out what his priorities are. Coaching would determine that without the need for therapeutic intervention.

But if they are indeed therapeutic issues, they can be resolved through REP – providing the person wants to make the change.

**Enquirer** My notion of a therapeutic problem has expanded.

I'm sure that people often think their problem is just the way they are made, and don't realize there's a reason for their behaviour and that they can change.

**Mentor** That's true. People often don't see their emotional limitations as therapeutic issues that can be resolved.

**Enquirer** So any time a person can't achieve what they want they should consider the possibility that they have a therapeutic problem.

But the practical achievement is not directly the concern of the therapist; the therapist's job is to identify and resolve the therapeutic obstacles which are stopping the person achieving his goals.

**Mentor** By definition, a therapeutic problem can be resolved – at least, in the philosophy and with the methods of Relearning Experience Process. Resolution of the therapeutic problem makes the practical problem achievable in a way that it wasn't before. The person still has to take the required action to achieve the practical goal; and achievement may still depend on external factors not in the person's control.

**Enquirer** And the thing that's in him that's holding him back – his problem with authority, problem with boundaries, or whatever the problem is – this is known to his employers, and that's why they don't promote him?

**Mentor** It may well be known to them, either consciously or unconsciously; but not necessarily.

**Enquirer** The reason that he's not getting a promotion might be something totally different; something that doesn't relate to a therapeutic problem at all. His employer might not like him, or has someone else lined up for the job. Or the employer sees limitations – real or imagined – that the person has no inkling of.

**Mentor** That's perfectly true. He might not even have the requisite skills or experience but just thinks he has. He might not even know what these are. The therapist should, where possible, interrogate all of this.

**Enquirer** Therapy is a complex business!

**Mentor** Helping the person to overcome his therapeutic problem may not necessarily lead to promotion, but it will certainly benefit him in other ways. By presenting for therapy he believes that there is something in him that's holding him back and needs to change. The therapist helps him to make that change. That's the therapist's responsibility. The practical goal is not the therapist's responsibility.

**Enquirer** The person recognizes that the problem is something in him, because we know these things unconsciously.

**Mentor** That's true. For this person the mistake would be to change jobs if the problem is internal to him. He would just be taking his problem somewhere else.

**Enquirer** I'm sure that people often do that.

**Mentor** Yes, they do. People try to run away from their problems. It's a form of projection. The problem isn't me. It's them. Or it's here. So I'll go somewhere else.

**Enquirer** If, after the therapeutic work is done, the person remains stuck in his post, then he should consider changing jobs. Maybe it is the others, not him!

## Key points

Feelings drive behaviour, overruling conscious thinking, because safety (physical and emotional) is too important to be left to the unreliable and whimsical conscious mind.

A practical goal is something that a person wants but can't seem to achieve because of an obstacle inhering in the person.

A therapeutic problem is the issue internal to the person stopping her from achieving the practical goal.

Resolution of the person's therapeutic issue is the task of the REP therapist. Achievement of the practical goal remains the task of the person herself.

# 19
## Psychotherapy descriptions

**Enquirer** You said, 'It's feelings that make you do what you don't want to do or stop you from doing what you want to do.' Is it feelings or emotions?

**Mentor** They are different manifestations of the same thing. The physical feeling drives behaviour. The emotion carries the information or message to consciousness. The feeling – if it's inappropriate – relates to a past experience. The consciousness required to apprehend the emotion helps to bring the person to a place of conscious choice.

**Enquirer** Because you speak specifically about psychotherapeutic problems, I thought I'd do a little internet research and see how they're described.

**Mentor** That's interesting. What is a psychotherapeutic problem, according to your research?

**Enquirer** Well, that's the interesting thing. Usually, a psychotherapeutic problem is not defined. Not only is it not defined, it doesn't even seem really to exist. Psychotherapeutic problems are discussed in the most general terms – as if they have no definition, or need no definition, or are not important. I also thought I'd look up 'psychological problem'.

**Mentor**  Oh, yes? What is a psychological problem, according to your research?

**Enquirer**  I found lists of 'disorders' categorized according to the *Diagnostic and Statistical Manual of Mental Disorders* (DSM). I don't think I want to be diagnosed with one of those disorders.

**Mentor**  And they wonder why emotional ill health is stigmatized. Who wants to be classified as having a mental disorder?

**Enquirer**  I have visions of officious-looking people in white coats. I don't get cold 'disorders' or viral 'disorders'; why should I have a mental 'disorder'? Maybe it's just to make it sound scientific. Unless it's scientific it can't be officially recognized – not in England anyway. Emotional problems sound normal and ordinary.

**Mentor**  Did you also look at how psychotherapy is defined?

**Enquirer**  Yes, I did. Primarily, psychotherapy is defined as a treatment for mental health problems – which are categorized as specific 'disorders'. I looked up these goals of psychotherapy, too.

**Mentor**  What did you find?

**Enquirer**  Broadly, the goals of psychotherapy are similar to the definition of psychotherapy.

**Mentor**  What are the goals? Is there much agreement?

**Enquirer**  Yes, there's a lot of agreement. 'One of the key objectives of psychotherapy', the UK National Health Service website says, 'is to help you gain a better understanding of the issues that are troubling you.'

These are the goals of psychotherapy according to psychotherapist Dr Bill Cloke of billcloke.com. It's a good example of a typical list of goals.

> (1) To know yourself better. (2) Alleviate emotional pain or confusion. (3) Assist you in developing a more complete understanding

of your psychological issues. (4) Establish more effective coping mechanisms. (5) Foster a more accurate understanding of your past and what you want for your future.

On the website sacramentopsychology.com the goals of psychotherapy are listed as 'abilities' under the three headings, *Healthy thinking, Healthy feeling, Healthy behaving.*

Here's another description of the goals of psychotherapy, by therapist Anna Frost, from psychcentral.com:

> From its inception through the present, the fundamental purpose of psychotherapy remains to strengthen the mind, the psyche and the soul. In the valuing of our words, talk therapy teaches us the value of taking ourselves seriously.

But maybe the problem is, rather, that we take ourselves too seriously. I'm not sure what strengthen mind, psyche and soul would mean.

How about this description, by Maharishi Mahesh Yogi, quoted on the psychologytoday.com site:

> The ultimate fulfillment of psychology lies in enabling the individual mind to tune itself and remain tuned to the cosmic mind, in bringing a fast coordination of the individual mind with the cosmic mind, so that all the activity of the individual mind is in conformity with the cosmic evolution and with the purpose of cosmic life.

I didn't really understand that one. Although it sounds rather like Abraham Maslow talking about transcendence.

**Mentor** Not much about resolving problems, then?

**Enquirer** Not that I could find. Psychotherapy apparently leads to understanding, alleviating, coping, managing – these were the words that came up repeatedly – and to personal development, which presumably comes about through greater understanding of oneself and is a result of the psychotherapy process.

**Mentor** Did that surprise you? Did you suppose that is what psychotherapy is about?

**Enquirer** No. Naively, I thought it was about resolving problems. Or maybe I have been influenced by your conception.

But isn't that why people present for therapy – to resolve emotional problems? People who don't have therapeutic problems – or, rather, people who don't have unachieved practical goals as a result of internal obstacles – don't go to a psychotherapist, do they? Nice to understand your problem, I suppose. But you really want to resolve it.

Maybe that's why some people think psychotherapy is self-indulgent – just a chance to talk about yourself and understand yourself better.

**Mentor** The purpose isn't to understand your behaviour; the purpose is to change it.

**Enquirer** Perhaps psychotherapeutic problems aren't conceived as being specific issues that require resolution. Or perhaps it's just that the goals of psychotherapy are more modest than I thought.

**Mentor** I suppose it doesn't help if you don't have a description of what a therapeutic problem is.

**Enquirer** You need to know what you're working with. You need a definition or description. Knowing what you're working with will help determine the work you do. But if psychotherapy doesn't know how to resolve therapeutic problems, there's not much point in defining them – they are not a direct concern of psychotherapy.

## Key point

Psychotherapy is generally considered to alleviate distress and develop self-knowledge, rather than resolve problems.

# PART II

## NEW FOUNDATIONS

# 20

# Responding to distressing events

**Enquirer** What is a psychotherapeutic problem? You seem to have a unique conception. You've said that it's where a person can't do what she wants to do or does what she doesn't want to do. That's a useful description, but it's not really a definition, is it?

**Mentor** A therapeutic problem exists when a person is prevented from achieving something she wants by something internal to her. The person's behaviour is interfering with achievement of her goals. This behaviour may involve doing something she does not want to do or not doing something she wants to do. The person is unable to change the unhelpful behaviour, because it is motivated by feelings deriving from something that happened in the past.

**Enquirer** How do feelings from the past motivate behaviour in the present?

**Mentor** I need your full attention here. People are, naturally, emotionally affected by what happens to them, and experiences that degrade personal dignity can have devastating emotional consequences. Through such experiences, people learn what circumstances to avoid; or, if the troublesome events cannot be avoided, they learn how to reduce the intensity of the impact by modifying their behaviour.

When something distressing happens to a person, what can she do to feel better? What response can she have that will reduce its impact on her? How can she respond to the event in a way that makes it not so bad, so that it is less degrading? The best choice might well be to avoid the event altogether. But this might not be possible; or she might not see the peril until the event is upon her. Alternatively, she might be able to take action to change the nature of the event so as to reduce its impact and the distress it provokes. If neither of these options are possible, is she able at least to learn from the experience, to prepare her better for the future? This would give her some mastery over it, reducing its negative impact and even making the experience positive.

When a distressing event occurs a number of times, a person is often able to develop management strategies to help her cope. The person might be able to try different responses to find out which one is most effective. But what happens if the person can't find any response at all to the event; if she can find no way to manage it, understand it, or make it less terrible? This is more likely to occur when the event is one-off, but can also occur in events that are repeated, especially if the person is powerless because she is young, for example. If the person finds no response that allows her to avoid, alleviate or intelligibilize the distressing experience, she becomes stuck in the experience, and this is the essence of trauma.

**Enquirer** You do have my full attention. But how is becoming 'stuck' in an experience the essence of trauma?

**Mentor** Imagine that a person can find no response that would make the distressing events more bearable: he has no control over events, and no way to make sense of them. If he can't find any response, or [as Langa and Ntando, discussed later, do] makes a response that is inappropriate, the event paralyses him and he feels utterly powerless. He might remain in this stuck state indefinitely.

In order to become unstuck and facilitate healing of the trauma, the person needs opportunities to understand and process the event, or events, retrospectively.

**Enquirer** I'm not quite sure what you mean by 'understand' and 'process' the event. Would you explain?

**Mentor** *Understanding* refers to finding meaning and learning something from the experience. *Processing* means situating or placing the event in a broader context of experience. If an experience is contextualized, it becomes mastered in some way. If the body does not get sufficient opportunities to contextualize it, the experience gets stuck in the body and has the characteristics of trauma. Situations that are subsequently encountered that seem comparable to the original trauma will trigger the trauma state.

**Enquirer** EMDR (Eye Movement, Desensitization and Reprocessing) is an excellent therapy for treating trauma.

**Mentor** Yes, it is very effective. The eye movements give the person an opportunity to make connections with other experiences and find a way to contextualize and so make meaning from what has happened.

**Enquirer** Now I understand why a traumatized person keeps reviewing an experience in his head but gets nowhere – he's trying to make sense of the experience, but is perpetually unable to.

**Mentor** In most circumstances a person does find a way to behave that enables her to handle the distressing events so that they are less distressing. The behaviour she adopts is less than the ideal because it is developed in the immediate circumstances of crisis and limited freedom. However, the behaviour is very significant for REP because it sets the precedent and blueprint for the person's behaviour in the future when faced with a similar circumstance. Where this behaviour later interferes with something the person is trying to achieve, it becomes a therapeutic problem.

**Enquirer** Explain how the behaviour becomes a therapeutic problem in the future.

**Mentor** The same behaviour that helped the person cope with a distressing situation in the past, may inhibit him in the future, when faced with a similar seeming situation, and stop him from achieving his goal.

**Enquirer** Let's have an example.

**Mentor** When he was a child . . . what shall we call him?

**Enquirer** Let's call him Usain.

**Mentor** Usain, as a child, received frequent and sustained disapproval from his parents and comparatively little affection, affirmation and encouragement. He tried hard to get his parents' approval, because of course he needed it, but failed, and usually received criticism instead. What did Usain learn from this?

**Enquirer** He learned that he doesn't deserve love.

**Mentor** Yes. He needs love, of course. If he doesn't get it, he believes it has to be his fault – as children do. The lack of love must be because he doesn't deserve it and needs to earn it. But his efforts are never enough. They can't be, because, however great his efforts, he still doesn't get the love he needs. He must always try harder and be better.

**Enquirer** Sounds like the psychological origins of the religious controversy of faith versus works.

**Mentor** These might sound like negative learnings. It would be much better if Usain could learn that he's lovable just as he is. But that's not what his experience teaches. He's not going to get his parents' love simply by wishing for it or believing he deserves it (though, of course, all children deserve love unconditionally).

To get what he needs, Usain understands he must take action. When he's helpful and does what he's told he discovers that he gets some love in exchange, or at least something closer to love. Even if it is meagre and inadequate, it's better than nothing. He learns that by being good he gets something approximating to love. So he understands that he's not worthy of love unless he is good; and that if he is not getting love it must be because he's not good enough. Being lovable depends on his good behaviour. If he is not well enough behaved he is not lovable. Is this an unhelpful learning, do you think?

**Enquirer** For Usain it's the best he can do. Behaving well has a certain, if limited, efficacy in helping him to get what he needs. Much better to get some love and approval than none at all.

**Mentor** Now, let's fast forward to the future. To when the behavioural response becomes limiting. Usain is grown up. How do you think he behaves as an adult?

**Enquirer** He's probably still craving love and approval.

**Mentor** Right. As an adult he is – or the love-starved child in him is – craving the love and approval he didn't receive as a child, and probably seeking it in inappropriate situations, possibly from friends and colleagues, and doubtless in inappropriate ways from his partner.

In his relationship with his partner he tries to be good, because being good means being lovable. The problem is that he never really believes that he's good enough, and so he never really believes his partner can love him. If his partner is not at every moment demonstrating love, he interprets this as want of love. But, essentially, he's unlovable: his partner cannot really love him, in his thinking. He doesn't deserve his partner's love, and his partner may leave at any time. So he doesn't trust his partner. His behaviour is needy, clingy, demanding, manipulative and controlling.

**Enquirer** All the ingredients of co-dependence and the basis for deeply unhappy relationships that are doomed to fail. Another example?

**Mentor** As a child a person was taught by her parents that she must please other people and avoid displeasing them.

**Enquirer** Her name is Leta.

**Mentor**  Leta's mother, in particular, was extremely concerned about the opinions of others and feared any disapprobation. Leta received approval not for her own qualities and achievements but rather when she behaved in a way her mother regarded as laudable in the eyes of others. And she received censure when her mother thought her behaviour would be unfavourably regarded.

As an adult, Leta's need to be approved of and to avoid disapproval became particularly acute in social situations. She dared not express her desires or opinions because if people didn't like them, she believed, they wouldn't like her. Being liked, or approved of, was all-important to Leta. So in public she had better keep her opinions to herself.

She's not really aware of this. What she's aware of is her fear of speaking out in social situations. It paralyses her. To avoid the possibility of disapproval, she remains silent. She can't say what she wants, what she thinks, how she feels. As a result, she is at the mercy of others – of what they want, what they think, how they feel – rendering her powerless. Consequently, not only does she fear speaking out, she's intensely anxious in social situations, especially with people she doesn't know well.

**Enquirer**  She has social anxiety.

**Mentor**  Yes. Is Leta's strategy successful? It certainly isn't. What she wants is approval. But what she gets is more disapproval. Her behaviour, pathologically modified in order to gain approval, has the opposite result.

**Enquirer**  Why is that?

**Mentor**  How can anyone like and approve of someone who they don't know, who doesn't express herself? And they might feel that Leta is hiding from them, and withholding who she is or what she really thinks. It almost seems as if she's judging them. As a result, they don't like her, they shun her; or, hardly better, they don't notice her or take no notice of her – exacerbating her social anxiety. As a result of the behaviour intended to mitigate her problem,

Leta's social anxiety intensifies, because she experiences herself as powerless, unable to express herself, and at the mercy of others. What could be an appropriate practical goal for her? How is it that Leta wants to behave?

**Enquirer** She desires to behave confidently in social situations and to express herself freely.

**Mentor** Yes. And what is the uncomfortable emotion that prevents Leta from achieving her goal – that stops her from being confident in social situations?

**Enquirer** Anxiety, of course.

**Mentor** So we have a practical goal, confidence to express herself freely in social situations; and we have an uncomfortable feeling, anxiety. Leta's presenting issue may have been a version of either or both of these.

**Enquirer** How do you resolve the problem? Because that's what it's all about, isn't it? Identifying the problem and finding out where it comes from is interesting, and maybe it can help the person to manage her behaviour better. But what she really needs is to resolve the problem.

**Mentor** The whole point, for Relearning Experience Process, is to resolve the problem, not to understand it, or learn to manage it – although, incidentally, the process of resolving the problem leads to a profound understanding of it.

We are not yet ready to resolve the problem – but we will get there. First, I want to explore with you the path from the problem experience to the manifestation of a therapeutic problem. Possibly the most striking thing about REP is its method of getting back to the original experiences that underlie the therapeutic problem, through a process called *tracking back*.

**Enquirer** Tracking back.

**Mentor** Yes. Or, simply, *tracking* – to the origins of the problem.

**Enquirer** I'm looking forward to learning how you do that. I still don't quite believe that it's possible.

**Mentor** I'm looking forward to showing you.

## Key points

From experience a person learns which experiences to try to avoid (because they degrade personal dignity).

If the difficult experience can't be avoided, a person learns how to ameliorate its impact (its degradation of personal dignity) by changing her behaviour.

This change in behaviour sets a precedent, a blueprint, for future responses to similar circumstances. Where this behaviour interferes with a person's goals, a therapeutic problem is precipitated.

If no response appears to make a situation more bearable or more intelligible, that experience produces an emotional response characterized as trauma.

Tracking back is the REP method to identify the origins of a therapeutic problem.

# 21

## Learning from experience

**Enquirer** There's something I've puzzled about for some time. I don't understand why emotional problems – therapeutic problems – are so difficult to get over. Why does problem behaviour seem so difficult to change?

Problem behaviour, you argue, is directed by feelings. The feelings come from experiences in the past. What makes these feelings so hard to change? My feelings change about all sorts of things all the time. My beliefs, which have feelings connected with them, also change. What can't I just change my behaviour through an act of will, or through talking about it in a counselling setting?

**Mentor** For survival, it's very important that the behaviour taught by experience cannot be overridden by an act of will. When you learn from experience something that is beneficial or detrimental to health and wellbeing, the feelings associated with that learning have to be powerful and not easily overcome. If feelings signifying threat or danger could be easily overcome you would not be well protected.

**Enquirer** That's true. But feelings can change about very many things, can't they? If my feelings can change easily enough about some things, why can't they change about other things – when I particularly want them to? Why are the feelings that drive unwanted behaviour so difficult to overcome?

**Mentor** There are certain kinds of beliefs that can be readily changed through an act of will. Learnings derived from experience and the feelings associated with them can't simply be changed by an act of will, however. But I will show you that learnings from experience can be changed, through the *relearning* – or resolution – work of REP.

Let's look at the difference between beliefs that can be changed readily and those that can't be changed readily. Give me an example of a belief that, in your experience, can be readily changed.

**Enquirer** There are lots of beliefs I have that, should evidence reveal that they are wrong, I would willingly change. Such as the distance of the earth from the sun; the age of the universe; the quickest route home.

**Mentor** They are all beliefs based on fact, and therefore – at least in theory – provable or disprovable. What would persuade you to change your belief, in these instances?

**Enquirer** I could be persuaded if an authority gave different information and other authorities agreed. I used to believe that planets were rare in the universe; now I know that they are common. I used to believe that elements were formed in the earth; now I know that they were formed through nuclear fusion and supernova explosions. Or I believe I know these things.

**Mentor** And what would make you change your mind about the quickest route home?

**Enquirer** If I found a quicker route.

**Mentor** Oh, so you wouldn't believe the authorities on that one?

**Enquirer** Not necessarily.

**Mentor** Is there a difference between your belief about the quickest route home and the other beliefs you mentioned, such as the existence of other planets?

**Enquirer** The things that are within the scope of my experience I prefer to decide for myself.

**Mentor** And when it's outside of your experience you rely on external authorities. If authorities have competing views, how do you decide which to believe?

**Enquirer** If I already have faith in a particular authority, or a particular type of authority, I will be predisposed to believe that authority; though my 'belief' might be conditional and not wholehearted, depending on how great my faith is in the authority. If I don't have faith in any particular authority, I might reserve judgement. No doubt, though, if I'm honest, my judgement would also be influenced by the media, and by people I know.

**Mentor** What would give you faith in a particular authority other than the media or people you know?

**Enquirer** I would base it on my knowledge about that authority.

**Mentor** What kind of knowledge?

**Enquirer** I don't really know. Perhaps agreement with other authorities and concordance with my own experience.

**Mentor** Which has more credibility for you, the agreement of authorities or your own experience? If the position of the authorities was at variance with your own experience, which would you be most likely to trust?

**Enquirer** I'd be more likely to trust my own experience.

**Mentor** You're saying that knowledge gained from your experience trumps knowledge received from other sources. Knowledge gained from other sources is second hand; it's not based directly on your own experience. In particular circumstances you are willing to let go of beliefs that are based on second-hand sources and adopt different beliefs – which you have done regarding the formation of elements. You're generally unwilling to let go of beliefs that are based on the evidence of your own senses. Is that right?

**Enquirer** Not just unwilling: unable. I would be unable to give up beliefs that are based on my experience – even if I wanted to.

**Mentor** Beliefs gained from other authorities are generally held intellectually; they are not generally strongly held on an emotional or feeling level – so they can be readily changed. Associations derived through experience, on the other hand, are held at the level of feeling and emotion. Such beliefs, or learnings, are involuntary and cannot simply be put aside by an effort of will.

**Enquirer** What about religious, political and social beliefs? They do not concern facts, and they are not really based on experience, but they are certainly held on the level of feeling.

**Mentor** Although we talk about political *beliefs*, such 'beliefs' are not a matter of truth or falsehood in the manner of intellectual beliefs (the earth goes round the sun or doesn't; elements are formed by nuclear fusion, or not) but, rather, a matter of *allegiance*. For example, a 'belief' in social justice is a support for the value of fairness in society; it is not a belief in the existence of such justice. Similarly, a 'belief' in integrity is support for the value of integrity; it is not a belief in the existence of integrity. This is true of all political 'beliefs': they are social values upheld as universal principles to be strived for.

**Enquirer** That's interesting. I'm thinking that *values* may be privately held, but *principles* are pursued publicly: principles are a manifestation of values expressed in a public forum or context.

**Mentor** The point is that what are called political 'beliefs' are voluntary and rational. Of course a person can feel strongly about his values. You should feel strongly. You invest emotionally in values and principles that are chosen freely. Political allegiances are freely chosen, even if a person feels strongly about them.

**Enquirer** What about religious beliefs? Belief in God is certainly a belief: God either exists or doesn't exist.

**Mentor** Yes, that's true. It is still voluntary, though – at least, in a free society – to believe in God. A person can choose to believe in God or not.

**Enquirer** So all beliefs can be charged with emotion; but some beliefs are voluntary and some – those based on experience, that you want to call 'learnings' – are involuntary. It's always possible to invest emotionally in a belief, even if the belief is voluntary.

**Mentor** Yes. In fact, all beliefs carry emotional investment, to an extent greater or lesser, and there is a tendency to uphold the rectitude of one's beliefs, no matter the nature of the belief, in the face of dissent or opposition. The greater the emotional investment in a belief, the more it is imbued with feeling and the stronger the 'belief' is held.

However, when a belief is not based on the learning of experience, it is not hard to change it through an act of will. Relinquishing rectitude can however be very uncomfortable; belief disinvestment can therefore feel like an injury to personal dignity, even if the belief is voluntary and changing it is entirely possible. In these circumstances the belief *per se* is not difficult to change, but the *consequences* of changing the belief may be difficult to accept.

Learnings that are formed from experience can't be changed through an act of will, and are involuntary. However, emotional investment in a belief, made voluntarily, can be withdrawn through an act of will. Persistent attachment to an object or viewpoint that turns out to be false or dangerous is pathological.

In short, providing you are willing to do so, you can change your beliefs about anything where the learning hasn't been formed from personal experience.

I prefer to use the word *learning* for ideas held involuntarily – whether or not they are apprehended on a conscious level – as a result of experience. This kind of learning is behavioural and serves to promote happiness and preserve emotional and physical safety. Beliefs, on the other hand, are held consciously and voluntarily invested in. Beliefs are ideational in nature and are likely to have been taken second hand from other sources or authorities. Beliefs imply the possibility of doubt and are conditional. Learnings are felt to be certain. Beliefs are voluntary. Learnings are involuntary. You can formulate any ideas you fancy in your mind; you can invest in the ideas emotionally; and you can believe the ideas of other authorities – but these beliefs will not have the emotional rootedness that learnings from experience must have, and so will be more fluid and changeable.

**Enquirer** Beliefs about homosexuality are a good example of how ideological or social beliefs can change – and have changed dramatically since the mid-1990s. Beliefs about gender have also changed a great deal. And, more lately, beliefs about the alignment of gender and biological sex have changed.

**Mentor** Yes. Prejudices are ideological and are not of course based on experience.

**Enquirer** Beliefs about the nature of the universe have also changed radically, as scientists have made amazing discoveries in the last few decades. These are second-hand beliefs. I can see how learnings gained directly through experience are different and much more difficult to relinquish. Does that mean affirmations don't work?

**Mentor** You can't change what experience has taught by stating what you'd like to believe – no matter how often or ardently you repeat it.

**Enquirer** You mean you don't think that if I say *I'm beautiful* a hundred times a day I'll eventually believe it? Well, then, I'll make a point to stop doing that.

**Mentor** People who repeat affirmations are trying to believe something they don't believe. At the level of feeling they have a contrary learning. If you affirm something often enough you may believe it earnestly on an intellectual level, but it won't erase any contrary learning on the level of feeling.

**Enquirer** I agree that you can believe something on a rational level but not believe it on the level of feeling. But why is the feeling level the most important? Isn't the conscious mind the authority on what you believe? If I believe something in my rational mind I believe it, don't I?

**Mentor** Can you truly believe something if you don't feel it?

**Enquirer** I don't know. Can't I? I can know something is true on an intellectual level but have contrary feelings.

For example, I may know rationally that I'm not ugly but still feel it. I may know there's nothing to be frightened of but still feel frightened.

**Mentor** What has the greatest effect on your behaviour: knowing there's nothing to be frightened of; or the feeling of fear?

**Enquirer** There's no question that the feeling will have the most impact on my behaviour.

**Mentor** This distinction between knowing something on a rational level but not (yet) feeling it on an emotional level is important in REP. It applies when setting goals. A person needs to know the truth of something *on a rational level* in order to set it as a goal. This is a prerequisite for changing a learning.

For example, on a rational level you need to know that you're perfectly attractive or that you are equal in value to every other human being if you're going to set one of these as a goal. You don't have to feel it yet – in fact, you won't be able to feel it yet. (If you did, you wouldn't need to make it a goal, obviously: it would already be true for you.) But you need to know it to be true on a rational level, or there's no chance of believing it on an emotional level. This is obvious, but fundamental. The work of REP will enable you to learn on the level of feeling, as if through experience, what you know to be true on an intellectual level.

**Enquirer** For therapy to be effective it has to work at the level of feeling. I can certainly see that. But how can the work of REP successfully intervene on the level of feeling if, as you say, learning from experience is involuntary and unconscious?

**Mentor** We give an imaginary opportunity to *relearn* experience.

**Enquirer** The original learning from experience was unhelpful.

**Mentor** It usually is helpful to learn from experience. The learning that is unhelpful is developed pathologically in response to difficult circumstances.

It is to our general advantage that we learn from experience and that such learnings cannot be forced aside by conscious will. Emotional and physical survival depend on learnings about the world gained through experience. It would not be good if you could persuade yourself that you can fly while standing at the edge of a precipice; or that being insulted or abused is harmless – even if some people do try to persuade themselves that insults don't affect them.

**Enquirer** If you are doing something dangerous you definitely should feel terrified. Nor is it ever okay to be abused or insulted. It's good that, as a principle, your body has no choice but to try to protect you.

**Mentor** Learning from experience safeguards physical safety and emotional safety. Safeguarding emotional safety is as important as safeguarding physical safety. Experience helps to protect a person from embarrassment, humiliation, disappointment, and so on. We don't need to be protected from other people's emotions, but we do need to be protected from harmful behaviour, whether the potential assault is physical or emotional.

**Enquirer** Perhaps human beings originally learned to protect against emotional threats because they can be the precursor to acts of physical aggression.

Second-hand beliefs, I think you are saying, is information received from external sources – such as parents, teachers, books, friends, the media and the internet. *Learning* is what we discover for ourselves, through experience.

**Mentor** That's right.

**Enquirer** And you're saying that learnings from experience are what motivate behaviour.

**Mentor** Learnings from experience generally *inform* behaviour. But when confronted with situations of danger, these learnings indeed motivate behaviour.

From experience you learn about your own nature, the world you inhabit and your role and standing in the world. Friends, teachers, parents, books, television, internet, or other agents, can do their best to influence you; but you won't be convinced at the level of feeling; and, if they succeed in motivating your behaviour, the change you make is voluntary.

Beliefs – or knowledge – gained from external sources are voluntary and conditional; they are something you buy in to. They are subject to the will and, with a change in will, can be changed. Interaction with the world and what you learn from this interaction leads to the wisdom of experience. Second-hand information doesn't lead to this kind of wisdom but to knowledge.

**Enquirer** I'm reminded of the old literary debates about whether more is learned through books or through experience. But some argue that art and literature can improve the moral being.

**Mentor** The arts, such as literature and fine art, have great power to work unconsciously and to open up the imagination and broaden horizons. Most received information doesn't do this. Art is more than information. Its purpose is metaphorical, not literal. It is not intended to be information; we approach it differently, as a collaborator in meaning and significance. I certainly don't want to underplay the significance of the arts, which interplays with experience more profoundly than information can. In fact, the relearning work of the resolution phase of REP has much in common with the endeavour of art.

**Enquirer** Clever advertising mimics the arts by working metaphorically and unconsciously. That's how it gets to you. If it worked on a purely conscious level its messages could easily be dismissed. So there is a blurring of the division.

**Mentor** Experience informs behaviour, inscribes personality and shapes identity. Secondary information doesn't do this. Information is ultimately to do with facts (of course 'facts' are always subject to the dialectical principle: they are always already interpretations) and ideas. The facts might be disputed, and so you may have beliefs about those facts, or different interpretations of them; but nevertheless information is about facts.

**Enquirer** You don't realize that much of your behaviour is learned – though not in the way behaviourism conceives. But you learn from experience how to behave; how others respond to you; what characteristics and personality you have; what you can get away with and can't get away with; how likeable, lovable, charming, or otherwise, you are . . .

**Mentor** That's right.

**Enquirer** You learn about what you're capable of, what comes easily and what your limits are. You learn what to feel frightened of and the circumstances in which it's okay to relax and let down your guard. You learn how and when to be confident. You learn how to behave and how not to and in what circumstances. You learn what's safe and what's dangerous – emotionally as well as physically. You learn whether you're okay or not. Whether it's okay to take risks or take chances or make mistakes. What kind of mistakes are okay or not okay. What expectations others have of you and what happens when you thwart those expectations . . .

**Mentor** Yes. All those things.

**Enquirer** That kind of learning – though strongly influenced by external factors – is peculiar to the learner. Everybody gets different lessons from life – even if the lessons of experience appear similar. These learnings help to compose a person's character.

**Mentor** Yes. It's only through experience that we can learn all those important life lessons. No one else can teach us. They can try! They do try – using reason, or examples of other people's experiences. Reason – the intellect – can't teach us the important lessons because there are always competing arguments. For any argument there's a counterargument. How can you judge between them if reason is all there is to go by?

**Enquirer** I agree. Anything can be argued with reason – just listen to the politicians! Do you remember those emotive television adverts years ago depicting drug addiction? It's as if the adverts were trying to teach learning that's received through experience. You are encouraged to learn through the experience of others. It doesn't work. You can't experience another person's experience.

We need, rather, balanced information to make informed choices; and, where the information does not convince us, we need to make our own mistakes, if necessary, and learn from them.

Better to give straightforward, unexaggerated and unemotive information about the effects of misuse of drugs, I think. No one wants to be told what to do – least of all young people. People have to decide for themselves. So give them good information.

**Mentor** Experience is the only way that we can learn the important lessons of life. And we can only be truly responsible for our actions if we base them on the knowledge we gain from experience. We use experience, not reason, to judge the information given to us.

**Enquirer** Are we travelling away from our purpose? I'd like to know how therapeutic problems develop.

**Mentor** This discussion is central to our purpose. It's important to understand how experience creates involuntary learnings that have a foundation in feelings and can't be overpowered by the will or conscious effort. It is when these learnings interfere with pursuit of a person's goals that therapeutic problems are formed. And it is by relearning the experiences that problems are resolved.

**Enquirer** Let me check my understanding. Learning from experience is different from information from secondary sources because it has the purpose of preparing you for situations you may encounter in the future. It warns against certain situations, and recommends others. It tells you how to behave in the face of difficult situations to enable you to cope with those situations. It also tells you which situations are safe and which are not, and what behaviour is okay in different circumstances. It enables you to know which situations are favourable to you and which you should avoid.

The learnings that inhibit behaviour are 'positive' in the sense that they protect from emotional degradation. That's their intention or purpose. But they have the potential of becoming a therapeutic problem if they impede your goals.

**Mentor** That is succinctly put.

**Enquirer** I've got a couple of examples of 'learnings' that don't seem to serve any positive purpose. A child learns he's unlovable, because his parents are not loving towards him. A child learns from his teachers that he's hopeless at English, when in fact he's dyslexic. These learnings are disempowering. Do you nevertheless want to insist that these learnings help the person to survive, or cope, or manage adversity?

**Mentor** People have disempowering experiences and receive disempowering messages. The task of the person is to find a resourceful response that reduces the indignity. If a child's parents are not loving towards him he experiences degradation as his emotional needs are being denied. He needs love; he's not receiving it. His challenge is to find the best action to take; to find a way of getting love. What behaviour would reduce this degradation and get him more love? He discovers that, if he's very well behaved, his parents are less harsh or, sometimes, more loving towards him. His solution is then: *If I behave well and am a good boy, then my parents will show me love.* He has learned that he needs to be a good boy in order to receive love. The corollary learning is, logically, if he's not receiving love it's because he's not good enough.

In your second example, the child who learns he's 'hopeless' at English, I'm not yet clear what the degradation is. What is he not getting that he needs?

**Enquirer** Let's say the child wants approval for his academic efforts and he's getting disapproval because of his dyslexia.

**Mentor** To reduce the personal dignity degradation, either he looks for a way to reduce the disapproval (a change in his behaviour), or he reduces his investment in approval (a change in his viewpoint). If he knows he's dyslexic he can decide that he doesn't need approval for his spelling and expression, and this will reduce the degradation and help preserve his personal dignity. To enhance his self-esteem he may want to find other areas where he can more readily gain approval.

**Enquirer** The needs of a person, then, aren't fixed. Consciousness comes into it. He can just choose something else for approval. In the first example, love is dependent on being good. If he doesn't behave well, or if his behaviour is construed as not good enough, then he's not good enough.

**Mentor** Exactly. And that leads to all sorts of psychotherapeutic problems based on the idea that *I'm not okay in myself (and I need to prove my worth through my behaviour).* This is why a parent's love should be unconditional. All children need and deserve unconditional love. It's the only earthly love for another person that ought to be unconditional. (One should also have unconditional love for oneself.) We should judge a child's behaviour, but not the child himself.

**Enquirer**  Your behaviour's bad, but that doesn't mean that you are bad; you are still okay.

**Mentor**  For a child who is not getting the attention he needs, the question is, *How do I get more attention?* The child discovers that being naughty brings attention. So his solution to not getting enough attention is to be naughty. The unconscious equation is formed: *To get attention, I need to be naughty.* The implied corollary learning is that if he's not getting the attention he wants it's because he's not being naughty enough.

This learning will probably not be empowering, because there will be negative consequences to being naughty – such as the attention he gets is not the type that he really wants; he gets picked on by teachers at school and get into trouble; he becomes antiauthority or anti-establishment. But there may also be positive consequences, such as getting the esteem of his peers for his courage in challenging the system.

**Enquirer**  You need to explain the concept of personal dignity.

## Key points

Learnings derived from experience are involuntary and cannot be overridden by an act of will. Such learnings help to keep us safe emotionally and physically.

Political or religious 'beliefs' relate to a person's allegiances, rather than to truth or falsehood, and are voluntary.

A person's feelings may contradict her rational beliefs. For example, a person may know she's perfectly attractive but feel ugly.

Reason can't be relied upon for the most important lessons of life, because compelling counterarguments can always be made.

Feelings deriving from experience, rather than the faculty of reason, provide the basis for judgement and, consequently, responsibility.

Where such learnings interfere with a person's goals, therapeutic problems are formed. Resolution is through Relearning Experience.

# 22

## Personal dignity

**Mentor** A therapeutic problem manifesting in the present has its origins in an experience in the past. To understand how therapeutic problems are created I'd like you to consider the emotional needs a person has and the extent to which they are being met. The significance of emotional needs is comprehended with the concept of personal dignity. The achievement of personal dignity requires the satisfaction of emotional needs.

**Enquirer** What kind of emotional needs are you referring to?

**Mentor** All those needs that have to be satisfied for a person to feel good about himself.

**Enquirer** Such as the need for love, respect, care, trust, consideration, affection, intimacy, sex, affirmation, acknowledgement, honour, play, companionship.

**Mentor** Yes. All of those.

**Enquirer** That sounds like a tall order.

**Mentor** Maybe. But unreasonable?

**Enquirer** I suppose it is perfectly reasonable to want all of those. But do you need to have them all to feel good about yourself?

**Mentor** Any individual may have particular needs peculiar to her at a given time. But most needs are shared by most of us, even if the individual expression of the need varies according to the person. If it is your emotional need, its possession is necessary for you to feel good about yourself. That's what makes it a need.

To the list you suggested I would want to add physical comfort, physical security and physical safety.

**Enquirer** You believe physical needs are also emotional needs?

**Mentor** When physical needs are compromised a person has an emotional response. Fear, anger, resentment, miserableness, self-pity, hurt – these are emotional responses to physical discomfort, insecurity and danger. If you live in fear for your physical safety and can't sleep comfortably in your bed at night; if you can't walk home after it gets dark; if you have to plan travel routes to guard against attack – your freedom is compromised, your self-respect is diminished, stress is increased, and personal dignity is degraded. So we have an emotional need for physical comfort, physical security and physical safety.

**Enquirer** How do these emotional needs affect personal dignity?

**Mentor** If a person doesn't receive one or more of her emotional needs – love, respect, affection, and so on – she feels less of a person; her self-regard is diminished: in other words, her personal dignity is degraded.

With degradation of personal dignity inevitably comes loss of confidence, inhibition of personal expression, impoverishment of thinking, and damage to identity.

**Enquirer** What about social injustice and inequality: would they also affect personal dignity?

**Mentor** Yes, certainly. Social injustice involves oppression, and oppression limits and degrades consciousness and capacities.

**Enquirer** Personal dignity is quite precarious, then.

How do you compare your idea of emotional needs with Maslow's hierarchy of needs, in his paper, 'A theory of human motivation'?

**Mentor** In this model, emotional needs aren't hierarchical. At any moment, any can be of great significance.

**Enquirer** But the physical need for food is greater than the emotional need for love.

**Mentor** Are you sure?

**Enquirer** I'm not sure. But if you're hungry won't that be more important to you than if someone is being disrespectful?

**Mentor** Do you think that hungry people aren't concerned about how people treat them?

**Enquirer** No. I'm sure they do care. In fact, suggesting that poor people don't care about the 'higher needs' because they are struggling with basic, or 'physiological' needs is patronizing. The hierarchy seems rather value laden.

**Mentor** The need for food is a physical need, but it's also an emotional need. Emotional needs are fundamental to everybody; so, even if they're not considered or recognized consciously, they are nevertheless felt to be an entitlement.

**Enquirer** They seem so natural; like a right. Any kind of oppression tramples on the personal dignity of people. Oppression is clearly wrong. But in order for people to be subjugated, they have to be oppressed, says Frantz Fanon. So perhaps there is a right to personal dignity. Why should there be a right to life and liberty, or to adequate food, shelter or sanitation, but not a right to other aspects of personal dignity?

But I suppose a person's needs cannot be guaranteed: people are not obligated to be respectful, or affectionate, or have any other specific regard, towards anyone. But it would be useful to recognize that people have emotional needs and how important these are. Perhaps personal dignity could be recognized as a personal right; a right to be respected and considered by others – even if it is a right that can't be underwritten by government.

**Mentor** Yes. When a person's emotional needs are compromised – a common experience for all of us – she feels her needs are being denied or blocked.

**Enquirer** And what if no one is in fact denying or blocking the person's needs?

**Mentor** It still feels to the person as if someone is or should be held responsible – or that the world is responsible. When personal dignity is compromised, people generally become resentful and angry and want to blame. It can feel devastating.

**Enquirer** Sometimes people deliberately set out to punish, ridicule or abuse a person, to sabotage her personal dignity.

**Mentor** Yes, they do.

**Enquirer** You can't feel good about yourself – you can't feel okay about yourself – when your personal dignity is degraded.

**Mentor** That's right. But when emotional needs are met a person experiences personal dignity and a sense of ease and comfort. Personal dignity is necessary for emotional wellbeing.

In every interaction the human being is concerned to maintain, safeguard and perhaps test personal dignity. Conflict threatens personal dignity, but is an unavoidable feature of everyday life.

In personal interactions there is often a battle between two or more people trying to assert their dignity. In ideal situations interactions are win–win for all parties. But for some people winning requires others to lose: defence of personal dignity in their perception is achievable only through denigration of others. People also misinterpret others' intentions, and some people abuse and denigrate others for their own power and pleasure. But the maintenance of personal dignity never requires the degrading of another.

**Enquirer** What about a person's need for adoration? Is the absence of adoration experienced as an affront to personal dignity?

**Mentor** The desire for adoration is not a need. Acceptance is a need; adoration is a hyperbolic desire or a pseudo-need. Any person may need acceptance; a person may desire adoration, but she doesn't need it. In the absence of a need there is an uncomfortable feeling; a person doesn't feel bad because she's not adored. A person does feel bad if her real emotional needs are unmet.

**Enquirer** Having needs met is good, I'm sure. But I would rather be adored than accepted. Who wants to live in a bungalow if you can live in a palace?

**Mentor** Hyperbolic desires are highly prized in marketing and can produce emotional highs. But having hyperbolic desires satisfied doesn't make people happy, and not having them satisfied does not leave people distressed. Hyperbolic desires appear to fulfil the criteria of a need, because they look like needs that are higher up the scale. However, hyperbolic desires, though pleasurable, are not emotionally satisfying – for a simple reason: they are not real. Adoration does not mean acceptance – or even respect. In fact, the other face of adoration is jealousy and suspicion (because the adored person possesses what the adoring person doesn't possess but desires) – which is why adoration can so easily give way to hatred and resentment. Tabloid news feeds on this duality. Adoration may produce a high, but it's not authentic and doesn't contribute to happiness. A person who is adored but not accepted feels no less degraded than someone not accepted or adored.

**Enquirer** The demand by a person that others serve his hyperbolic desires is narcissistic.

**Mentor** You're right. Where hyperbolic desires become perceived 'needs' for a person, the 'need' is pathological, and the behaviour of the person to serve these desires by imposing his will on others is characterized by narcissism.

With respect to emotional needs, absence of evidence is evidence of absence. If a person does not feel (for example) respected, cared for, accepted, she feels disrespected, uncared for, unaccepted. Personal dignity is fragile. Threats to personal dignity are ever present and imminent. No one is immune from them. Degradation can be devastating. It's a small step from feeling unrespected to feeling unvalued, and a small step from there to feeling worthless. Self-esteem is a subjective measure of personal dignity. Because it is so fragile and volatile, it is jealously guarded.

**Enquirer** The stronger the fortress built to defend it, the more fragile is the self-esteem.

**Mentor** Fragile in emotionally healthy people, personal dignity is still far more precarious in emotionally unhealthy people who are trying in vain to satisfy the unsatisfied needs of their childhood. When personal dignity is compromised, people become angry, resentful and jealous. In this we are all human and all equal. Whether a person feels good about herself depends on whether she is presently having her emotional needs met. This unremitting quest for personal dignity underlies all human interaction.

**Enquirer** The quest for personal dignity is the quest for emotional nourishment. Is this true also of children?

**Mentor** Children's need for personal dignity is no less than that of adults, even if their emotional needs are different and they lack the understanding and ability to articulate them. Children don't automatically know how to get their needs met, and have to learn how to do this. During early childhood it is the duty of parents and caregivers to ensure that all the emotional needs of children are met. Children are wholly dependent on others to uphold their personal dignity.

Adolescence is the period when the child learns appropriate strategies to safeguard emotional needs, and this takes time and requires the support and guidance of parents and guardians. With the onset of practical and financial independence at the end of adolescence, individuals must shape their own circumstances to ensure their emotional needs are met. This constitutes emotional independence.

The crisis of adolescence, or the struggle between adolescent and parent or carer, should be understood in terms of a striving for emotional independence – that is, self-established personal dignity. The adolescent, with growing vigour, attempts to assert her own criteria for personal dignity, casting aside protection externally imposed.

When there is a failure to meet the emotional needs of a child or adolescent, her personal dignity is degraded, and an exaggerated demand to have this need met is generated. If unhealed, this will lead to codependent relationships in adulthood, as the adult person will attempt to get her needs met in inappropriate – that is to say, pathological – ways.

**Enquirer** Emotional needs have to be satisfied for a person to feel good about herself – or perhaps just to feel normal. Happiness requires it – or maybe personal dignity is synonymous with happiness. But why is money so important to people if personal dignity should be the top priority?

**Mentor** Personal dignity is the top priority, but not necessarily consciously. Money isn't an emotional need. But with money comes public esteem, which looks very much like self-esteem, and seems as if it will lead to personal dignity. The promise of money is that it will satisfy emotional needs. That's why people want money. That's what advertising promises. Buy this, the advertisers declare, and your emotional needs will be satisfied: it will give you the dignity you crave. So people believe money will bring about the satisfaction of emotional needs. But, at the same time, people also know that it won't.

Material riches, which buy social prestige, appear to create additional opportunities for emotional needs to be satisfied, but don't necessarily do so. Similarly, fame appears to give extra potential for emotional riches, but may instead lead to degradations of personal dignity. And, of course, money, or fame, can be distractions from the dirty business of having real emotional needs met.

**Enquirer** It's a dirty business, having emotional needs met.

**Mentor** It requires continual work and is always under threat.

**Enquirer** Any interaction will probably give you some of what you need emotionally and some degradation.

**Mentor** Yes. Many degradations, such as minor disappointments and disagreements, will however be routine and unremarkable. Most adults learn to cope with them well. If they don't, they may be considered immature or narcissistic.

Through experience we learn the causes of dignity degradations and how to reduce and, where possible, eliminate them; and we learn how to sustain or augment personal dignity. We also learn how to cope emotionally with minor degradations. Beneficial experiences are those that bring personal dignity; detrimental experiences are those that bring degradations. Behaviour is driven by the attempt to maintain or enhance personal dignity.

**Enquirer** Is personal dignity then in conflict with personal integrity? If you're seeking love, respect and affirmation, won't you want to do what pleases people; what decreases your discomfort; what pleases you – not what is morally right?

**Mentor** On the contrary. I believe integrity and personal dignity are entirely consistent with each other. Behaving dishonourably degrades personal dignity; behaving honourably enhances it. As well as needing love, respect, affirmation from others, we need it from ourselves. Regard for self is not very different to regard from others. Perhaps it is more important. Behaving without integrity leads to dignity degradation that is deeply uncomfortable.

But it's true that acting with integrity can risk attacks from others. It certainly takes courage to assert an opinion that is not shared by the majority and to act in a principled way that might be perceived as disagreeable or offensive.

**Enquirer** Okay. How is all of this relevant to therapeutic problems – specifically, to how therapeutic problems are created?

## Key points

Personal dignity relates to satisfaction of emotional needs, which are not hierarchical but include physical safety and nourishment from food.

Personal dignity degradation leads to loss of confidence, inhibition of expression, impoverishment of thinking and damage to identity.

Emotional needs should not be confused with hyperbolic desires, which may lead to narcissistic behaviour.

Children need adult carers to protect their personal dignity and require support as they learn to maintain it themselves.

Personal dignity and integrity are consistent with each other.

# 23
## Strategic behaviour

**Mentor** At the origin of any therapeutic problem is a personal dignity degradation; or, more accurately, an attempt to reassert personal dignity and combat degradation. That's how a therapeutic problem originates – although at this stage the behaviour that develops serves as a solution, not a problem.

Something is happening in the person's life that is degrading his personal dignity, sabotaging his emotional needs, and causing deep emotional discomfort. In order to ameliorate the discomfort created by the personal dignity degradation, the person modifies his behaviour. To the extent that he is successful in reasserting his person dignity, his discomfort is diminished.

**Enquirer** By changing his behaviour he finds a way to regain personal dignity and feel better about himself.

**Mentor** That's right – at least somewhat better. And the more significant or pronounced the degradation, the greater the efforts a person will be compelled to make, in terms of behaviour modification, to restore his personal dignity. As we interact in the world we respond behaviourally to what we encounter to enhance wellbeing and to minimize threats to wellbeing. We do this habitually, at every moment, usually without any conscious awareness that this is the intention behind our actions. But the desire to maintain personal dignity informs how a person responds in any interaction.

**Enquirer** How does a personal dignity degradation lead to the creation of a therapeutic problem?

**Mentor** Behaviour is modified in an attempt to redeem personal dignity. This is remedial or adaptive behaviour. It isn't ordinary or natural consequential behaviour. Behaviour adapted specifically to cope with difficult circumstances is strategic. This strategic behaviour leads to the creation of therapeutic problems if in the future it interferes with what the person is trying to achieve.

We'll see later how resolution of therapeutic problems is achieved through transforming the originary experience in imagination.

You look like you need some convincing. Let's look more carefully at how behaviour gets modified. How do you respond to a situation where you are threatened, either emotionally or physically?

**Enquirer** It depends on the nature of the threat.

**Mentor** What's the aim of your behaviour when you feel that you are under threat?

**Enquirer** Obviously, it's to reduce the threat as far as possible. If I see a group of rowdy and ill-tempered men in my path, I might cross the road.

**Mentor** Better to avoid the threat if you can. Crossing the road is a way of taking evasive action. What if you can't avoid it and have to walk right through the group of rowdy men?

**Enquirer** I would act confident but non-aggressive.

**Mentor** You would be taking action – strategically modifying your behaviour – to reduce the threat that you can't completely avoid. And you're putting into action learnings that you've previously made: looking confident, rather than nervous; and looking neutral and non-aggressive. You want to look like you're not easily intimidated, but you're not posing a threat. What alerts you to the threat? How do you know there's a potential threat?

**Enquirer** If the people look aggressive. But – if it was late in the evening and I suspected they'd been drinking, for example – I might avoid them even if they don't really look aggressive. They could become aggressive quickly. How do I know that there's a potential threat? It seems obvious. I suppose I know from previous experience.

**Mentor** Do you remember specific experiences?

**Enquirer** No, I don't remember any specific experiences. Maybe there aren't specific experiences. But I know that a group of rowdy men can be dangerous. I have enough experience of that. And I get a feeling . . .

**Mentor** You get an uncomfortable feeling. The feeling warns you of a potentially threatening situation.

**Enquirer** Yes. Apparently some people with autism don't get this feeling and have to be taught explicitly about dangers.

**Mentor** The feeling that warns you of a threat – is it comfortable or uncomfortable?

**Enquirer** Obviously, it's uncomfortable.

**Mentor** Is this uncomfortable feeling useful?

**Enquirer** You want to avoid threatening situations. If you can't avoid the situation, then you need to find a way of dealing with it that reduces the level or intensity of the threat. You will find a behaviour that reduces the threat. Best option: take away the risk. If that's unavoidable, reduce it. If that doesn't work, do what you can to not get hurt; or do what you can for the hurt to be less.

**Mentor** That's right. The strategic behavioural response is designed to reduce the intensity of the threat in the best way the person knows at the time, depending on his knowledge, experience and capacities.

Embarrassment, shame, ridicule, humiliation, physical injury – these are degradations to personal dignity that the body wants to avoid, or at least manage. The body is always alert to threats to physical and emotional wellbeing and wants to help the person to manage them and, where possible, avoid them.

The body wants to guard against active threats to personal dignity. It's also striving to gain love, respect, friendship, and so on, because the absence of these also diminishes personal dignity.

**Enquirer**  What about boredom and fear? Are these also threats to personal dignity?

**Mentor**  Boredom is not a significant threat; but boredom can be a signal that emotional needs are not being met. Boredom is not so much a degradation of emotional needs but an indication that needs are not being satisfied. Boredom can motivate people to do something. However, people often claim that they're bored when actually they're feeling something else – such as unmotivated, or out of their depth.

Similarly, fear is not a threat but a warning of a threat. We need to avoid the threatening situation to which we are alerted by fear.

**Enquirer**  To maintain personal dignity, you have to protect yourself from the carelessness and malignity of others, but you also have to court favourable responses, such as love and respect, and establish favourable and safe environments in which to live and work.

**Mentor**  Both are necessary to sustain and uphold personal dignity: emotional wellbeing requires both protection against threats from others and positive regard from others. Paradoxically, to achieve positive regard you need to put yourself in situations that risk emotional degradation, such as embarrassment and rejection. That's why we're never safe.

**Enquirer** Right. The very same opportunities that have the potential to satisfy emotional needs also have the potential to dash them. To find love you need to risk rejection; to be successful in work you may need to fail many, many times and even then may be ultimately disappointed.

**Mentor** The unconscious body learns from experience. This enables you to recognize potential threats. It's impossible to avoid threats completely; and circumstances that are the richest in opportunities are often also the riskiest. If you try too hard to avoid threats, you miss out on opportunities. It's a perilous path: how do you get your emotional needs met without at the same time putting personal dignity in grave peril?

**Enquirer** That is the dynamic challenge of living. Very often the most feared activity is at the same time the greatest opportunity.

**Mentor** Where people have put themselves at risk and not succeeded, they may become shy about taking further risks. When a person's dignity is degraded he develops behaviours in response to the degradation to ameliorate the damage done. And, when it is helpful to do so, he develops viewpoints and rationalizations to change his perspective of the world in order to reduce the intensity of the degradation. If you can't change the circumstances, at least change the way you regard the circumstances.

The behavioural response to a particular degradation has a chance to stand or fall – to be permanently adopted or not – depending on whether it works and whether future events reinforce or contradict the learning.

**Enquirer** The strategic behaviour becomes 'maladaptive' as circumstances change and the behaviour becomes a problem. But originally the behaviour may have worked very well; or, at least, was the best the person could do in the circumstances.

**Mentor** That's right. The adaptive behaviour may be consolidated if one or more of these conditions are met: (1) the person sees no other possible choices; (2) it subsequently works for the person; (3) it is not significantly challenged; (4) there are secondary benefits; and (5) the severity of the original circumstances makes the adaptive behaviour particularly compelling.

This is why, to resolve a therapeutic problem with REP, there may be a number of past experiences to visit and relearn. A number of experiences may have reinforced or contributed to the original learning.

**Enquirer** Let's see if I can sum this up. A person learns how to behave through experiences that preserve or degrade her personal dignity. Generally, she tries to forge experiences that satisfy her emotional needs; that is, that enhance her personal dignity. Where she experiences a degradation, she adapts her behaviour in an attempt to avoid feeling so bad. If this works, it constitutes a 'learning' that sets a precedent for future behaviour.

This learning is unconscious and, generally, very helpful because it allows a person to manage threatening experiences automatically, without interference from the ponderous conscious mind.

**Mentor** In the future, when a similar situation is encountered, the original behavioural response is activated. The mechanism for its activation is the uncomfortable feelings experienced during the original event, which motivated a specific behaviour that seemed to help.

The learning from the original event, this strategic behavioural response, may become a problem in the future if it limits or constrains the person's behaviour in a way that prevents her from getting something that she wants. If this happens, the behaviour has become disempowering and has led to the development of a therapeutic problem.

The body is at all times alert to potential physical and emotional threats. When it perceives one that has been encountered previously, the behaviour learned from the past experience, with a motivation proportionate to the severity of the original experience, is automatically activated. In most circumstances this behaviour seems natural to the person. It may not be a problem and may not be perceived to be a problem. The person's attention is drawn to it and it becomes a problem only if she is pursuing something that she wants (which we have called a *practical goal*) that requires a change of behaviour. When the impelled behaviour prevents the person from achieving something she wants, an internal struggle ensues and a therapeutic problem is generated.

## Key points

At the origin of every therapeutic problem is an attempt to rescue or redeem personal dignity by changing behaviour to ameliorate a difficult circumstance.

In future, this 'adaptive' behaviour is triggered unconsciously (by feelings) in potentially dangerous circumstances considered similar.

The greatest opportunities to satisfy emotional needs often also have the greatest potential to denigrate personal dignity. Reducing such risks also means reducing opportunities for promoting personal dignity.

Behaviour that is adapted to ameliorate personal dignity degradation may become a therapeutic problem, and 'maladaptive', if it later interferes with attaining something that the person desires.

# 24

# Responsibility and the role of reason

**Mentor** I'd like us to look at two issues of consciousness for a moment: self-responsibility and the use of reason.

**Enquirer** You said earlier that self-responsibility is the most important principle for emotional health and wellbeing. What do you mean by that?

**Mentor** We've already talked about how important it is to take responsibility for your own feelings and actions; not to assume responsibility for the feelings of others; and to hold people accountable for their actions. But it's also important to take responsibility for your beliefs and values. A common problem in the therapeutic context is when people take on, without examination or question, the beliefs and values of other people – often those of their parents, but also those of their cultural group, class, caste or gender, or any other type of group they identify with. Abdication of responsibility for beliefs leads easily to the abdication of responsibility for actions, and to therapeutic problems when those actions clash with the person's interests.

**Enquirer** That would be difficult in many cultures. Shouldn't you do what your parents want?

**Mentor** Certainly not as an adult. But you're right that in many cultures going against the wishes of parents can be very difficult. Is it difficult in actuality, because it creates problems for the individual in relation to others; or is it difficult ideologically, because honouring the wishes of parents is an internal imperative? But your life is your experience and should belong to you. Your decisions should belong to you. Your parents' interests may not cohere with yours. When you don't do what you think is best (based on your experience), and when you try to please someone else, such as a parent, you get caught in a no-win situation. If you do what your parents want and it goes wrong, or you don't like the consequences, who's responsible? You have chosen to follow your parents' will. Should you blame them? But it was your decision to make; and, as an adult, doing what your parents want is your decision, not theirs. Holding other people responsible for your actions or the consequences of your actions is not helpful, and is unjustified because no one else has control over your body. You can blame yourself for blindly doing what your parents want; but you can hardly blame your parents if what they want for you isn't right for you: it's your responsibility to do what's best for you.

Furthermore, and most importantly, if you choose to delegate your decisions to others, you can't learn by experience. If it goes well, you're not responsible, because you didn't choose it. And if it goes badly, you don't even know the reasons behind the decision, because it was made by someone else. Immaturity is characterized by the abdication of responsibility.

**Enquirer** You can't learn from experience if you don't make decisions for yourself. Let your mistakes be your own.

**Mentor** When people abdicate decision making, they lose sight of who they are. A lot of people who present for therapy have this problem. You'll usually find that a person who says 'I don't know who I am' has abdicated responsibility for her decisions.

**Enquirer** That's another reason therapy can only really be successful in a (relatively) free society, where taking an independent viewpoint is permissible. In time, the person doesn't even know what she wants for herself, because it is so long since she did something that was based on what she thought was the right thing for her. So she loses her identity. Is this a problem that is more characteristic of women? Don't women more often sacrifice their own viewpoints and put others' viewpoints ahead of theirs?

What if you make your own decision, but it doesn't turn out well; and your parents' choice would have turned out better? Didn't they make the right decision and didn't you make the wrong one?

**Mentor** Even if your decision turns out badly, it was still the right decision, providing you made the best decision you could have made at the time, based on your experience and any information that you needed and were able to acquire.

The fact that you made your own decision is far more important than whether it turned out well, providing – and this is the crucial point – that you choose to learn from your experience. From your decision, and the experience you gain as a result of your decision, you continue to learn. You can learn nothing from a decision made by someone else.

Choosing your actions and determining your life path is solely your responsibility. You can't delegate it. It's the primary responsibility of every one of us to take care of ourselves and be self-responsible. This involves making the best possible choices for ourselves. It's a vital responsibility. It can be scary, but the consequences of abdicating that responsibility are profound.

**Enquirer** It sounds like you're saying that you should put yourself first. Isn't that self-interested and selfish? Isn't selflessness what we should be aspiring to? The absence of ego; being of service to others . . . ?

**Mentor** I know it is claimed by many that selflessness and absence of ego should be the aspiration. But that's not a helpful or healthy idea, in my view. Your first duty is to yourself. That's very important. Everything stems from that principle.

**Enquirer** But is it not selfish and arrogant to put yourself first?

**Mentor** Is it selfish or arrogant to look after yourself; to protect your own interests; to develop yourself; to fulfil your potential?

**Enquirer** It's self-interested.

**Mentor** Self-interest is not the same as selfishness. Let me ask you: what is your purpose; what are you here for?

**Enquirer** Surely, to serve others.

**Mentor** Really? Your purpose is to serve others? Should you do this at your own expense? Because it would be at your own expense if you are not taking care of yourself.

**Enquirer** I don't know. It's confusing. You're told about the importance of taking care of yourself, but you're also told that you should abandon your ego and serve others. And that you shouldn't be conceited or proud of yourself.

**Mentor** I agree, it's very confusing. I want to help you to look at it differently. Your purpose has to relate directly to yourself.

Let me ask you to consider this. Did you create yourself? Did you give yourself the talents and capacities that you have? Are you responsible for your body, your capabilities?

**Enquirer** No. I didn't create myself and I didn't give myself the capacities that I have.

**Mentor** Nature – or God, or the universe – bestowed these on you. Isn't that right?

**Enquirer** Yes.

**Mentor** Since you were given the talents and capacities that you have, and didn't create them yourself, it would be foolish to be arrogant, don't you think? It's hard to be arrogant about something that you didn't create for yourself but received as a gift. Shouldn't you rather be grateful for what you have been given?

Gratefulness is incompatible with arrogance. You cannot be arrogant about a gift you are grateful for. Gifts make us humble, don't they?

And what is the purpose of these gifts – your talents and capabilities? Isn't it incumbent on you to develop them and use them? In developing and using them, you are taking care of yourself and fulfilling your potential. Is this not true?

**Enquirer** Yes. I can't argue with any of that. You should not hide your talents under a bushel.

**Mentor** How would you do the greatest good of which you're capable in the world? Would you do this by sacrificing yourself, denying your interests, and neglecting your skills and capacities? Or would you do this by developing your skills and talents – fulfilling and empowering yourself – and utilizing them in the world?

**Enquirer** It is much better, paradoxically, to develop and utilize your skills. And it isn't selfish to do this?

**Mentor** Selfishness implies that you are serving yourself at the expense of other people. Taking care of yourself shouldn't ever directly harm other people. Others might not want you to take care of yourself; they might disapprove of you doing so and even feel offended that you're taking time for yourself.

**Enquirer** Such people should be avoided.

**Mentor** Taking care of yourself makes you a far greater asset to the world. Have I persuaded you?

**Enquirer** Self-care is a prerequisite of doing good in the world. I am persuaded. The faculty of reason is indeed important.

**Mentor** It can be very helpful to use reason to argue the case for a particular goal – but only ever as a *suggestion* to a client, of course. Sometimes the person has rejected a goal that could be good for him, for he believes it to be faulty, flawed or immoral –

just as you thought that self-care and self-interest were selfish and arrogant and therefore not acceptable.

An appealing and appropriate goal is vital to the success of REP – as, you'll remember, we discussed earlier. The therapist needs to help the client to find a practical goal that is preferable to what he's already doing. Sometimes this involves offering the person some ideas he hasn't thought of, or has rejected without adequately thinking through them.

If he thinks – as many people do – that the extreme opposite of what he is currently doing is the only alternative to what he is currently doing, the therapist should help him to consider other alternatives. Reasoned arguments can be helpful in persuading a person of the merits of particular goals.

**Enquirer** Isn't it better for the goal to come from the client?

**Mentor** Yes, certainly. But people often need a lot of help to formulate a positive and appealing goal The difficulty in doing this may have made the problem protracted. The crucial element is not who thought of the goal, but whether it is something the person actively chooses.

It's obvious, I know, but not always appreciated and worth repeating: you can't help a person go towards any goal she doesn't actively choose. The person will not take a single step towards a goal that the therapist thinks is wonderful if it doesn't appeal to the person herself. Reason may be very usefully applied in persuading a person of the merits of a particular goal. She must then embrace the goal with her will.

Reason is also required to counter clients' unhelpful beliefs that interfere with therapeutic progress. The belief you expressed a little earlier, that caring for others should take precedence over taking care of yourself, is commonly encountered. There are a number of commonly held beliefs that interfere with healing and change and contribute to people being thwarted in pursuit of their goals. Since these beliefs are ideological in nature (that is to say, not founded on experience), they can be readily changed if the person so wills.

Earlier I referred to Jayden who, in the role of the party-going drug dealer, felt he had status and esteem. He was cool; he was somebody. People were interested in him and seemed happy to see him. When he wasn't high and dealing, he considered himself boring and without appeal. This young man was attending Twelve Steps residential rehab, paid for, with some sacrifice, by his mother. With these beliefs about himself and his role, do you think Jayden was going to stay sober for long? Definitely not. The last thing Jayden wanted was to be a boring nobody. He needed to find a way to like and value a sober version of himself at least as much as the drug dealer version.

In order to like his sober self Jayden might need to change his viewpoint. The achievement of this may involve a greater investment in his own estimation of himself and less regard for the estimation of others. Achieving this subsidiary goal would require persuasion on a rational level of the merits of this goal and, probably, therapeutic work to establish the belief at the level of feeling.

Whatever the alternative chosen, the goal has to be more appealing than the present behaviour, or it won't be sustained. The behaviour which has the greatest motivation will always triumph.

**Enquirer**  What if the person has a strong belief, perhaps motivated by religion or culture, that prevents him from adopting an empowering goal and he's unwilling to change his belief? What if he thinks his belief has a moral imperative? For example, he takes the Christian view that he should put others before himself . . . ?

**Mentor**  I would explain to him how this belief may be contributing to the therapeutic problem he is experiencing, and suggest that challenging the belief could enable him to overcome the problem and achieve his goal. I would add that it's his life, and it's completely up to him.

**Enquirer**  Why would you say that?

**Mentor** The person needs to take full responsibility for his decisions and own them. He can't passively go along with someone else's proposals. But I would earnestly challenge any belief that is creating a problem for the person. It's important to take great care, of course, when challenging a belief that someone holds dear. If you appear to rubbish someone's beliefs you are going to lose rapport with that person. Without trust, you can achieve nothing.

When I have the person's agreement that it is worth changing his belief – or, at least, that it is worth *considering* changing it (a much easier step to take, which doesn't require commitment, but nevertheless pretty much assures the change) – I'll help him to find a goal he's comfortable with. This may well involve delivering some rational arguments.

**Enquirer** And it's possible for him to change his belief.

**Mentor** Yes. As we discussed earlier, ideological beliefs are readily changed. The change requires intention and will – that is all. That's why therapy is most successful in a free society. If however the person wants to change his belief, but finds he can't because the belief is underwritten by feelings, then this belief is addressed as a therapeutic problem. Something happened in the past that made this belief a learning for him.

**Enquirer** I'm glad reason has a place in REP. Do you have other examples where you need to deliver rational arguments to help someone to choose a useful goal?

**Mentor** This is a very common one: the person is unwilling to let go of anger towards her transgressor. You might think it's strange that so many people seem to want to hold on to their anger.

**Enquirer** The anger is vengeful. It feels like it exacts some kind of revenge or punishment.

**Mentor** Yes. She's confused the emotion associated with the desire to punish – anger – with punishment itself. It's as if by holding on to her anger she is continually punishing her transgressor.

**Enquirer** In fact, the transgressor is probably long gone and has forgotten all about it.

**Mentor** So who does the victim's anger actually hurt?

**Enquirer** It only hurts the victim. It doesn't hurt the transgressor in the least.

**Mentor** That's right. That's the argument I put to the person who claims to want to hold on to anger. I add that the lingering anger means she is stuck, holding on to the experience, and the transgressor is actually still winning. I say to the person: *Is your anger hurting the other person in any way?* She has to agree that it isn't. Next, I'll say: *Is your anger benefiting you in any way?* Again, she has to agree it isn't. The person is usually very clear that the anger isn't benefiting her. Then: *If you could let go of it, would you?* At this point, any answer other than yes would be patently irrational.

**Enquirer** Do people always accept that argument?

**Mentor** Yes, they do. People are susceptible to reason when it's in their own interests. It would make no sense to want to hold on to something that punishes oneself and not the transgressor. This is the reverse of what the person wants! The logic is compelling.

**Enquirer** Are there other common examples where you give a reasoned argument to persuade someone to change his goal?

**Mentor** Guilt is a common example. People seem to believe that by holding on to guilt they are somehow making up for their wrongdoing. But of course they are not. I would ask similar questions to those about anger. *Does holding on to your guilt help the person you have wronged?* In most circumstances it clearly doesn't, unless the other person wants to keep punishing him. This may occur in families. If the person's spouse or parent wants to keep punishing him, I ask: *Is it helpful to your relationship with your spouse* (or other family member) *for you to hold on to your guilt and allow the person who was wronged to keep punishing you?* It obviously isn't helpful. The presence of guilt turns the relationship between spouses (or family members) from one of equals into wronged and wrongdoer, punishing and punished, perpetrator-victim and victim-perpetrator. The guilty person will eventually become resentful for being the recipient of punishment and will start attacking his spouse, if he's not doing so already.

I also ask, *Does it help you to hold on to your guilt?*

**Enquirer** The guilt may be a reminder to the person not to transgress in that way again.

**Mentor** Yes, the person might suggest this as a reason to hold on to the guilt. I agree with him that it's very important to learn from this experience, and I enquire whether he has learned all he needs to learn from what he did. Nearly always, he has already learned all he needs to learn. If he hasn't, and perhaps even if he has, we just make explicit the learning he should take from the experience. I check whether, without the guilt, he would be able to remember and act on the learning. And of course he will be able to. I ask again: *Is your guilt still helpful to you now?* The answer will almost certainly be no. Then I say: *If you could let go of the guilt would you?* It would be irrational for him not to want to let go of the guilt if it is not helpful in any way.

Remember, the person has to want to let go of the guilt before you can help him to do this. But no one will resist an argument that is clearly in his own (and, where relevant, the other party's) best interests.

I'll ask the person to say that he's ready to let go of the guilt.

**Enquirer** You ask him to state it out loud.

**Mentor** Yes. I want him to say it and hear himself say it. He's making a declaration of intent. I'll often ask a person to make an undertaking to himself out loud.

I'll explain that since on a conscious level he wants to let go of the guilt, his body will help him to do it. Having completed the work on the conscious level, we address the issue at the level of feeling.

Here's another example. A common theme among people who come for therapeutic help is the desire to please and the fear of others' disapproval. For these people, to do anything that might disappoint or upset others is wrong and should be avoided – even when such behaviour is detrimental to the person's own interests. The consequences of this belief is often social anxiety.

Again, rational arguments will be employed. The person cannot heal his social anxiety without changing his beliefs about the need for approval – first on a rational level; then on the level of feeling.

The need for approval is framed (or rationalized) by the person with social anxiety differently to how it is framed by the therapist. In his way of thinking, by not disappointing other people he's sacrificing himself for their benefit. He believes his behaviour is commendable and for the benefit of others. Through self-sacrifice he's trying not to be the problem.

**Enquirer** How does social anxiety result from the need to avoid disapproval?

**Mentor** If you are desperate to avoid disapproval you will not advocate your own viewpoints, or wishes, for fear that they will invite others' disapproval. This puts you at the mercy of others' opinions and plans – including their plans for you and their opinions about you. Being at the mercy of others in this way is strong grounds for anxiety.

What is the goal that would help the person? On a conscious, rational level, the person needs to decide that he wants to believe that it's okay if others are upset or disappointed by his actions. He doesn't have to like it if others are upset; that would be perverse. But he must believe, on a rational level, that expressing his legitimate viewpoint should (in many contexts) take priority over the sensibilities of others. He won't believe this on an emotional level yet, because we haven't yet done the work, and a change on the emotional level is the result of the resolution work; but he can have, and must have, the intellectual belief, and the conscious, rational intention and desire to believe it.

**Enquirer** How do you persuade someone of that? I think I share that issue! I want people to approve of me. I don't want to disappoint anyone. Isn't that natural?

**Mentor** There's no harm in wanting people to approve of you. That's not the same as needing approval from everyone, and behaving in a way that compromises your own desires and values to get that approval.

**Enquirer** Actions need to be consistent with values. Trying to please others compromises your values and leads to inconsistent behaviour.

**Mentor** Your values and behaviour should be in alignment.

**Enquirer** What would you say to persuade someone that it's okay if others are disappointed in you or disapprove of you when you're behaving according to your values? What rational arguments would you make?

**Mentor** First, I'll ask: *Which is more important to you, your experience, or the experiences of other people?* Clearly, your own experience is the most important. You have direct access to your experience; in fact, it's all you ever have. You have others' accounts of their experience, but never direct access to their experience. It follows that behaving in a way that's right for you is more important than others' opinions or emotions about your behaviour.

Second, I'll suggest: *You are not responsible for the emotions of others.* If someone becomes upset because of something you say or do, it is not that you are making that person upset. You are responsible for your behaviour, but not for the emotions of someone else. When you behave in a way that is true to your principles (but it's also commendable to be tactful and sensitive), if someone gets upset because of your behaviour, that is not your problem. You are responsible for your own behaviour, not others' emotions or responses. There's no telling how anyone will emotionally respond to anything; or even whether the response they claim to have is genuine or relates to your behaviour at all.

**Enquirer** We should judge others' and our own behaviour; we should not judge emotions. If someone is upset, the emotion is his responsibility; my behaviour is my responsibility, his emotional response is not.

**Mentor** People sometimes need a lot of convincing before they understand or are willing to accept this point – especially people who have more than an ordinary share of emotional disturbance. But, when explained clearly, I haven't come across anyone who insists that he is responsible for the emotions of others, or that others are responsible for his emotions. No one can dispute that a hundred people might have a hundred different emotional responses to your words and behaviour. It makes no sense to claim responsibility for each person's emotional response.

**Enquirer** Nobody's that important.

**Mentor** Third, I'll offer an analogy. Although the person who is the queen of England seems generally to be approved of, the heir to the throne is roughly approved of and disapproved of in equal measures. What accounts for this? The queen says nothing controversial; but the prince readily expresses his beliefs publicly. It may or may not be a good idea for a monarch to speak her mind, or for an heir to the throne to speak his mind. The queen can rely on her position for esteem, but most of us cannot.

The point is this: if you do or say anything of value, anything that has significance, it's going to be controversial and some people are not going to like it, and therefore may well not like you. So it's a good sign if some people don't like you; it means you're doing something significant.

**Enquirer** Unless you are in a hurry to wear a crown!

## Key points

It's your primary duty to act in your own true interests and take responsibility for your decisions.

By taking responsibility for your decisions you are able to learn from your experience.

Self-care is a prerequisite for doing good in the world.

The use of reason can help the therapist to persuade a person of the merits of a particular practical goal.

Beliefs that are contrary to a person's interests should be challenged. For example, that the person's anger is (somehow) hurting the perpetrator; that guilt helps to right a wrong; that disappointing others has to be avoided.

# 25

## Connecting present and past

**Enquirer** It would be helpful to me if you would very briefly summarize your theory of how a therapeutic problem originates in the past and comes to manifest in the present: the aetiology of an emotional problem.

**Mentor** All right. Let's begin with the origins of an emotional or therapeutic problem.

A person – very often but not necessarily a child – encounters a difficult situation that degrades his personal dignity. He needs to find a way of responding to this difficult situation that will lessen the severity of its impact on him; that will reassert as far as possible his personal dignity. To this end, he finds a way of behaving that provides some sort of solution to the problematic situation.

The original events that incur personal dignity degradations we refer to as problem experiences; and we call a person's strategies to cope with or manage these experiences his behavioural responses (or remedial behaviours). The behavioural response may be a far cry from an ideal solution, but it is the best way the person can find to cope with or reduce the severity of the degradation.

From the original experience the person learns behaviour that helps him to manage or cope with similar circumstances. The behaviour learned in one context is activated automatically in the future, whenever the person is faced with a potentially perilous event similar to the one encountered previously. This behaviour is too important to be left to the deliberations of the conscious mind and is activated involuntarily by feelings, the agency of action.

The remedial behaviour – developed originally as a solution to difficult circumstances – isn't necessarily a problem, unless and until it comes into conflict with how the person consciously wishes to behave to achieve something he wants. When such a situation arises, the conscious mind wants to behave one way, but the unconscious body insists on behaving in a different way. The conflict between the body's learned protective response and the desire of the conscious mind is what constitutes a therapeutic problem.

**Enquirer** A therapeutic problem occurs when the body wants to do something and the conscious mind wants to do something else.

**Mentor** That's right. Feelings are impelling the person to behave in a way he doesn't like or is contrary to what he's trying to achieve.

When presenting for therapy, the person may therefore identify either the feelings (interfering with the desired behaviour) or the problem behaviour (which the person wants to change) as her problem. She might alternatively present a symptom or aspect of the problem.

**Enquirer** Okay. Let me check if I understand you correctly. A person has an experience that degrades his personal dignity. To attenuate this emotional disturbance, he finds a way of coping with or managing the situation to reduce its negative impact on him; that is, to restore his dignity as far as possible. He finds a way of behaving that achieves this more or less successfully.

From experience he learns unconsciously that, faced with a particular kind of threat, a particular kind of behaviour will help him to reduce its impact. In future, when he finds himself in a situation his body recognizes as similar to the original experience, he'll behave in the way he's learned to behave. He will do this automatically, without thinking, impelled by his feelings.

He won't know why he behaves in the way he does, and won't question it, because his behaviour seems natural and inevitable. However, if the behaviour interferes with a goal, he will regard this behaviour as a problem. He will try to behave in a different way, in a way that will enable him to achieve his goal. But he fails, because the feelings – whether he's aware of them or not – compel a contrary behaviour that he learned some time before.

**Mentor**  That's right.

**Enquirer**  And it doesn't matter how long ago the problematic experience was. There's no expiry date?

**Mentor**  The body doesn't forget.

**Enquirer**  There's no time in the unconscious, says Freud.

**Mentor**  We will doubtless be given many opportunities to resolve our problems. If we don't take these opportunities and resolve them before old age they will become more and more difficult to manage, because our coping resources and compensation strategies will decline as brain cells die.

**Enquirer**  Now that I've got a better idea of how a therapeutic problem has its origins in the past, would you give me an actual example, showing this connection of past experience and present manifestation?

**Mentor**  Sure. I'm thinking of someone who came to see me for help with his career.

**Enquirer**  Let's give him a name. Ashton.

**Mentor**  Ashton had had a series of jobs that had all led nowhere. They often involved working in isolation, sometimes in remote places. Really, he wanted to be a consultant, but said he had a fear of working for himself. He knew what he needed to do to be a consultant, and he had the skills and experience. So why hadn't he done it? It was, he said, because of a lack of belief in himself.

We learned that the problem was about being visible. The idea of being visible created fear. The feelings of fear that came up in relation to being visible took him back, through the tracking process, to the age of sixteen. The problem material was a difficult relationship with his stepfather, who was very critical of him. After the resolution work he was able to be visible without any uncomfortable feelings. This meant that, if he chooses, he would be able to pursue his desire of becoming a consultant without fearing visibility. That's the quick summary.

**Enquirer** Why did the criticism Ashton received from his stepfather as a teenager mean that he found work in isolated places rather than the kind of work he wanted?

**Mentor** At the historical origin of his problem, what do you think was degrading Ashton's personal dignity?

**Enquirer** He was getting criticism from his stepfather, rather than the approval and understanding he no doubt needed.

**Mentor** Yes. What behaviour helped him attenuate the situation?

**Enquirer** He probably kept his head down, staying out of his stepfather's way.

**Mentor** That's right. He kept out of the way, out of sight. As long as he's visible, he's subject to criticism. The strategy of being invisible defended him from this. How does this remedial behaviour create a problem in the present?

**Enquirer** Ashton really wanted to work as a consultant, but that would mean working for himself. Working for yourself means being visible. Being visible, for him, means getting criticized. He took and remained in posts he wasn't happy with in order to be invisible and avoid the criticism that he feared he'd get if he did what he really wanted.

**Mentor** Yes. That's the conflict at the heart of his therapeutic problem: he wanted to work as a consultant, but doing this would mean being visible, and experience had taught him that he must remain invisible (to avoid criticism).

You see how the helpful learning of keeping his head down to avoid criticism has now become an unhelpful learning, because it stops him from achieving his goal. Sure, if you want to avoid criticism, better to keep your head down and not do anything noticeable. But that's not helpful if you are ambitious and really want to achieve something. Hence the conflict between how Ashton behaves and what he wants. The pursuit of his desired practical goal was thwarted by an uncomfortable feeling impelling a contrary behaviour.

Did you notice that he seemed completely unaware, on a conscious level, of the connection between being visible (and the fear of criticism) and working for himself, and had no notion of the cause of his difficulty? To him it seemed that the problem was a fear of working for himself; and he rationalized this – he explained it to himself – with the idea that he lacked belief in himself.

**Enquirer** But lacking belief in himself wasn't the real issue.

**Mentor** In many respects he did believe in himself – except that he had cause to doubt his self-belief because of his fear of criticism. It was confusing for him. He didn't understand why he couldn't go for what he wanted.

Does this explain a little more clearly how the feelings from a past issue affect behaviour in the present?

**Enquirer** Yes, very well. But I don't know how you got to the original experience.

**Mentor** We get to the sources of the problem via the tracking back process: the means to travel in imagination from the present problem to its origins in the past. The transit involves identifying the uncomfortable feeling in the present that impels the undesired remedial behaviour.

To identify the troublesome feeling and track to the origins, it will help us if we can articulate an appropriate practical goal, and an appropriate *therapeutic goal*.

**Enquirer** We've talked a bit about practical goals, but what are therapeutic goals?

## Key points

A therapeutic problem occurs when the unconscious body wants to do something and the conscious mind wants to do something else.

You will be given many reminders about your emotional issues. Resolve them before you lose your compensation strategies in old age.

# 26

## Getting started

**Mentor** When a Relearning Experience Process therapist begins working with a person, what's the first thing to identify, do you think?

**Enquirer** Is it the presenting problem?

**Mentor** That's the person's starting point. What do you need to find out next?

**Enquirer** I'm not sure.

**Mentor** You need to identify the practical goal. That is to say, you need to find out what the person wants that he's been unable to achieve. The problem and the practical goal are interrelated: one cannot exist without the other. The problem points to the practical goal, and the (seemingly unachievable) practical goal points to the problem. The person may be aware of one, the other, or both. The practical goal may not yet be clearly identified by the person; or the problem might not yet seem clear to the person. Often a discussion of the problem will lead to a more clearly articulated practical goal.

If the practical goal isn't clear, it may be that you haven't yet got a clear sense of the problem. When the person's initial focus is on the problem (rather than the goal), the therapist needs to understand clearly why it constitutes a problem.

Sometimes it's not clear what the practical goal is, because the therapeutic problem manifests in many different ways, and none of the manifestations are a definitive articulation of the problem. The practical goal may then be very difficult to articulate. I'm thinking of the case of a particular person [discussed later: named Brooke], where I was unable to ascertain the practical goal; and it was equally difficult to pin down the therapeutic problem. Eventually we settled on a therapeutic goal which allowed the therapy to progress. However, most of the time the practical goal is articulated easily enough.

Clarity about the practical goal is important for the therapeutic process. If the person's goal is not appropriate, she needs to understand why it's not appropriate and be given the opportunity to find and formulate an appropriate practical goal – which may well require the guidance of the therapist.

An inappropriate goal might be the reason why the person has remained stuck in the problem. We discussed this earlier, when we talked about the importance of formulating appropriate goals.

**Enquirer** Yes. The goal also needs to be appealing to the person – more appealing than his present behaviour.

**Mentor** Again, the person may have become stuck because the goal he envisages is not appealing to him.

**Enquirer** But it's also possible that the person presents a well-formed goal but hasn't been able to achieve it.

**Mentor** Yes, certainly: the person might have an appropriate and appealing goal. It often happens that people know what the problem is and what they want; but they still can't change the undesirable behaviour. This is often the case with people who have previously received psychotherapy or counselling. The person may have learned to understand or 'manage' the problem, but the problem has not been resolved.

To reiterate. Problem and goal are interdependent. They're two sides of the same coin. Without a goal there wouldn't be a problem; and the existence of a problem implies a (frustrated) goal. So the first therapeutic task is to identify the practical goal. This will often be determined through an exploration that includes a discussion of the problem the person is encountering.

**Enquirer** Yes, I understand that. Let's say the practical goal has been established. What next?

**Mentor** Once the practical goal has been identified, the therapist needs to determine what is stopping the person from achieving his practical goal. For it to be a therapeutic problem, the behaviour the person is unable to perform (to achieve his goal) needs to be behaviour that the person is perfectly capable of performing, but cannot because of something internal to him. Helping the person to change his behaviour to make the practical goal possible is the task and purpose of REP therapy.

What is lacking in the person so that he is unable to behave in the desired way let's call a *quality* or *attribute*. This quality or attribute is not a material resource, such as money, or a skill that needs to be learned; it is something that is already latent in the person and has the potential to be accessed in the immediate present. Through the restoration of this quality or attribute, the person will be able to behave in a way consistent with achieving his practical goal. We shall refer to this quality or attribute as the *therapeutic goal*. Achievement of the therapeutic goal therefore resolves the therapeutic problem, and is the task of the relearning or resolution work.

**Enquirer** The person is at the same time capable and incapable. That's paradoxical.

**Mentor** It's the paradox of internal conflict: the conscious mind and unconscious body are at odds. The conscious mind wants to do something; the body has a contrary orientation.

**Enquirer** The unconscious is trying to protect the person from harm. It's acting in the person's own interests.

**Mentor** Yes, exactly. It's acting in the best interests of the person, according to his experience.

**Enquirer** What are some examples of therapeutic goals?

**Mentor** The goal could be confidence; or the ability to say no; or the ability to prioritize self-care. But therapeutic goals need to be articulated carefully – as I shall explain.

**Enquirer** For REP, the agency that stops the person from being confident, saying no, or taking care of himself, is feelings. Feelings drive people to do what they don't want to do or stop them doing what they want to do. The unconscious of the person has learned from previous experience that the actions the person wants to take are potentially dangerous. They might lead to embarrassment, humiliation or ridicule (for example). Even if these feelings can be overcome by an act of will, it is only temporarily.

**Mentor** It's possible to behave in a way that is contrary to the unconscious body and overcome feelings through an act of will. But such a 'victory' is going to be limited and temporary and achieved only with great effort. Feelings will always win. As they should.

**Enquirer** That is true in my experience. Willpower always ultimately fails. Feelings are certainly stronger than the will. When feelings motivate undesired behaviour and interfere with what the person wants, a therapeutic problem develops. The facilitation of a certain 'quality' or 'attribute' – that is, of the therapeutic goal – is the required solution.

**Mentor** The therapeutic goal is what the person requires, and needs to acquire, to behave in the way she wants. The therapeutic goal is the antidote to the therapeutic problem. It's the remedy. Its achievement resolves the problem. If the therapeutic problem is fear of rejection, for example, the therapeutic goal may be self-approval. If the therapeutic problem is self-loathing, the therapeutic goal may be self-acceptance. If the therapeutic problem is fear of failure, the therapeutic goal may be acceptance of mistakes as an important and helpful learning stage en route to success. If the therapeutic problem is fear of disapproval, the therapeutic goal may be being true to oneself or one's principles, even when this displeases others.

**Enquirer** There are of course a great many possible issues that bring people to therapy, but in fact it looks like there aren't so many distinct therapeutic problems – and therefore not really that many therapeutic goals.

**Mentor** That's quite right. Just a few therapeutic problems underlie the majority of issues.

**Enquirer** What's the relationship between the therapeutic goal and the practical goal? Are you saying that the achievement of the therapeutic goal means the practical goal is achievable?

**Mentor** The achievement of the therapeutic goal means that the practical goal is much more achievable – provided that what had been identified as the therapeutic problem was in fact what was getting in the way of the achievement of the practical goal.

It doesn't mean the practical goal's achievement is assured, however. To achieve his practical goal the person still needs to take the appropriate action. Achievement may also – and often does – depend on the actions of others, which are outside of the person's control. And it's possible that there are additional therapeutic problems interfering with the achievement of the practical goal; and these other problems may not yet have had a chance to be recognized because they had been occulted by the current manifestation of the therapeutic problem. With the resolution of this therapeutic problem, others might begin to reveal themselves.

Achievement of a practical goal can therefore involve the resolution of a number of therapeutic issues.

## Key points

Initial investigation of both the therapeutic problem and practical goal should clarify both and ensure the practical goal is appropriate.

The therapeutic goal is the quality or attribute the person needs to make possible the achievement of the practical goal; it is therefore the remedy for the therapeutic problem.

Facilitating the therapeutic goal is the aim and outcome of REP.

# 27
## Inappropriate goals

**Enquirer**  You stress how important it is that the practical goal is 'appropriate'. How do you know if a goal is inappropriate? What makes a goal appropriate or inappropriate? Is it simply a matter of judgement?

**Mentor**  People frequently have inappropriate goals without realizing it. It isn't necessarily apparent whether a goal is appropriate or not to the therapist until it has been discussed. Various possible goals might need to be explored and interrogated. Ultimately, it is a matter of judgement.

I was attending a hypnotherapy training once when the trainer described a case he was currently working with. His client was married but having an affair with a woman who lived in a different town – shall we give him a name?

**Enquirer**  He's called Miyoko.

**Mentor**  Miyoko's presenting problem was difficulty urinating. All the time he was visiting his lover, and while he was in the town in which she lived, he was unable to urinate. This was clearly very unpleasant and inconvenient for the man.

The trainer asked for suggestions about how he might find a way to help Miyoko get over his urination problem. The trainer was making a classic error: identifying the client's presenting problem as his practical goal. The trainer's intention was to help his client to be able to urinate when he visited his lover in the nearby town. No doubt this was what the person expressly wanted. But it was not an appropriate goal for Miyoko. The highly significant message the man's body was trying to give him needed to be acknowledged and explored.

**Enquirer** Miyoko was clearly in conflict with himself. He wanted to be with his lover, but his body wasn't happy with the idea. What would have been an appropriate goal?

**Mentor** It's not possible to know, without talking to him. Miyoko himself most probably didn't know without discussing it. His body was giving him a message it was impossible for him to ignore, related directly to his sexual organs. No doubt, his body had previously given him this message more subtly in the form of feelings, but he had refused to attend to it. The conflict raging in the body of Miyoko had to be addressed. Addressing this conflict through discussion may well have resolved the problem. If it did not, an appropriate practical goal would need to be formulated.

**Enquirer** Therapy is not about trying to defeat the unconscious. That's a common mistake that therapists make.

**Mentor** The therapist has to work with the messages of the body. However apparently unpalatable the message, it's there for a reason. You can't overcome a problem by trying to defeat the unconscious. The issues underlying Miyoko's problem needed to be explored. He was in denial about what his body was trying to tell him.

The therapist should have helped Miyoko to address his body's messages and explore why his body was responding in such an extreme way. By colluding with the person's attempts to suppress or quell his unconscious, the therapist was exacerbating Miyoko's problem and compromising his rapport.

**Enquirer** What kind of issues should the trainer have explored?

**Mentor** He could have started with any of the following.

> *Did Miyoko want to stay with his wife or leave his wife for his lover?*
>
> *If he wanted to leave, what was preventing him from doing this?*
>
> *If he didn't want to leave, what was the purpose of his affair?*
>
> *What is his moral position about what he is doing?*
>
> *What are some of the possible reasons that were leading the body to react so extremely?*

**Enquirer** It could be Miyoko's body's way of telling him that an affair with this woman was a big mistake; or that she's the wrong woman for him. It could be that he is trapped in an unhappy marriage but has moral beliefs that prevent him from leaving. It could be that his affair reminds him (unconsciously) of a traumatic event in his childhood. And there are, of course, any number of other possibilities.

**Mentor** The work of establishing appropriate goals – both practical and therapeutic – may well illuminate the nature of the conflict between what his body wants of him and what he's doing or wants to do. You can see how determining an appropriate practical goal is really important in this case. Does Miyoko want to leave his wife or not? He may not know. He's clearly conflicted. He may need help to work out what he wants.

The job of the therapist may be to help Miyoko to find the answer by resolving the emotional issues in him that are interfering with his judgement. It's often the case that the client doesn't know what he wants. The therapist obviously doesn't know what the person wants. But by healing the person's emotional issues, the person's true wishes and desires can emerge, which had been obscured by pathology.

Without determining the practical goal it's not possible to establish the therapeutic goal. You don't know how to resolve an issue unless you know what the issue is; and you don't know what the issue is if you don't know what the person wants.

**Enquirer** Miyoko – and his therapist – thought his goal was to conquer his urination problem, but actually it was something else. The therapist didn't bother to find out – or, more likely, was ill equipped to find out.

**Mentor** Miyoko's presenting problem was a symptom that could lead to the real issue – if the trainer had the skills to get there.

**Enquirer** I can see how people can easily have mistaken goals. Can you give other examples of mistaken goals?

**Mentor** Sometimes a person will state that his desired goal is not to care when others disapprove of him; or when his boss rebukes him; or when his girlfriend leaves him. To not care isn't a plausible goal. Even if it were possible (and it's not), it would not be desirable. Nor would it be ethical.

**Enquirer** It's neither possible, desirable nor ethical not to care!

**Mentor** You need to know what the person wants, or thinks he wants; but, where this is in conflict with his real interests, the therapist needs to help him to understand the problem and determine an appropriate goal.

**Enquirer** But is it permissible not to help the person to get what he wants? The trainer was at least trying to do that. Isn't that what the client is paying you for? And who is the therapist to arbitrate about what is good for the person?

**Mentor** Good questions. The job of the therapist, in my view, is to find a solution that brings the conscious and unconscious into alignment. That's about helping the whole person to get what he wants, not just the conscious part. The therapist would be acting unethically in supporting a person to achieve something that is contrary to the client's own interests (as perceived by the therapist). Integrity and congruence are central to the therapy process.

**Enquirer** I see. By aligning the conscious and unconscious, the person will be able to be congruent and emotionally at ease. Maybe this is what the yogi meant about the individual mind conforming with the purpose of cosmic life.

**Mentor** If you only help the conscious part of a person to get what he wants – supposing this to be achievable – the person will still be in conflict with himself. The body would find another way to express the issue, so he'd still have a psychotherapeutic problem.

**Enquirer** If the person was successfully helped to urinate in the town of his lover, the underlying problem would still be there and would manifest in a different way.

**Mentor** Yes. But, as I say, I don't think the therapist would be able to help him to urinate against the wishes of the body. If this was the therapist's aim, the person's unconscious would doubtless lose trust in the therapist and not want to work with her.

**Enquirer** So the therapist needs to listen to the presenting problem, and then establish what the person wants to have (instead of the problem). If this goal is not appropriate, the therapist needs to help the person to formulate an appropriate practical goal.

**Mentor** To establish an appropriate practical goal you might need to challenge the person's values.

**Enquirer** To be popular is an example of an inappropriate goal.

**Mentor** If someone's practical goal is to be popular, the person is likely to believe that popularity will solve a problem for him. So the therapist needs to find out what the problem is that he believes popularity will solve and help him to find a better way to solve the problem that is within his own control.

**Enquirer** How would you go about changing the belief that being popular is important?

**Mentor** I'd ask what's so important about being popular. I think you'd soon get to the real issue.

**Enquirer** What about the goal of being appealing to women? Sounds like there is something wrong with that too.

**Mentor** Yes. It's worth challenging. Is the goal to be appealing to women, or is it to find a partner? The person may believe he needs to be appealing to women in order to find a partner, or that this is necessary for him to feel good about himself. Of course he has to be appealing to someone – but not necessarily generally appealing – whatever that would mean. Pursuing that sort of goal may well make him even more unappealing to women.

**Enquirer** He could look phoney or, worse, smarmy. Trying to be appealing to women might be exactly what's putting them off!

**Mentor** Here are a couple of examples of inappropriate goals from a training I delivered recently. I need two South African men's names.

**Enquirer** Langa and Ntando.

**Mentor** Langa volunteered to be a demonstration subject. He had been attacked a few years previously by a person from a different South African clan. He hadn't fought back and viewed himself to be a coward. He also developed the idea that his attacker's clan was characterized by racism.

I asked him what he wanted to believe instead. He said that he wanted to believe he had been brave by not fighting back.

**Enquirer** That's a good reframe, isn't it?

**Mentor** It couldn't have worked as a goal – for very good reason: it wasn't true. You can't have a goal you don't believe in. You can't believe to be true something that you know not to be true. This goal was entirely inappropriate for Langa because he didn't believe his actions had been brave. This was the goal that he thought he wanted because it is how he would have liked to have seen it. Maybe this was how he explained his behaviour to others. His restraint may certainly be considered wise; but, according to his own assessment, it was not brave. Langa had identified for himself a false and therefore impossible goal – which is why he had remained stuck in that trauma.

Langa decided that he wanted to believe that the character of people from the attacker's clan was no different from that of any other group of people. While considering this new outlook, he spontaneously remembered that the friend of the attacker had tried to stop the attack and had actually ended up in a physical fight with his friend.

The incident was a problem for Langa because of the two conclusions he came to: that another racial group was disposed to racism (a view that didn't sit well with him); and that he had lacked courage in not fighting back. Langa needed an alternative understanding of what happened in order to let go of it. I helped him to formulate a new goal – which was simply to heal from the trauma of the attack. Letting go of his impossible goal allowed him (with a little further therapeutic work) to let go of the trauma.

Ntando, another participant at this training, as a young teenager had witnessed the death of a child, and had remained stuck in the trauma. He was on a school trip when a child had struck his head diving into the swimming pool. Although Ntando had had some basic first aid training in resuscitation, rather than attempt to help the injured child himself, he ran off to find a teacher. He returned with a teacher, who attempted to resuscitate the child, but the child tragically died.

Ntando had become stuck in this experience because he had chosen an inappropriate goal. He said that he wanted to believe – he wanted to persuade himself – that he had made the right decision in going to find a teacher (rather than use his training to try to resuscitate the child himself). But this goal wasn't appropriate. Although there was no way of knowing whether the alternative course of action, attempting to resuscitate the injured child himself, would have been successful, the decision he made was evidently unsuccessful, and so can't necessarily have been the best decision. He himself did not believe that the goal he proposed for himself was true, but had stuck with it because it was what he wanted to believe.

**Enquirer** He was stuck for the same reason that Langa had been stuck: he wanted to believe something that he couldn't possibly believe about his own behaviour.

**Mentor** I suggested that, instead, he could choose to understand and forgive himself. That worked well as a goal for him. It was appropriate. As an adult, it was easy for him to understand and forgive the actions of his child self.

**Enquirer** Are you saying that you can't, or that you shouldn't, help someone to achieve an inappropriate goal?

**Mentor** You probably can't and you definitely shouldn't. You probably can't because the body in all probability won't agree. You definitely shouldn't because it wouldn't be desirable. It would not be a responsible act.

**Enquirer** It would be unethical.

**Mentor** Yes. It wouldn't be serving the person's highest interests. Serving the person's highest interests doesn't mean imposing your values on someone else; but it might well mean challenging whether the person's own values are serving him well. This is a therapist's duty, I believe. Ultimately, though, it is his life, and he must take full responsibility for his decisions. The therapist can put forward counterarguments as possibilities to consider, and make suggestions – but that is all.

**Enquirer** You make 'suggestions'; you don't advise the client?

**Mentor** The therapist definitely shouldn't give advice. The person may burst into your office declaring that taking your advice was a dreadful mistake and his life is ruined! Whenever I make a suggestion to a client – which I do very often – I always add that it is his life and his decision, and that I'm only making a suggestion.

**Enquirer**  Earlier we were talking about Ashton, who needed to avoid being visible. Now that I understand the concepts of REP, I'm interested to know how he described his presenting problem and what his practical goal was.

**Mentor**  His presenting problem was this: *I put my energies into things and don't leave with anything.* The same lesson kept repeating itself: *I work hard and am dedicated, but I get no rewards. I feel stuck and frustrated.* He said that, in the companies that employed him, he tried to create a position for himself that would allow him to contribute more, but the companies wouldn't allow it. Actually, discussion revealed the companies were not in a position to allow this, or clearly would have perceived no advantage in doing so.

**Enquirer**  He was wasting his time and effort.

**Mentor**  Exactly. He needed to resolve his therapeutic problem, rather than find ways to pretend it didn't exist. Most of his recent work had been in African animal sanctuaries, very far away from any kind of visibility – far away from virtually anybody.

The presenting problem did not in itself suggest his practical goal. What is it that Ashton wanted?

**Enquirer**  He said he wanted to contribute more. Is that a practical goal? He also said he wanted to be a consultant.

**Mentor**  To contribute more is a practical goal – although you might want to find out what that means more specifically. The role of consultant would be an example of contributing more and could equally be the practical goal. Either of these practical goals would bring out the therapeutic problem of visibility; both will become achievable with the achievement of the therapeutic goal. The person should choose what he considers to be the most significant of the two goals.

**Enquirer**  All right. We've established the practical goal and the therapeutic goal.

## Key points

A person's presenting problem should not be mistaken for his practical goal.

Resolving a problem involves bringing conscious and unconscious into alignment, not trying to defeat the unconscious.

Helping someone to achieve an inappropriate goal is impracticable, undesirable and unethical.

Sometimes it is necessary to help a person to heal emotional issues before her true desires and wishes can be known.

# 28
## Questioning

**Enquirer** How do you get from presenting problem to where you need to get to? What kinds of questions do you ask? What did you ask Ashton, the would-be consultant?

**Mentor** I asked Ashton what he wanted and he told me that he wanted to be a consultant. I would never have guessed that that was what he wanted from the work he was doing. He assured me that he had all the knowledge he needed to be a consultant. So I asked, *Why haven't you become a consultant?* His answer was that he lacked belief in himself.

**Enquirer** But that wasn't entirely accurate. It was the explanation he gave to himself.

**Mentor** That's right. It was his rationalization. That's what you get if you ask *why questions* – rationalizations! So it wasn't a good question.

**Enquirer** But aren't you trying to find out why? Why shouldn't you ask why questions?

**Mentor** Why questions can sound aggressive. The response may be defensive and you risk losing rapport.

But perhaps more importantly, the client doesn't know why. If he really knew why (as opposed to thinking he knows why) he probably wouldn't have the trouble in the first place. Asking why is going to get the conscious thinking and reasoning processes going – which will not lead to a useful answer. I often say: if the client is thinking during therapy, he's doing the wrong thing. He is not going to get to the answer through conscious thought. No doubt he's tried that before himself, numerous times.

When I asked Ashton why, I got a rationalization. That's the conscious mind's answer. It wasn't exactly wrong here – although it often can be completely wrong – but it wasn't very helpful. We want an answer that is communicated from the unconscious body. Better to ask *what, when and how* questions; such as:

*What does that mean?*

*How do you know?*

*What would happen if . . . ?*

*When do you/don't you do that?*

*What makes you do it/not do it?*

These questions encourage specific answers rather than generalizations, and encourage the person to turn inward to consider his own experience.

**Enquirer** In NLP those are called meta-model questions and encourage a person to 'chunk down' to specifics. They take a person out of his problem 'trance' – just as the Milton [Erickson] model utterances are generalizations that put a person into trance (as the person makes 'transderivational searches' to find meaning in the generality: hence the trance).

**Mentor** Right. The real issue for Ashton wasn't so much that he lacked belief in himself but that he had a fear of visibility. To get from lack of belief – his rationalization – to visibility, I asked that type of question to get more specific information.

**Enquirer** What questions did you ask, specifically?

**Mentor** Remember that unconsciously the client knows exactly what the problem is. So his answers come as no great revelation to him; it's a matter of bringing out of him what he already unconsciously knows. My questioning went something like this.

> Therapist: *What needs to happen for you to be a consultant?*
>
> Ashton: *I need to put myself out there.*
>
> Therapist: *It's hard to put yourself out there?*
>
> Ashton: *I don't like being visible.*
>
> Therapist: *It's uncomfortable if others see you.*
>
> Ashton: *It's terrifying.*

This is how we got to the therapeutic problem of visibility, the fear of being visible.

**Enquirer** The aim of your questioning is to get more specific information about the problem. How do you know when to stop questioning?

**Mentor** I'm looking for the most specific answer possible, but I don't need detail. I'm also looking for the emotion. His 'lack of belief' in himself just begs the question: *What is the belief that you lack in yourself?* Lacking belief is vague. I don't know what he means by that. When he expressed his fear of being visible, I didn't need to go any further. He has the fear of being noticed, of being seen, of being exposed publicly.

**Enquirer** Could you have asked, *What do you mean by 'visible'?* Or *Who do you want to hide from?*

**Mentor** I could have asked those questions. But Ashton would have said something like, *I don't want to be visible to other people.* I might have said, *What's the matter with being visible?* But he would probably have just answered that it makes him fearful. Further questions would not have got any more useful information. I had identified the feeling (terror) and the instigator of that feeling (being seen) – that was what I was looking for.

I know the practical goal: to become a consultant or to do work that allows him to contribute more. I know the therapeutic goal: *I'm comfortable being visible to others.* I know the feeling that interferes with progress towards his goal: terror.

I don't yet know why he has this fear of visibility or where it comes from. Further questioning probably won't reveal these. We need to identity the original problem material, which will require the process of tracking. Identifying the problem material will give a clearer understanding of the problem; and, most importantly of course, it will enable us to resolve the problem.

**Enquirer** I'm not sure what else there is to learn by going back to the original experience in the person's past. Why do you need to know where the problem comes from? Can't you resolve it now that you have the issue and the feeling?

**Mentor** Until we travel back to the origins of the problem and find out what was going on then, we don't know what the problem behaviour in the present is all about and, without that information, we don't know how to resolve it.

**Enquirer** What did you learn at the origins?

**Mentor** We learned that underlying the problem of being seen was criticism Ashton received from his stepfather. This is what we call the problem material. As a result of this criticism, he learned to keep his head down and not be visible. This was his remedial behaviour.

**Enquirer** The decision he made to not be visible was unhelpful for him.

**Mentor** It's not helpful to him later on – it's the cause of his problem of not being able to become a consultant – but it was certainly helpful at the time he developed the behaviour.

We don't want to judge negatively the strategy the person developed in the original circumstances. (Of course we never want to make those kinds of judgements in therapy.) Being invisible may not be the ideal response – who knows? – but it was the best that Ashton could come up with at the time, based on the knowledge and experience he had gained. I believe that to be true. At the time that it was developed, this behaviour was resourceful.

**Enquirer** Ashton's practical goal was to contribute more, or become a consultant, which is about being visible. His therapeutic goal is to be comfortable being visible. If he can overcome his inhibitions and be comfortable being visible, then his practical goal becomes possible. The problem is that being visible is exactly what he has learned he mustn't be. He was in a place of contradiction.

**Mentor** Exactly. That's why it's so difficult (if it's possible at all) to resolve a problem without resolving the origins of the problem. He was fighting against himself: *I want to be visible; but being visible exposes me to criticism and is therefore dangerous.*

To be comfortable being visible is a perfectly usable therapeutic goal, and was the best goal we had before tracking back. (It allowed us to get to the problem material, which is the primary purpose of the therapeutic goal.) But when we got to the origins of the problem we could identify an even more precise therapeutic goal. We amended the goal to: *I'm okay even when I'm criticized.* It could equally have been: *I choose to do what I think is best even if others criticize me.* If Ashton can be okay with criticism, he will have overcome his fear of being visible.

**Enquirer** So you can change the therapeutic goal.

**Mentor** Yes, if you identify a better one.

## Key points

Questioning should aim for specificity, rather than detail.

The therapist is helping the person to express what she unconsciously knows.

# 29
## Terms and concepts

**Mentor** I think it would be helpful to make a list of our specialist terms and define them.

*Therapy complex* is a concept that encompasses all aspects of the psychological or emotional problem: practical goal, therapeutic goal, manifest problem, remedial (or adaptive) behaviour, problem behaviour, problem feelings, and problem material.

*Presenting problem* is the client's initial description of the problem. Interrogation of the presenting problem normally leads to delineation of the practical goal.

*Practical goal* is an appropriate and appealing formulation of what the client wants to achieve in the world but is unable to achieve because of something in herself.

*Therapeutic goal* is the personal quality or capacity that will make it possible for the person to achieve her practical goal (or, at least, remove an obstacle to its achievement that is internal to the person). The therapeutic goal is not something exterior to the person; it is latent within the person and is potentially realizable right now, in the present moment. Achievement of the therapeutic goal is the task and outcome of the therapy consultation.

*Manifest problem* is a description of how the person experiences the problem in the present. It will be what has prompted the person to seek therapy. The problem, manifested in the present, has its origins in the past and will have further manifestations in the future (unless and until it is resolved through the relearning work).

*Personal dignity* is the result of having emotional needs met. Personal dignity feels like an entitlement, and its frustration can lead to desperate bitterness. The struggle for personal dignity is however a constant and unremitting challenge and an aspect of the human condition.

*Personal dignity degradation* is the experience of having emotional needs frustrated or denied. Any assault on or undermining of the integrity of a person has the effect of lowering the person's self-regard. The greater the degradation, the more pronounced the emotional discomfort. To reduce this discomfort, and to redeem or salvage personal dignity as far as possible, a change in behaviour is required (or, possibly, a change in the person's interpretations and understanding of events). The behaviour modification is termed remedial (or adaptive) behaviour.

*Emotional needs*, which confirm human beings' essentially social nature, are individual to a person, though a great many are shared in common, and may include, for example, love, comfort, safety, recognition, respect, admiration and sex. The satisfaction of emotional needs is required for the achievement of personal dignity. Having emotional needs satisfied is a perpetual human challenge. When emotional needs are not met it is experienced as a personal dignity degradation. The satisfaction of emotional needs produces happiness. Much human energy is expended, however, in the pursuit of objectives that are not emotional needs and do not produce happiness.

*Problem feelings* are the uncomfortable feelings that directly drive remedial behaviour – that drive a person to behave in ways contrary to what she wants, or (which is to say the same) stop her from behaving in ways consistent with what she wants.

*Remedial* (or *adaptive*) behaviour is the strategic behaviour that a person develops in response to a personal dignity degradation. This behaviour is characterized by its being adopted specifically to ameliorate a problem situation. When this behaviour is transposed involuntarily to a new situation, and dictates behaviour that is against the person's wishes (because it has come into conflict with a practical goal of the person), it becomes the problem (or manifest) behaviour, constituting a therapeutic problem. Remedial behaviour is considered pathological.

*Problem* (or *manifest*) behaviour is the undesired behaviour manifesting in the present.

*Problem material* is the difficult experiences in the person's past identified as the origins of the problem. These experiences lead the person directly to develop remedial behaviour. It's the problem material that requires the resolution work.

*Amelioration* (or *attenuation*) of emotional discomfort is the intention underlying the person's attempt to restore personal dignity through remedial behaviour.

*Resolution* (or *relearning*) *work* is the intervention that counters the remedial behaviour and brings into realization the therapeutic goal. As a result of the resolution work, the problem feelings are eliminated, the manifest behaviour loses its driving force, and the therapeutic problem is resolved. The problem complex dissolves permanently – unless there are additional problem experiences that contribute to the manifest behaviour. If there are additional experiences that contribute to the therapeutic problem, these also need to be resolved for the problem behaviour to be completely transformed.

*Tracking* (or *tracking back*) is the process that transports the person (in imagination) from the present to the origins of the therapeutic problem in the person's past.

# PART III

## RELEARNING THERAPY

# 30
## Preparation phase

**Mentor** As you know, in REP the key to being able to resolve the problem at the origins is the tracking or tracking back process. The tracking process is simple, but it's only possible if particular elements of the therapeutic problem are accurately articulated.

There are three main phases to REP:

(1) The preparatory work, which establishes the practical goal and therapeutic goal and brings online the feelings required for tracking back.

(2) The tracking process.

(3) The relearning work.

At the end, the results of the work are tested.

The most challenging and time-consuming element is usually the preparation work. The tracking process is generally very straight-forward and only takes a few minutes. The relearning work will sometimes require imaginative dexterity on the part of the REP therapist, but is rarely time consuming.

**Enquirer** I'm beginning to understand the different elements of a therapeutic problem. But it would be helpful to have an example of the preparation phase: going from presenting problem to the point where you are ready to track back to the origins of the problem.

**Mentor**  Yes. Here's an example.

A person enters my office and says he's really stressed at work and this is affecting his sleeping, eating and work performance. That's his presenting problem . . . What shall we call him?

**Enquirer**  Call him Augustus.

**Mentor**  I want to find out what it is about work that is stressing Augustus so much. He says it's volume of work and expectations placed on him. This is more specific information, but I need to chunk down further and find out what the expectations actually are and who has them.

But Augustus is unable to give a convincing answer to either the what or the who. He can't say what the expectations are of him that are so stressful, and he can't say who has these expectations of him. He can't actually recall his managers expressing any dissatisfaction with his work, or making any particularly onerous demands.

Where, then, does he get the impression that the expectations on him are beyond what he could reasonably expect of himself? The expectations are in fact his own: his managers' unrealistic expectations and demands are his own construction. I suspect that his stress is therefore entirely self-imposed.

**Enquirer**  How did you know the expectations were just his own construction?

**Mentor**  He could give no evidence at all in support of the idea that his managers demanded or expected more than he was presently delivering. But his anxiety about this was intense.

I needed to find out more about where these expectations came from. I had in mind that he had unrealistic expectations of himself;

possibly that he demanded impossible perfection from himself. If his expectations of his own performance were unrealistic, we would need to help him to change them.

**Enquirer** Why do you say 'we'?

**Mentor** It is a joint endeavour: the client and I are working together.

Augustus finally reluctantly admitted that he feared losing his job.

**Enquirer** Reluctantly?

**Mentor** He was reluctant to declare this because on a rational level he had doubts that it was in fact the case. But he felt it.

**Enquirer** He didn't think he was actually at risk of losing his job?

**Mentor** When he articulated it, he had no doubt that the fear of losing his job was the cause of his anxiety. But that doesn't mean he believed it on a rational level. When I questioned him about it, he acknowledged that his job wasn't at risk. He confirmed that his work was valued by his managers and he was considered very competent. He knew himself that he was doing a good job. There was no real or imminent danger that he might lose his job. He knew all this on a rational level. And yet, the fear of losing his job was creating intense anxiety and stress.

Here again is the distinction between what a person knows on a rational level and what is felt on an emotional level. Because the feelings are involuntary (and come from the past), no amount of rational thinking can extinguish them. This kind of contradiction is very uncomfortable and to articulate it clearly is often very difficult – without the help of the therapist.

However, the rational knowledge that his job was not under threat is a precondition for Augustus to let go of this idea on the level of feeling. If on a rational level he maintained that his job really was under threat, obviously he wouldn't be able to relinquish any of his anxiety.

**Enquirer** If his job had really been under threat, it would not be helpful for him to feel otherwise!

**Mentor** That's right. There might still be a therapeutic problem there somewhere, but it wouldn't be the fear of losing his job. Augustus' fear of losing his job was not based on any external evidence. In other words, the fear came from within himself and was misplaced and inappropriate. It was this fear (not, as I had mistakenly suspected, a desire for perfection) that was behind his construction about the expectations of his managers. He felt (but hadn't vividly articulated it to himself, because it was so irrational) that he might lose his job. In order to retain his job, he must work harder (rationalizing, but again rather vaguely, that this was his managers' expectation of him) – because this is how you keep your job (isn't it?): work harder; do better.

The stress arose from the idea that his job was under threat. But his solution – working harder – did nothing to diminish the fear of losing his job.

**Enquirer** It couldn't, because the threat didn't derive from real circumstances in the present; so it wouldn't be alleviated by greater achievement. Whatever action he took was not going to diminish the threat. In fact, the fear may acquire some justification because the stress may well begin to affect his performance adversely.

**Mentor** The presenting problem is – what?

**Enquirer** Work stress. And the effects of this stress on his eating, sleeping and work performance.

**Mentor** What is the practical goal?

**Enquirer** He thinks his practical goal is to save himself from losing his job – although this is not an appropriate goal because his job wasn't actually under threat. He thinks he has too much work and is demanding too much of himself in an effort to keep his job. But that is not the real issue. He wants to overcome the work stress – which is real enough.

**Mentor** That's right. If we tried to work with an inappropriate goal our therapeutic attempts might lead nowhere, because we'd be trying to help with something that wasn't actually the problem. But I did check that working too hard wasn't a problem in itself. I said, 'If you weren't afraid of losing your job, would you still feel that you need to work extra hard?' And the answer was no.

**Enquirer** So what is an appropriate practical goal for Augustus? Is it to overcome his work stress?

**Mentor** That's what we needed to consider. I asked him: *What do you want instead of this fear of losing your job?* He replied, 'I want to feel absolutely secure in my job.' What do you think of that goal?

**Enquirer** Absolute job security is not a reasonable expectation. It's another example of an inappropriate goal.

**Mentor** I suggested this was an unreasonable expectation and explained why. I asked him to consider a different goal.

He said: 'I get on with my job without fear of losing it.' That was a perfectly good formulation of an appealing and appropriate practical goal. Ideally, we use positive terms for the practical goal, but it's not always possible. This goal at least had a positive phrase.

**Enquirer** It seems that some goals can't be stated positively. It's hard to formulate positive goals about addiction, for example. Any wording about addiction is going to have a negative element. The best I can think of would be something like: *I am liberated from this addiction*; *This addiction has no appeal for me*; or *I get on with my life happily without this addiction.*

**Mentor** That's true. Occasionally we have no choice but to use a negative formulation for the practical goal. We now have a practical goal. What's the therapist's next task?

**Enquirer** To articulate a therapeutic goal.

**Mentor** Yes. And unlike the practical goal, the therapeutic goal must be stated in positive terms. If the therapeutic goal can't be formulated in positive terms, it's not an appropriate therapeutic goal. Similarly, the therapeutic goal needs to be capable of being true right now, in the immediate present. If it can't be true right now, it's not an appropriate therapeutic goal.

We further discussed his therapeutic goal, and finally Augustus settled on: *I'm confident that the work I do is good enough.*

If, after the resolution work, he is able to feel in the present moment that this is true (rather than just think it and believe it on a rational level), he won't have an unrealistic fear of losing his job and his stress (at least in relation to this issue) will no longer be there. In other words, the problem will have been resolved.

**Enquirer** Why do you need to articulate a therapeutic goal? Remind me of the purpose of doing that?

**Mentor** The articulation of the therapeutic goal by the person, when it has been correctly construed, brings up the problem feeling. This is crucial to the therapeutic process because the problem feeling is the agency that leads back to the origins of the problem.

**Enquirer** What do you mean by that?

**Mentor** I mean that, when the person states the therapeutic goal, the uncomfortable feeling associated with the problem will present itself. If the therapeutic goal isn't correctly expressed, the uncomfortable feeling won't be there. This feeling is indispensable for the tracking process to operate: it enables the person to go back to the origins of the problem.

**Enquirer** I see. Where did the tracking process take Augustus?

**Mentor** He travelled back to ten or eleven years old. This is the origin of the problem; and it is here that we find the problem material. At the age of ten or eleven Augustus began to realize, or realize with greater clarity, that he was gay; and, at the same time, he was acutely aware that if his sexuality was discovered (in the conservative rural community in which he was brought up) the consequences would have been dire and he would have been vilified. So at the same time as the realization of his sexuality was dawning, so too was his need to conceal it; and, alongside this need for concealment, the fear that his secret would be discovered.

Throughout adolescence Augustus felt a high degree of fear and insecurity. He had to conceal an essential aspect of himself and some of his activities. This required a high level of vigilance that he maintained until he left his home country as a young man and came to London – where he could be more free to be himself. Some aspect of this was surfacing in the present and had created a problem at work.

In his youth, Augustus had learned that by working hard he could be thought of as clever, and this brought him the rewards of appreciation and esteem. He used his cleverness, he said, to get approval and gain acceptance – compensating for the disapproval that he feared regarding his hidden sexuality. But he didn't feel that he was very clever, and was constantly worried about being uncovered as a fraud.

The concern about being discovered as not being clever was similar to his fear about his sexuality being discovered. The two issues (being exposed as gay and being exposed as not clever) became confused and conflated. He had to hide not being clever just as he had to hide his sexuality. (In reality, of course, he was perfectly clever; but of relevance is his feeling that he wasn't – which may have been a displacement of his fear of being exposed as homosexual.)

An aspect of Augustus was socially unacceptable, and he'd be in danger if this aspect of him was found out. But he learned that if he worked hard enough, and was vigilant enough to hide the real truth, he could make himself socially acceptable. His learning could be stated in this way: *To avoid vilification I must work hard and be super-vigilant (and not be exposed as gay or as a fraud).* This is exactly what was going on in the present, and had become a therapeutic problem. He explained it to himself in a way that made more rational sense (as long as he didn't think about it too carefully): *I must work hard or I'll lose my job.* But how hard is hard enough?

**Enquirer**  Hard enough would be when the threat of vilification wasn't there any longer. And this can only be achieved through resolution of the therapeutic problem, not through hard work.

**Mentor**  That's what made it so stressful. However hard he works, the threat is still there, undiminished.

**Enquirer**  What was the solution?

**Mentor**  The solution was tricky because Augustus still kept his homosexuality secret from his family and community at home. Ideally, he would have (in his imagination) explained his sexuality to his family and been accepted. But the ideal is not always possible: his family would still not be accepting of his sexuality.

We found a way of helping his younger self to understand that the danger did not come because of something bad in himself, but because of something wrong in his community. In his imagination, trustworthy, supportive and loving people talked to his child self about his sexuality. He learned to be open with them, safely, and accepted that there was nothing wrong with him. Knowing he was perfectly acceptable as he was, he didn't need to be thought clever to be accepted. Augustus therefore no longer needed to maintain secrets, or fear being exposed as gay or as not so very intelligent.

## Key points

Both the therapeutic problem and practical goal should be accurately articulated for REP to be successful.

A person's explanation of the causes of his behaviour may be completely at odds with the real causes.

Practical goals should be stated in positive terms wherever possible; but this isn't always possible.

# 31

# Articulating the therapeutic goal

**Mentor** The practical goal, integral to the Relearning Experience Process, has to be appropriate and appealing for the individual.

**Enquirer** Yes, we have established that.

**Mentor** When the focus of the therapeutic issue is on the problem rather than the goal, as it often is with addiction, for example, the person may not have given much thought to what she wants instead of her problem behaviour.

**Enquirer** Twelve Steps keeps the addict focused perpetually on the problem.

**Mentor** Even if she has considered what she wants instead of the problem, the goal she has in mind might not be appropriate and might be decidedly inappropriate.

**Enquirer** Yes, we have talked about that.

**Mentor** Often the person's declared goal is simply the opposite of what she is currently doing, as if this is the only alternative. But the opposite of the current behaviour is usually impracticable and almost certainly highly unappealing to the person.

**Enquirer** We are very clear that the person may need help to elucidate an appropriate and appealing practical goal.

**Mentor** By articulating what the person wants, it becomes clear what is stopping her getting it, and the problem is clarified.

**Enquirer** Quite so.

**Mentor** We have also seen that it's acceptable if the person's practical goal is not completely in her own control. In fact, usually it won't be. The person who wanted a promotion is an example.

**Enquirer** That's right.

**Mentor** It's even okay for the practical goal not to be stated in the positive, if a positive expression is not possible.

**Enquirer** All of that is agreed and understood. I have been attending carefully.

**Mentor** Yes, and you have helped me to explore and articulate the arguments. But I am getting to the point.

When a person presents for therapy, it's because he can't achieve his practical goal and has acknowledged that there is something in himself that's preventing him from achieving it. The person feels impelled to behave in a way that is inconsistent with attaining his goal. Overcoming this problem does not require the outside world to change. Nor does it require new skills or knowledge. If these were required, therapy would not be the answer. The need for therapy is indicated by an internal obstacle; something within the person that needs changing. I appreciate that you know all this.

When the requisite internal change is achieved, the person will be able to behave in a way consistent with attaining his goal. This doesn't necessarily mean the person will attain his practical goal (since attainment of a practical goal is likely to depend not only on the requisite action being taken by the person but also at least in part on external forces); but the goal becomes possible as the internal obstacle to its achievement is removed.

Let's consider further the therapeutic goal. As an antidote to the problem behaviour – traditionally described as 'maladaptive' behaviour, but which we have called remedial or adaptive behaviour – the therapeutic goal needs to be postulated. The therapeutic goal is a quality that the person already has, or a capability already in him, that would make possible the behaviour required for the person to pursue his practical goal unencumbered. Unlike the practical goal, the therapeutic goal must therefore be something entirely within the person's own power, not requiring anyone else.

The therapeutic goal takes the form of a statement and must be (able to be) stated in the first person, in positive terms, in the present tense, and have the possibility of being true right now.

**Enquirer** I understand. The therapeutic goal is something the person is capable of right now, but achievement is inhibited because of uncomfortable feelings. Articulation of the therapeutic goal will bring up the feelings associated with the problem. These feelings are required for tracking back.

**Mentor** Exactly. There are specific requirements of an appropriate therapeutic goal statement. The therapeutic goal statement needs to be:

- Stated in the first person, using the personal pronoun *I*.
- Stated in the present tense.
- Stated in positive terms – what the person wants (not what she doesn't want).
- Entirely within the power of the person and not dependent on the cooperation of anyone else.
- Capable of being true right now.

**Enquirer** Some examples would be helpful.

**Mentor** Here are some examples of therapeutic goal statements.

*I'm lovable just as I am.*
*I'm perfectly attractive.*

*I'm confident in social situations.*

*I'm okay even if other people don't like me.*

*I'm comfortable being visible.*

*I'm okay even when I make mistakes and others criticize me.*

*I approve of myself even when others don't.*

*I am able to express what I feel even if others don't like it.*

*It's okay for me to have and express my own ideas.*

*I choose to put myself first and take care of my interests.*

*It's okay for me to make mistakes (and learn from them).*

*I'm comfortable not being in control of circumstances or other people.*

*I allow myself to trust trustworthy people.*

*I survive/am okay if others don't support me.*

*I recover even if I am betrayed.*

**Enquirer** I'm not clear what you mean when you say the therapeutic goal should have the possibility of being true right now.

**Mentor** Let's compare some of the examples I've just given of therapeutic goals with formulations that aren't suitable and wouldn't work. The statement, *I am lovable just as I am*, is good; but the idea that *my parents love and care for me* may be false and not capable of being true right now. The statement, *I'm perfectly attractive*, can be made legitimately by just about everyone; but the claim that *I'm appealing to women* may be far from true right now. The statement, *I'm confident in social situations*, has the possibility of being true in the present; but the idea that *I am popular among my peers* might be false and is not in the person's control.

The following statements may be impossible in the present: *I am in a good relationship*; *I am highly regarded at work*; *I am successful in my career*; *I am wealthy*. These may well be legitimate practical goals, but they could not be therapeutic goals and they don't point directly to therapeutic problems. If a client offered up one of these practical goals for therapeutic intervention, the therapist would need to find out what the person's not doing that she could be doing that would enable her to have a good relationship, make her wealthy, and so on; and then find out what (if anything) is stopping her from behaving in the manner required. If what is stopping her is internal to her, then she has a therapeutic problem.

**Enquirer** What about these statements, *I have overcome my social anxiety*; *I have overcome my fear of social situations*? Are those acceptable therapeutic goal formulations?

**Mentor** Those statements are not okay because they put the therapeutic goal in negative terms and they need to be stated in positive terms. If you were to overcome your anxiety, what would or might you be doing, or what would you be feeling?

**Enquirer** I would be feeling confident in social situations.

**Mentor** That is a much better therapeutic goal: *I am confident in social situations.* Can you be even more specific? How would you display that confidence?

**Enquirer** I would be confident speaking out in front of others.

**Mentor** That's better still, because it's even more specific. The therapeutic goal would be: *I am confident speaking out in front of others.*

**Enquirer** Can you say, 'I want to be confident'. Or, 'I wish I was attractive'?

**Mentor** Those sound more like whimsical statements than therapeutic goals. 'I wish I was attractive' is very different from *I am perfectly attractive.* Even 'I wish I believed I was attractive' is not a satisfactory therapeutic goal, because you wish that you believe you are attractive at the very same time as feeling that you're not attractive. A wish never needs to be realized. A wish is weaker even than an intention. The therapeutic goal must establish the desired reality, not defer it. Similarly with the statement, 'I want to be confident in social situations.' You desire it because you haven't got it. The statement, *I am confident in social situations*, is perfectly possible and achievable in the present moment.

The therapeutic goal has to be believable to the person. If some-body thinks she's ugly she may postulate a goal statement that asserts, 'I'm physically beautiful.' Put it to the person: *Is that cap-able of being true right now?* (If she does think it could be true right now, of course don't argue with her. She will realize herself soon enough if the goal is impossible.) Help her to choose a goal that is credible to her. She doesn't have to be beautiful to get a part-ner or to feel comfortable in herself (for example): being perfectly attractive is enough.

**Enquirer** Give me another example or two of therapeutic goals that are not appropriate.

**Mentor** An inappropriate therapeutic goal would be: 'I don't care what others think of me.' Not needing others' approval is not the same as not caring what they think. A person shouldn't depend on the approval of others for her own self-regard, but a properly functioning human being cannot be indifferent. Much better could be something like: *I have the courage to say what I believe even if other people don't like it.* Another inappropriate therapeutic goal: 'I am super confident' (about my abilities in whatever it is).

**Enquirer** Super confidence lacks humility and the possibility of error. Super confidence also sounds like it excludes any doubt or nervousness at all – which I'm sure isn't realistic or helpful.

**Mentor** Not caring at all, not being in the least nervous – these are commonly wished for, but are inappropriate therapeutic goals.

Once you've determined the therapeutic goal, write it down, be-cause you're going to want to check it again at the end to make sure it has been realized. This is part of case note taking. Don't worry about interrupting the therapeutic process to do this: recording it emphasizes the importance of the goal.

**Enquirer** You check the therapeutic goal again at the end?

**Mentor** Yes. In fact, that's a key feature of REP. After the reso-lution work is done in the imaginary past, the person returns to the present. She is asked to try to bring back the uncomfortable feelings that were accessed for the tracking process.

**Enquirer** You actually ask the person to try to get the uncomfortable feelings back?

**Mentor** Yes. If the problem has been resolved she will not be able to get the feelings back. Remember that feelings are involuntary. If she can't get the uncomfortable feelings back, her behaviour will no longer be directed by those feelings, and she has regained freedom of choice. This is the test that the work is complete and has been successful. If some uncomfortable feelings remain, there is more work to do to resolve the problem completely. Of course, the client will want to test the success of the therapy in the world.

**Enquirer** Might the feeling still be there at the end?

**Mentor** It won't be the same feeling unless you've really been on the wrong track completely – and I don't know how that would be possible. If the person still has an uncomfortable feeling, it will have changed in form or intensity, indicating that you have done some of the work, but that there is more work to do – more experiences in the past to heal.

## Key points

Therapeutic success enables the person to pursue her practical goal unencumbered by internal obstacles; it does not assure its achievement.

Therapeutic goal statements need to be in the first person, present tense, use positive terms, not depend on anyone else, be possible right now.

Inappropriate goals, such as not caring or having super confidence, are undesirable and unachievable.

# 32

## Accessing problem feelings

**Mentor**  Once the therapeutic goal has been established, the person is asked to state the goal out loud. She does this and the therapist asks what she's feeling.

**Enquirer**  What's the purpose of stating the therapeutic goal out loud?

**Mentor**  A very interesting thing happens when the therapeutic goal is proclaimed. If the therapeutic goal has been accurately identified and correctly articulated, an uncomfortable feeling will accompany the statement. This feeling is crucial to our inquiry.

**Enquirer**  An uncomfortable feeling occurs when the person articulates her positive goal? That seems surprising. I would have thought she would have a good feeling.

**Mentor**  You might have thought so. A good feeling might also be there, because it can feel good to imagine having what you desire. Sometimes the person believes the therapist is asking for a positive feeling in response to stating the positive goal statement and will report that it feels good. But, if the therapeutic goal has been articulated correctly, there is predominantly an uncomfortable feeling, and it's this uncomfortable feeling that we're looking for. If necessary, this is explained to the person.

**Enquirer** Why would the person feel bad when articulating something that she wants? Does she feel bad because she hasn't got it?

**Mentor** Stating the therapeutic goal is like being in the problem situation. The body reminds the person that this situation is perilous. It's the bad feeling from the past coming up again as a warning. The person has learned that a particular behaviour is dangerous; so if the person makes a statement that suggests the behaviour is not dangerous, the body alerts her to the danger by reproducing the bad feeling.

I'm thinking of someone who had difficulty celebrating her own attractiveness, and felt deeply uncomfortable when she stated the therapeutic goal, *I am perfectly attractive.* As a teenager, her stepmother undermined and denigrated her whenever she dared in any way to suggest (either verbally or through her body language) that she considered herself attractive. Even wearing attractive clothes or showing off her figure led to negative remarks. When she said, *I am perfectly attractive*, her body would hastily remind her that considering herself such was dangerous, because denigration may be the response.

How do you think she deals with this problem as a teenager? What is her adaptive behaviour?

**Enquirer** I imagine that she hides her attractiveness. She makes sure she doesn't look attractive.

**Mentor** Yes, and she persuades herself that she is not attractive. The idea that she was perfectly attractive seemed so ridiculous to her that she just laughed when I asked her to state the therapeutic goal out loud. If the client laughs, you know you've found the appropriate therapeutic goal. Some people are reluctant to say the goal out loud because it sounds so wrong. But I still like to encourage them to say the words. They'll experience how different it is to make the statement after the resolution work is done.

**Enquirer** Now I understand why it is that if you don't have the appropriate therapeutic goal, there won't be an uncomfortable feeling.

**Mentor** The uncomfortable feeling provides confirmation that the goal is appropriate. It's also – vitally – the mechanism to take the person back in time to the origins of the therapeutic problem, via the tracking back process.

An appropriate therapeutic goal will definitely bring up the uncomfortable feelings. However, you need to be a bit careful because the person may have trouble accessing her feelings or has anaesthetized herself to her feelings. So it's possible to have the appropriate therapeutic goal, but apparently without uncomfortable feelings. Additionally, if the person smokes, he may well not be able to access his feelings without some effort and guidance. The same is true of many people with other difficulties who have learned to dissociate themselves from what they feel.

**Enquirer** Such as people who were abused as children.

**Mentor** Yes. Any trauma where the person has learned to cut herself off from her feelings. You need to have the feeling itself to work with – not the remembered 'feeling'; not a thought about the feeling; nor anything else that is in the head rather than palpable in the body.

**Enquirer** How do you help people to access their feelings if they're having difficulty?

**Mentor** If someone has difficulty accessing her feelings, I'd explain the process in the same way as I did earlier – I'd just take longer going through the steps. Do you remember we talked about that earlier?

**Enquirer** I don't really remember. Please remind me.

**Mentor** First, and most important, in order to feel, the person must be relaxed, and that means breathing freely. Tension involves holding the breath; so relaxing involves breathing freely. Not deeply, but freely.

Second, I find that it's helpful for the client to stand up rather than to sit. Sitting is fine for talking, but it's not a great position for accessing feelings. It's easy to dissociate when sitting. There can be a tendency to get too comfortable, and therapist and client should not get too comfortable sitting and chatting. Also, when the client is sitting, he's normally looking at the therapist. That's polite, but not helpful. His focus needs to be turned inwards on himself, not outwards to interact with the therapist. So I prefer the client to stand in order to access the feelings. When I'm standing up with the client, I stand alongside him, not opposite. I'm not in his space. I'm out of his way, but close by; an ally, in support.

Third, this is about feeling, not thinking, and the client needs to focus attention on his body. I check that the client is looking down while contemplating; if he's looking up, I know he's thinking rather than accessing feelings.

If the client tells me he has a feeling that isn't in his abdomen or chest but in his back or his head or his legs, I say, *Let's acknowledge that feeling* . . . And, after a few moments, *What else are you feeling?*

I may say, *Pay attention to this part of your body*, and indicate the abdomen and thorax. *Relax and breathe and focus you're awareness here.*

**Enquirer** So the client needs to be relaxed and to breathe; to be standing up; to be paying attention to himself, not to the therapist; and to be focusing on his body, rather than thinking. What if he still feels nothing?

**Mentor** It's very unlikely. I'll ask whether he feels nothing, or whether he feels numb. He does, after all, have feelings. Has he become so good at ignoring his feelings that he doesn't recognize them and has lost awareness of them; or is he numb?

If it's lack of awareness, then he needs to be still and quiet and give himself time to allow himself to notice his feelings again. They are there. If he feels numb, he should focus on the numbness. Ask him where he feels that numbness, and to describe that physical feeling. The numbness is a feeling, and it's a cover for the uncomfortable feelings. Work with the numbness and, if necessary, resolve that, as the first issue. If the feeling of numbness doesn't directly relate to the problem you're working with (which it may well do), at least by resolving the issue of the numbness you will be able to access other feelings.

**Enquirer** Could you do EMDR with the numbness?

**Mentor** Yes. The numbness is because the person is stuck in the trauma, so EMDR would be a good option. I've had many clients who've lost their awareness of feeling, but I've never had a client who isn't able to regain that ability.

## Key points

Stating her therapeutic goal will bring up an uncomfortable feeling, reminding the person that this situation is perilous.

In order to feel, the person needs to be relaxed and breathing, preferably standing up, focusing inwards and not thinking.

This feeling is utilized in the tracking back process to return to the origins of the problem.

# 33
## Associating into the problem situation

**Mentor** There are two ways of bringing up the uncomfortable feelings which will lead to the origins of the problem through tracking. The first we were talking about a few minutes ago: the therapeutic goal statement.

**Enquirer** Stating the therapeutic goal out loud brings up the uncomfortable feelings. And there's another way of bringing up those same feelings?

**Mentor** That's right. The person simply imagines that she is in the problem situation; or she imagines being in the problem situation doing the desired behaviour.

**Enquirer** An example or two would be helpful.

**Mentor** A man has a fear of public speaking.

**Enquirer** That's Benedict.

**Mentor** Benedict's agreed to give a talk to a group of chief executives, and he's very anxious about it. He knows his subject and, if his audience were two or three friends, he'd have no problem at all in delivering the talk very proficiently. His knowledge isn't in question; nor are his skills: he can articulate his ideas well enough. His feelings are the problem, because they prevent him from presenting confidently or coherently. To Benedict, his anxiety seems irrational, but anxious he is.

**Enquirer** He sees all those people in front of him and his mind empties because his body has gone into frustrated fight or flight.

**Mentor** Exactly. His therapeutic goal could be, *I am relaxed and confident when speaking publicly.* Saying this out loud would bring up the uncomfortable feelings.

**Enquirer** What would his practical goal be?

**Mentor** He wants to have the confidence to perform competently when speaking publicly.

**Enquirer** The practical goal and the therapeutic goal are pretty much identical.

**Mentor** You're right. Perhaps the emphasis is slightly different: the therapeutic goal (the target of therapy) relates to feelings; the practical goal (Benedict's primary concern) is focused on performance.

**Enquirer** Benedict states the therapeutic goal, and this brings up the uncomfortable feelings. But he can do something else instead?

**Mentor** Yes. He can simply imagine being in the problem situation, or being in the situation and behaving as desired. Here is Benedict, in the board room. The executives are in front of him, looking up at him. He begins to speak.

Imagining being in the situation will bring up the uncomfortable feelings. In fact, the feelings might be more intense than when the therapeutic goal is stated. (But the degree of intensity is not important; we just need the feelings to be there.) When imagining being in the problem situation, it's very important that Benedict is in his body, looking through his own eyes. This is referred to as *associated*. It's the first-person position; as distinct from the third-person position (or meta-position), referred to as *dissociated*, which is when the person is looking at himself from the outside. The distinction between associated and dissociated is important because the ability to feel depends on being associated.

**Enquirer** Some people who have been severely traumatized are dissociated much of the time, because they have learned to avoid their pain by emotionally stepping away from the body.

**Mentor** Dissociation can be helpful as a short-term measure, but it's not a solution, because the trauma remains in the body, influencing the person's behaviour and using, and depleting, the body's resources. The longer and more vigorously the traumatic experience is suppressed, the more internal resources it usurps.

**Enquirer** Leading eventually to physical illness.

Are there any advantages in imaginatively associating into the problem situation, rather than stating the therapeutic goal?

**Mentor** Being associated in the problem situation can be helpful in clarifying and delineating aspects of the therapeutic problem. By imagining being in the problem situation Benedict is able to use his feelings to evaluate precisely where the difficulties lie.

For example, he sees negative judgement in the eyes of his imagined audience and realizes that his anxiety is because of fear of negative judgement. Or in his imagination he sees that individuals look bored and are not paying attention, showing that he fears that he or his presentation is not interesting enough. Or he sees the audience stifling laughter, showing his fear of ridicule.

**Enquirer** Would you give another example of putting yourself imaginatively in the problem situation to bring up the problem feelings.

**Mentor** A very common issue among people who present for therapy and coaching is difficulty saying no.

Saying no isn't physically difficult, of course. But to say no to some-one who is expecting you to say yes; who wants you to say yes; who is pressurizing you to say yes; who will be very disappointed and possibly angry and disapproving if you say no – or if you believe any of this to be true, even if it isn't – can be extremely difficult.

The person who has trouble saying no is very keen not to disap-point or upset people. She feels that other people's points of view are more important than hers are; or that she doesn't have the right to her own viewpoint; or even that she shouldn't take up any space or any oxygen in the world. Her name?

**Enquirer** Her name's Elsie.

**Mentor** Elsie's therapeutic goal could be: *I am comfortable saying no to people, even if it disappoints or upsets them.* Saying this would bring up the uncomfortable feelings required for tracking. In-stead, Elsie can imagine a situation in which it is difficult for her to say no. This could be a likely or typical situation, one that has occurred recently, or one that is anticipated. It needs to be im-agined as if it's happening in the present. Elsie imagines that her line manager is asking her to stay at work late one evening to com-plete some work. If the work was really pressing, she'd willingly stay late. She's committed to her work and to the company out-comes. But she strongly suspects it's really not necessary to work late and the work can wait.

As Elsie imagines being in this situation, she says to her manager, perfectly reasonably (even if she needed the guidance of her thera-pist to know that it is perfectly reasonable): 'I'm sorry, I can't stay late this evening.' Elsie says it feels wrong to say this and has an uncomfortable feeling in her body. This feeling is what we use for the tracking back process.

**Enquirer** I've been in that situation! My manager kept giving me reasons why it was so important and asked me what I was doing that could possibly be more important. But I knew the work could wait. Guess who won the argument?

**Mentor** What did you say when your manager asked you what you were doing?

**Enquirer** I think I told her I'd arranged to meet some friends.

**Mentor** Saying that wasn't a good idea.

**Enquirer** Why not? What should I have said?

**Mentor** You mustn't give a reason. Your reason, however good it is, will not be convincing to your manager. Answering the question allows her to argue with you. You don't want to argue with your manager. You definitely don't want to initiate an argument when you say no.

**Enquirer** How do I avoid it?

**Mentor** Just keep repeating what you've already said: 'I'm sorry, I can't stay late this evening. I've already made arrangements.'

**Enquirer** She'll ask what I've arranged.

**Mentor** Don't answer the question. It's none of her business. Just repeat the answer you've already given.

**Enquirer** Don't answer the question but repeat what I just said? Surely not word for word.

**Mentor** Yes, word for word. Several times if required. It's very effective. Even the most obtuse of persons won't ask more than three or four times when she gets exactly the same answer each time. It's called the stuck record technique. I came across it in the work of Gael Lindenfield. The technique also works very well with sales agents. You just say, 'I'm not interested, thank you' – the 'thank you' is optional – and repeat the words 'I'm not interested' as many times as necessary when challenged with further interrogations or arguments.

Repetition of your intention, but not your reason, is very important. The moment you give somebody a reason for your answer, you're offering an opportunity for a counter-argument. It doesn't matter how good your argument is, any argument can be countered. The salesperson, like your manager, is not interested in the cogency of your argument or the import of your reasons, but only in countering them in order to engage you and wear you down. But if you refuse to elucidate any further on your perfectly reasonable answer, you've offered nothing to argue against. You've offered no material for the salesperson, manager, or whoever it is, to work with; there's no argument to counter. You won't need to repeat it more than three or four times, at most.

**Enquirer** I'll try that. But I'm not sure I'll be able to do it. I think I'm a people pleaser.

**Mentor** You don't need to wait until then. You can just imagine being in the situation now. If it feels like it's really difficult to behave in the way you want, then you know it's a therapeutic issue for you. We would find where the feelings come from in your past and resolve them. The feeling would then be gone and you'd be free to respond as you wish.

**Enquirer** I want to believe you. But no, thank you. Let's have one more example of bringing up the feelings for the tracking process by putting yourself in the situation.

**Mentor** A businessman, who has to travel frequently for work, has a fear of flying, and particularly of turbulence.

**Enquirer** His name is Cormac.

**Mentor** Cormac flies a great deal on business – especially over the Atlantic, where there's often a lot of turbulence. His therapeutic goal is, *I am relaxed and calm during turbulence while flying.* Articulating this will bring up the uncomfortable feelings.

Alternatively, he can imagine being on the plane and experiencing turbulence. Here he is on the aircraft. He feels the plane shaking. The seatbelt sign is illuminated. There's an announcement that all passengers should return to their seats. As he imagines being in the situation – remember, he needs to be in his body, associated, as if it's happening right now – he gets some of the feelings he would get in the situation itself.

**Enquirer** When he does that, is Cormac remembering a situation from the past?

**Mentor** In fact, it doesn't matter whether the thing that is being imagined has happened, is going to happen, is a typical example of what has happened, or is something that might happen. The person is not really 'remembering' it, because that situates the event in the past, and we need to situate it in the present. The important point is that, in imagination, it needs to be experienced as if it's happening right now. So just remembering an experience, or remembering the emotion of an experience, won't work. The emotion has to be experienced in the present. The feelings won't be as strong as they would be if the person really was in the situation. That doesn't matter. The feelings don't need to be intense; they just need to be there.

**Enquirer** You also said something about not just being in the problem situation but also performing the desired behaviour.

**Mentor** It's a problem situation because the person is having difficulty behaving in a particular way in that situation. For example, if you have a fear of speaking your opinion to a group in a social setting, it's no use imagining you're in a social situation but not saying anything. That may not be a fearful situation. You need to imagine you're in that social situation speaking out. This is what brings up the feelings. Cormac is going to feel the fear by imagining just being in the shaking plane. But in many situations you need to imagine doing the desired behaviour, because it's the desired behaviour that creates the fear or discomfort.

**Enquirer** Imagining being in the situation or articulating a therapeutic goal may only bring up very mild feelings of discomfort.

**Mentor** Thank goodness the feelings are not as strong as they would be in a real situation. If subtle feelings are what we have, subtle feelings are all we need.

**Enquirer** So you can state the therapeutic goal, or you can imagine yourself being in the problem situation behaving in the way you'd like. Either method will bring up the bad feelings. Neither method is preferable; it doesn't matter.

**Mentor** Yes, it doesn't matter – whichever seems most suitable.

**Enquirer** I'm curious: where did Cormac's fear of turbulence come from?

**Mentor** He'd experienced emotional turbulence in his family when he was a child. After addressing those experiences, he was okay with the air turbulence – even though he still wasn't keen on it, he reported a week or two later, after a flight. Ideally, there was probably more work to be done on the childhood turbulence.

**Enquirer** I'm not sure many of us are very keen on turbulence. The fear was his body's way of telling him he needed to address that childhood issue.

Okay, the emotional feelings are present in the body of the client, either through articulating a therapeutic goal or by imagining being in the problem situation. What happens now? How do these feelings guide back to the origins of the therapeutic problem?

## Key points

In addition to stating the therapeutic goal, imagining being in the problem situation and behaving as desired will bring up the uncomfortable feelings required for tracking.

Whether the problem situation happened in the past, is forthcoming or is imagined doesn't matter, but the person has to be associated.

# 34

## The path to the origins

**Mentor** Tracking, the method to go back to the sources of the therapeutic problem, is really very straightforward. Although it is this discovery that has made the new methodology possible, it is probably the simplest aspect of the Relearning Experience Process.

**Enquirer** This is what you promised you'd explain when we first met. You said it's central to the methodology. We've finally got here! But I can't believe it will be as simple as you suggest.

**Mentor** You have been patient. To reach this point we have listened to the person's presenting problem; established an appropriate practical goal; articulated the therapeutic goal; and identified the somatic feeling associated with the therapeutic problem.

**Enquirer** Yes.

**Mentor** The feeling will have been elicited either by the person stating the therapeutic goal or by imagining being in the problem situation performing the desired behaviour.

**Enquirer** Right.

**Mentor** When the person has focused attention on and has tuned in to the physical feeling, she is asked what the emotion is that relates to the feeling. Do you remember that we talked about how to do that earlier?

**Enquirer** Yes, I do. It was important not to think about what the emotion might be but to focus awareness on the feeling and allow the emotion to reveal itself.

**Mentor** That's right. The person directs all her attention on the physical feeling and the therapist asks, *What's the emotion that goes with that physical feeling?* The person will then state what the emotion is – or try to, because it's not always easy to put it into words.

**Enquirer** Okay. We have a feeling and a corresponding emotion. What's next?

**Mentor** For the tracking process we need to represent the history of the person's life in the consultation room. We'll imagine a straight path that represents the person's life, going from the present time back to her biological conception. In the consultation space, this imaginary path might be just a few paces, from one side of the room to the other.

**Enquirer** So one end of the path represents the person in the present, and the other end represents the person's biological conception. The path between these two ends represents the years between conception and the present.

**Mentor** That's right. I may also suggest we reserve a little space in front of the present to represent the imaginary achievement of the practical goal in the future.

I ask the person to stand in the present space and face forward, with the past behind her. I explain that this space represents the present. I point to the wall behind her and tell her that next to the wall represents her biological conception. And I say that the path between where she is standing and her conception represents all the years of her life between conception and the present.

So let's imagine this is a consulting room. Come over here and stand near to the window. Take a small step or two back from the window. Face forward. This space represents the present. The wall behind you, at the other side of the room, represents your biological conception. Between conception and the present is the path representing all the years of your life.

**Enquirer** This 'path' obviously needs to be straight and un-obstructed. I can see why it's nice for the person, standing in the present, to look out of a window, rather than being faced with a wall. The window gives a view, as if into the possibilities of the future, rather than an obstruction. How much space do you need for this life path?

**Mentor** You don't need much. I've worked in tiny spaces with no windows. It's even possible to do it all in imagination – but there's no reason to do it like that.

**Enquirer** What next?

**Mentor** The person is asked to focus on the physical feeling and not to think about anything; and then to walk backwards and stop at the point along the path of the past where the physical feeling is most intense. The therapist places the palm of her hand lightly on the person's back to give safety and support as the person walks backwards.

**Enquirer** It gives reassurance. And you don't want the person to worry about walking off at an angle or bumping into something.

**Mentor** You want her to know you're with her and supporting her physically and emotionally so she can just focus on her feelings.

She walks backwards and, somewhere along her life path, where the physical feelings are most intense, she stops. The therapist then asks the person to confirm that this is where the feelings are most intense. When this is confirmed, she asks the person what age she is at this point – immediately suggesting that she should trust the first thing that pops into her head. (The therapist doesn't want her to start thinking about when it might be or start doubting the age that comes to mind. The age has to come from the unconscious body, not the conscious mind.)

The person states her age here. She is now at the origins of the problem behaviour. When the therapist asks the person what age she is, she should use the present tense, saying, *How old are you here?* The person needs to be associated, in her body, living the experience, not remembering it.

**Enquirer**   Is that all there is to it?

**Mentor**   That's all there is to the tracking process. We've got to the age we need to work with. We're ready to find out what was going on during this time and then do the resolution work.

**Enquirer**   It sounds very simple. What if the person doesn't know how old she is in the place she stops?

**Mentor**   She will know. When I ask how old she is, I always say, *It's the first thing that pops into your head.* And an age always pops into the person's head. But it could be a period of time, a few years rather than a single year. So she might say, for example: *I'm seven*; *I'm about 12*; *Between 11 and 13*; *I'm 15 or 16*; *I'm in my mid-twenties.*

**Enquirer**   Could she have got the age wrong?

**Mentor**   There's no reason for it to be wrong. The person has tuned into her body. She not using her rational mind. She's not thinking. She's letting her body communicate with her. The unconscious body is not going to do anything arbitrary (supposing this were possible); and the body knows where this feeling comes from and wants to help the person resolve the problem.

**Enquirer**   The body knows where the feeling comes from?

**Mentor**   Yes. You can look at it entirely physiologically, if that helps. The uncomfortable feeling developed at a particular point in the person's past, because something difficult happened that degraded the individual's personal dignity. Before the event occurred there was no specific feeling. The feeling was created at the time of the occurrence. The uncomfortable feeling persisted later, but the feeling is naturally most intense when the problem occurred.

The person may express doubts that she has arrived at the right age, because it may feel like a guess to her. The therapist just assures her that she's doing the right thing and to assume the age is correct. It's important to trust the body and to trust the process. If the therapist trusts the process, the person will too. If the therapist doesn't trust the process, it's not possible for the person to do so.

Occasionally, the person will start relating an experience and then begin to question whether the experience she's relating is consistent with the age she specified. The therapist should reassure the person that the experience is likely to be relevant (or it wouldn't have occurred to her), and not to worry about whether or not the event occurred at the specified age.

**Enquirer** Is the experience you're looking for a single thing, such as being shouted at or being hit over the head, for example, or can it be a number of things?

**Mentor** The experience that we are looking for might be a specific event, or may be a number of occurrences. The one-off event could be a visit to hospital, for example, or an incident that occurred at home, at school, or anywhere else. Or it could be something that was endured over time, such as being continually picked on, being undermined by a parent, or repeated sexual, physical or emotional abuse. If more than one thing seems relevant, there'll be a clearly identifiable theme, and the person may have stopped on her life path at a particularly significant moment. If the therapeutic problem relates to a relationship, the body might go back to the beginning of that relationship, or to a significant occurrence during the relationship.

The important thing isn't the exact age (people are often not clear about the exact age they were when something happened and may contradict themselves), but what was happening during that time. Don't be concerned about the precise age. The age is simply a guide to find out what was going on at that time. You should – and this is important – trust the events that the person relates, even if she doesn't trust their accuracy herself. Remember that historical chronicling is not our concern.

The body's aim – and the aim of tracking back – is to uncover the problem material. The body may do this indirectly – for example by starting with one memory and leading to another, more significant one. So the therapist needs to be flexible rather than mechanistic or overly procedural. The person's unconscious body is doing its best to help.

You might not understand immediately what the body wants to say, but it's always trying to say something; so never dismiss it. It may direct you to the relevant experience via an indirect and circuitous route.

**Enquirer** The body might have many choices of where to stop.

**Mentor** You need to trust that the body will take you where you need to go. Sometimes the person hovers at one spot in her life path, and then goes back further. If she does this, or seems to equivocate about the place, you can invite her to go backwards and forwards, if that's helpful, until she finds the precise location where the feeling is most intense. You're just giving her permission. She'll let her intuition guide her. It's not a scientific experiment; it's a communication from the unconscious. Trust the person's unconscious. Encourage her to trust herself.

**Enquirer** The feeling will be most intense in one particular spot on the life path? It's that specific?

**Mentor** Yes. One tiny step further back or further forward and the feeling is less intense.

**Enquirer** This establishes the age of the person at the problem experience, but you still need to find out what's going on at this time, don't you?

**Mentor** Yes. The body knows what the problem experience is and will help you to articulate it. You have narrowed it down by establishing the age. Now you need to find out specifically what was going on.

## Key points

The person focuses on the physical feeling and walks backwards, stopping where the feeling is most intense.

The place where the person stops may be a specific moment or a period of time.

The intention is to identify the problem material and, to do this, the body may need to find an indirect route.

# 35

## Probing the antecedents

**Mentor** The person is standing at the origins of the psycho-therapeutic problem: the site of its antecedents. We have learned how old the person is here. We are now tasked with finding out what's going on at this time: to identify the problem material.

**Enquirer** Remind me what problem material refers to.

**Mentor** The problem material is the difficult event or occurrences underlying the problem's manifestation in the present. It's the experience that led to a behaviour modification at the origins of the problem.

**Enquirer** You refer to a 'manifestation' in the present presumably because there could be other manifestations of the problem.

**Mentor** Yes. Unless and until the origins of the problem are resolved, the problem is likely to manifest in many different contexts at different times.

**Enquirer** Now that you've arrived at the antecedent age, how do you elicit the problem material?

**Mentor** The therapist simply asks: *What's going on at this age?* Note the use of present tense: the idea is that the person has travelled (imaginatively) back in time. The person may know immediately what is going on at this time; or he may need prompting. I say to the person that he should trust anything that pops into his head, without censoring it or trying to work out whether it's relevant. I might even remind him that this is his one responsibility in therapy – to let me know what's going on with him.

If he seems hesitant to say what's on his mind, I again encourage him to say anything that occurs to him, even if it doesn't make sense or seems irrelevant. If appropriate, I tell him I don't need details of anything embarrassing; just the general idea is fine.

**Enquirer** How can you be sure you have arrived at the relevant experience?

**Mentor** We trust that the feelings will lead to where we need to go. If he is focusing on his feelings he will arrive at the right time. It could be any age, of course, and the problem material could relate to anything. The proof will be resolution of the problem.

**Enquirer** Will the problem material be obvious and immediately evident?

**Mentor** Not necessarily. It often is; but often enough it isn't. Usually it's really not difficult to uncover, though. The body knows and wants to communicate – that's why it has brought you here. Exploration needs to continue until the material emerges. The material might not appear to be particularly dramatic. It might even seem surprisingly ordinary. A considerable issue can develop from something that might seem trivial to someone else.

**Enquirer** What if the person doesn't come up with anything?

**Mentor** If we've arrived at the antecedent age and the person isn't volunteering anything, the therapist needs to ask questions.

**Enquirer** What kind of questions?

**Mentor** You can start by asking, *Where are you living at this time?* If it's during the person's childhood or adolescence, you can then ask any of the following questions:

*How are things at home?*

*How are you getting on at school?*

*How are your friends towards you?*

*How are your parents getting on with each other?*

*How are you getting on with parents/friends/teachers?*

*Who is important in your life at this time?*

*Is anyone ill?*

*Has anyone died?*

*Is anything new or different?*

If the person is an adult, you might ask:

*How are you getting on at work?*

*Are you married or do you have a partner?*

*What is your relationship like?*

*Do you have many friends?*

*Has something changed?*

*Has something happened?*

*How's your home life?*

*What's going on with your family?*

If the relevant issues are still not apparent, discussion about what was going on at this time might at first touch on a number of different areas, but the discourse will begin to find a focus and the problem will gradually reveal itself.

**Enquirer** Will you give a few examples of problem material?

**Mentor** Criticism from a stepfather; not being listened to by mum; being ridiculed by a teacher; being picked on or bullied at school; the end of a relationship; and so on. Anything, really. Those are summaries of the problem material. The person will be relating experiences, of course, not giving summaries.

**Enquirer** Do you always find the problem material?

**Mentor** Nearly always you'll find the problem material.

**Enquirer** But not always? Is the person sometimes unwilling to talk about what has happened and chooses to hide it from you?

**Mentor** That could happen, but I'm sure that it's extremely rare. The person would be wasting his money. The family therapist Virginia Satir says that much of the effort of a therapist is to encourage the client to trust so that he can express himself without fear of judgement. Trust is the basis of all real communication.

If the antecedent age is very young, it can be more difficult to establish the problem material; but generally it is quite straightforward. You might need to keep talking for a few minutes after you arrive at the relevant events to apprehend their relevance. The person may need questioning, prompting. He may be hesitant to tell you: the material that pops into his head may seem to him to be trivial, irrelevant, embarrassing. The therapist doesn't need the details; it's always worth reminding the person of this; but the therapist does need a general idea about what is going on. Something was happening. The person was alive and doing something. It may require some prompting before you get to the problem material, but you will get there. You can ask the person to guess. There may well be an emotional exclamation as the person finally remembers the significant event – *Oh! My mother died that year* (to give a real example). Or what occurs might not seem very significant to the person, and you have to encourage him to disclose what's occurred to him. Keep a close eye on the person: you'll see when something occurs to him. Press him to disclose it.

For all the work you do when the person is on his life path in the past, it's important to use the present tense, as if you are speaking directly to the person at this earlier age. You want to help the person to be associated in his body at this age. Encourage him to reply in the first person and in the present tense. This is important, because if the client is dissociated he is likely to be thinking, not feeling, and he will lose connection with his body and the communications from his unconscious.

You don't want the person to start rationalizing, justifying, explaining – in other words, making it up. Don't allow the thinking, conscious mind to start interfering.

**Enquirer**  How can you tell if the person is dissociated?

**Mentor**  He'll use the second person instead of the first person to describe himself (saying *you* instead of *I*), and may use the past tense (instead of the present). It's important to correct this. Just ask him to use *I* and speak in the present tense, as if he is the younger self. His physiology and posture will also reflect whether he's associated or dissociated.

**Enquirer**  How will his physiology and posture reflect this?

**Mentor**  If he's associated, he will be looking down, accessing feelings; his body will be fairly symmetrical, and his weight distributed equally on both feet. He will be standing squarely in his life path, looking forward. If he's dissociated, he will have shifted his weight on to one side. He won't be fully in his life path but will have stepped slightly out of it – as if he doesn't really want to be there; as if he's intellectualizing about it rather than experiencing it. He may be facing the therapist, looking at her and trying to engage her; or standing at an angle, rather than properly inhabiting his life path and facing forward towards the future. He may also be touching his face with one hand in the manner of someone giving thought to something, or leaning to the side. His words might seem designed to divert you from your task.

If he's dissociating it is because it is more comfortable or more habitual for him to do this. But if you let him stay like this the work you're doing will unravel and you'll find yourself just talking.

Some clients are very practised at talking about their problem because they've done it so many times before.

**Enquirer** What can the therapist do if the person is dissociated?

**Mentor** If the person is dissociated, just ask him to come back inside his body, step properly into his life path, access his feelings, and face forward.

The therapist should be modelling how she'd like the person to be so he can naturally mirror her physiology and posture.

**Enquirer** It's very important for the person to be associated on his life path.

**Mentor** It's very important. He needs to be associated while he's accessing the experience. If he's not in the experience, he's distancing himself from the experience, and from his feelings (and therefore from his unconscious body): this will prioritize his conscious, rational mind and he'll be of no help to himself.

**Enquirer** What should the body language of the therapist be?

**Mentor** The therapist should be standing beside the client; that is, at his side, not opposite him or in his visual or physical space. The therapist should be supporting him and allowing him to be with himself, rather than engaging outwardly with the therapist – which could easily distract him from his purpose. When necessary, step away; give him space. The therapist's posture should be the model for the client: standing evenly on both legs; balanced, upright and relaxed.

**Enquirer** From this associated position the client describes his experience. Then what?

**Mentor** After the client has described what's going on and the problem material has been identified, the therapist invites the person to step out of his path, on to the sidelines, facing the path, as if looking at his younger self. From this dissociated position he has a better vantage point to consider the options. This is a task therapist and client will do together. Being outside of his life path also helps the person to keep the two roles separate.

**Enquirer** What two roles are you talking about?

**Mentor** The role on his life path, of being his younger self, and the role off the path, of being an observer considering the options for his younger self.

When looking for solutions it is better to take the position of a third party, a meta-position (the client as the older, wiser, expert of himself), than remain in first position as a younger person or child, immersed in the situation and with many fewer resources. From meta-position he can contemplate his younger self using all the experience and wisdom he has gained throughout his life, and more easily come up with ideas and solutions for the younger person. Therapist and client both talk about the younger person as if he is right there before them on his life path.

**Enquirer** This is where you find a resolution to the problem.

**Mentor** Yes. First, we will decide what the best relearning experience would be. Then we observe (in imagination) the proposed new experience as it unfolds.

When this is done, if all seems well, the person steps back in to his life path and experiences, or *encounters*, the resolution from inside the body of his younger self, associated.

**Enquirer** The therapeutic problem is then resolved?

**Mentor** Yes. The inappropriate feelings should now have cleared. The person returns to the present. Back in the present the person restates the therapeutic goal, or imagines being in what had been the problem situation and behaving in the desired way. He can now do this with no uncomfortable feelings. If he is unable to get the uncomfortable feelings back, the problem is resolved and the therapy complex will have dissolved.

**Enquirer** You check that the person can't get the uncomfortable feelings back?

**Mentor** The therapist asks the person to try to get the uncomfortable feelings back by restating the therapeutic goal or imagining being in the problem situation behaving resourcefully. That is the test that the work is complete and has been successful. Of course he can remember the bad feelings; but, if the problem has been completely resolved, he won't be able to experience them.

If he does still have uncomfortable feelings – and this is quite possible – it simply means that there is more work to be done. But if the work has been done properly, the specific issue that you've been working on will have been resolved, even if the wider problem requires more work. If there is more work to do, the feelings will be different.

**Enquirer** Explain this.

**Mentor** It depends on the issue. If you are working with a person on her eating problems (or eating 'disorder'), for example, you might find there are a number of childhood incidents to resolve before the eating problem is finally resolved. In this case, you will resolve each incident you work with, but the broader eating issue won't be resolved until you have reached a tipping point with the many childhood occurrences. You would confirm each childhood incident has been resolved by checking that the feelings related to that specific incident have been cleared.

There are some experiences that need to be addressed in various contexts before they are finally resolved. For example, the death of a close relative may have pathological effects on a person in a number of different contexts. Each context may need to be addressed separately before all the issues associated with the death are finally resolved. This may include, for example, the news of the death; the manner of death; the absence of appropriate grieving; anger with the person for dying; coping with the responses of other members of the family.

## Key points

The tracking process leads to the origin of the therapeutic problem, where the problem material is identified.

The therapist doesn't need details, but does need to understand what was going on at this time that created the therapeutic problem.

The person should be addressed as if he really is at the antecedent age and is encouraged to speak in the present tense and using the first person.

If the peson is dissociated, he needs to be encouraged to come back inside his body, stand fully in his life path, and face forwards.

After the problem material has been expounded, the person steps off his life path to resolve the problem from meta-position.

# 36
# Tracking process

**Enquirer** I'm very keen to find out how you go about resolving the problem in the past. But I have a few questions about the tracking process.

To go back to the origins of the problem, the person needs to access the problem feeling by stating the therapeutic goal or imagining himself in the problem situation performing the desired behaviour. With the feelings engaged, he steps backwards along his life path. Could the uncomfortable feelings simply vanish the moment the person steps backwards?

**Mentor** That does sometimes happen. First check that the person is focusing on the present task and hasn't been distracted. If he loses the feelings temporarily, ask him to restate the therapeutic goal or imagine the problem example to reactivate the feelings.

The client is often sitting down while the preliminary work is done. By the time the tracking process has been explained to him and the path mapped out in the room, he may have lost the feelings that were there a few moments earlier. So just remind him of whatever it was that brought up the feelings for him. In fact, it's a good idea to check that these feelings are still palpable before the person takes his first step backwards.

But it is possible for the feeling to be there in the present but for it to disappear the moment the person steps backwards. When this happens, there are two possibilities.

The first is that you haven't set up the task correctly. The feelings are there, but the therapeutic goal isn't quite right, or the example situation isn't quite right. There may be more information that is required which you haven't taken into account, and the body wants you to identify this information before it's ready to go back.

The second is that the problem you have to deal with – or have to deal with *first* – is situated in the present. If this feeling relates to the present and not to the past it will vanish the moment the person steps away from the present. Find out what's going on in the present and resolve this. There may also be something in the past that needs work but, if something is going on in the present, this should be addressed first. It may not be possible to resolve a problem at the origin until the situation in the present is addressed.

**Enquirer** What if you go back to a time in the past but just can't work out what the problem is? The person is giving you information about this time, but you just can't identify a problem experience there?

**Mentor** The body has brought you back to this time for a reason – even if the reason isn't immediately apparent. It's possible, occasionally, to come back to a time where you don't need to do any resolution work. You need to trust that the body is finding a way to tell you, and you need to follow where the body leads. The body will guide you to the relevant material. But it's possible it might not take you there directly, and might take you via some strange turns. I'm thinking about an intelligent woman, successful professionally, who came to see me in a desperate state –

**Enquirer** Mia.

**Mentor** Mia wasn't coping professionally or personally. She was a single parent whose job – she was self-employed – made great demands on her time and energy. Her children were demanding her attention, but she wasn't able to give them any real attention. She wanted to give them attention, she said, but her relationship with them wasn't working. This was her presenting problem.

Our first port of call when tracking back was the time when Mia started a relationship with a man who was a paedophile. She married him and had children with him, even though, she told me, she had known intuitively about his paedophile tendencies from the beginning. He went on to sexually abuse her children and was violent towards her. Years later, Mia finally escaped from him and changed her identity. That was when she came to see me.

There was no healing to do at the point where tracking first led. But tracking back to the start of her relationship with a paedophile gave important information about her behaviour: she had chosen an exceptionally unsuitable man to be husband and father of her children. This was information her therapist needed to know.

We followed the feelings back further in time to her childhood, where we would learn why, as a young adult, she chose such a man and why she had been unable to extricate herself from the relationship early on, even though she knew what he was like.

**Enquirer** So you didn't need to do any resolution work at your first stop; you just found out useful information.

**Mentor** Without that information I may not have been able to work out the significance of the problem material when we arrived at the problem's origins. The information was crucial.

**Enquirer** So why did Mia choose such a person?

**Mentor** Mia had not been cared for by her parents, She hadn't received their affection or love. She had not been listened to. Nor had her interests and viewpoints been considered by them.

**Enquirer** A clear contravention of her emotional needs and attack on her personal dignity. What age did you travel to?

**Mentor** Tracking back took Mia to age twelve. After a car accident she was taken to hospital. One of the medical staff took an interest in her and sexually molested her. He was the only adult who had paid her any real attention.

**Enquirer** Even though his behaviour was wrong and no doubt made her feel bad, his attention gave her something that she needed emotionally. She discovered a way to be cared for – through sexual attention, though in an abusive relationship.

**Mentor** Yes. That sums it up well. It's not so surprising that, as an adult, Mia chose someone who would sexually abuse her children and physically abuse her. She wants love, but the only way she knows to get love, or something approximating to it, is in an abusive relationship. She doesn't know what it's like to be loved in a caring way. She has no experience of that. She learned from her parents that she is not worthy of love and care. But there is a kind of attention that she can get. It's better than nothing. She recognized, in the man she was to marry, an abuser who would give her that attention.

**Enquirer** She recognized him as an abuser even from the start.

**Mentor** She says that she did – even consciously. People convey so much information about themselves in everything they do: unconsciously you have a very good idea about how people are. If you are in touch with this unconscious knowledge (through the faculty known as intuition), and if you trust it, and heed it, you can make good choices. She received the information, but she didn't heed it, because of her overwhelming emotional need for love and attention.

**Enquirer** She craved love and care. We all do, of course. But her need was the greater because she didn't receive it when she most needed it – as a child. From the man she married she found a way of getting something that was an approximation of what she needed emotionally and, because of the strength of her need, she was unable to resist it, despite her better judgement and the terrible risks. This semblance of love was all that she believed was possible for her; it was the best she'd ever had.

**Mentor** You understand very well. Consequently she felt enormous guilt for what she had exposed her children to, and felt unworthy of their love. Because of her guilt, she avoided her own children and didn't give them attention. She didn't understand why she was behaving as she was.

**Enquirer** So that's why she wasn't giving her children the attention they needed. But this could change?

**Mentor** Certainly.

**Enquirer** I'm intrigued to know what happened with this person.

**Mentor** I helped her to overcome her shame about not protecting her children. To achieve this, she needed to overcome her shame about being sexually used by the medical man. After this, the uncomfortable feeling she had had in her chest was clear; she could forgive herself and no longer feel guilty about not protecting her children; and she was able to develop more intimate bonds with them.

**Enquirer** Did she later confirm all that to you?

**Mentor** Yes, she did.

**Enquirer** Another question. What if there's nowhere along the life path where the feeling is most intense?

**Mentor** There usually will be. If the feeling doesn't change in intensity at all, the client keeps walking backwards until she gets to her biological conception. The problem would then have developed at conception.

**Enquirer** That's incredible. Does that happen often?

**Mentor** More often than you might think. If the person travels back to conception, we find out what's going on with mum at the time. Any difficulties occurring at conception are likely to have a profound impact.

**Enquirer** How do you find out what's going on at conception?

**Mentor** By asking questions. Even if she doesn't know exactly what was going on, she will probably have a good idea if and why her mother was unhappy; if her father was being unfaithful, or drinking, or about to leave the family; if her mother had doubts or fears about her relationship or the future; if there was a death or some upheaval in the family; or if the child was planned or welcomed, or otherwise.

**Enquirer** I find it hard to believe that a person can experience anything at the time of conception or soon after.

**Mentor** The unborn being is intimately bound with her mother and is subject to her mother's emotions. If her mother is stressed, fearful, sad or miserable, she is affected by it. If her mother doesn't want her, she'll feel it. If the mother's relationship with her partner is difficult, she'll experience it. Any of this may affect her emotional development profoundly.

People don't just return to biological conception, of course, they'll stop anywhere between conception and birth, at birth – or, of course, at any other time.

**Enquirer** But not before conception?

**Mentor** No.

**Enquirer** All of these eventualities are really significant to the yet-to-be-born person?

**Mentor** I understand your scepticism. The foetus or infant body will have no understanding of the events themselves; but these events could have highly significant and long-lasting effects on the person. So we explore possibilities and trust what feels right for the person, even if we don't have reliable knowledge of this history. Ultimately, in our therapy work, we're not interested in what 'really' happened (even if the client understandably is); the task of the therapist is to help the client resolve the problem, not to verify a version of history.

**Enquirer** We've travelled back to the origins of the therapeutic problem. We've learned what was going on at that time to create the problem. Now I'm very curious to learn how you go about resolving the problem. But first, would it be helpful very briefly to summarize the Relearning Experience Process?

**Mentor** Yes, I think it would be a good idea to give a summary.

(1) The person relates what is called the presenting problem.

(2) An appropriate practical goal is identified and articulated, and the therapeutic problem is clarified.

(3) The therapeutic goal – the quality the person needs to behave in such a way that his practical goal becomes achievable – is formulated.

(4) The problem feeling – the feeling which drives the person to behave in the way he doesn't desire or prevents him from behaving in the way he desires – is activated. This is done either by stating the therapeutic goal or by imagining being in the problem situation and behaving in the desired way.

(5) Guided by the feeling, the person travels back to the origins of the problem via the tracking process.

(6) The problem material, which connects with the problem experience, is identified.

(7) The problem experience is resolved through the relearning (or resolution) work. The relearning work dissolves the entire therapy complex by providing the person with an alternative experience to learn from. The new learning, or relearning, replaces the old learning (the remedial behaviour) and neutralizes the uncomfortable problem feeling that had underpinned the remedial behaviour of the manifest problem.

(8) The person returns to the present and checks that the uncomfortable feelings are no longer accessible and that the

therapeutic goal is now realized. Stating the therapeutic goal now feels very comfortable; and imagining being in what had been a problem situation is now accompanied by appropriate feelings which are no longer contaminated by past events.

(9) Optionally, the person then steps forward into the practical goal achievement space and imagines that he is achieving (or has achieved) his practical goal.

## Key points

If the feeling vanishes as the person steps backwards on his life path, check that (1) he hasn't been distracted; (2) the therapeutic goal is correct; (3) there is no issue relating to the present.

The problem might have its genesis in the person's biological conception. Events occurring at this time need to be acknowledged and understood.

The therapist is not concerned with history or biography, but only with resolution of the therapeutic issue.

# 37

# Relearning work

**Mentor** I'm now going to briefly explain, for the first time, how to resolve a therapeutic problem at the origins. I hope that it will make sense to you.

**Enquirer** I'm very interested to hear.

**Mentor** The purpose and outcome of the resolution or relearning work is to transform or reconfigure in imagination the historical experience of the person so that, instead of the problem behaviour, the person is able to behave in the way she chooses. The resolution work provides an opportunity to relearn experience: to provide a healthy learning by reconfiguring the original experience, or by modifying the response to that experience. The response is then non-pathological – that is to say, healthy.

**Enquirer** Are you trying to modify the memories of the person?

**Mentor** We're giving the person a different reference for the problem experience; a new way of approaching or understanding that experience. By modifying the reception of her experience in this way, she is able, in imagination, to change her behaviour in the past. Through this modified 'experience', the remedial behaviour she originally learned will no longer be applicable in the present: she will have an alternative way of responding that will be more natural to her. This (retrospectively) obliterates the old, pathological, precedent and sets a new, healthy, precedent for the person's present and future behaviour.

**Enquirer**  So that's what you meant when you said at the beginning of our conversation that the best way to overcome a therapeutic problem is not to have it in the first place.

**Mentor**  Yes. I wasn't intending to be facetious. We're adjusting the scenario to one in which the therapeutic problem would not have developed; where the behaviour in response to a situation is not fixed, and the person remains flexible and resourceful.

**Enquirer**  But I'm still not clear what you actually do with the memory.

**Mentor**  In imagination the person will modify the historical experience so that it ceases to be a problem. How this is done depends on the nature of the experience and the original response to it. The outcome is that the person is able to behave in a way consistent with achieving her practical goal.

**Enquirer**  Replacing the client's experience doesn't change what really happened, does it? You can't make something that happened not happen; and you can't make something happen in the past that didn't happen!

**Mentor**  The adjustment to experience, or the reconfiguring of experience, happens only in imagination. However, it provides an opportunity for the person to undo the old learning and relearn, and the relearning is inscribed in the history of the person where the old learning was.

Obviously, there's no suggestion that this new experience will replace the real one, but it does displace it. The client won't forget what really happened. What changes is that the original experience no longer has power to affect the person's feelings or behaviour in an unhelpful way.

The guiding principle of the reformulation – and this is crucial – is that the reconfigured experience is credible to the person. The new experience doesn't have to be possible in a practical way, but it does need to be credible. Credibility, a test made at the level of feeling (not intellect), is the guarantee that the unconscious body is assenting to the process.

The details of the reconfigured experience are agreed between therapist and client. In practice, in fact, the client will probably need to be guided quite explicitly. But the guidance needs to be in the form of suggestions and options (as it should be in all therapeutic work): the client needs to be fully engaged in the process, and she advises whether the reconfigured experience is acceptable to her. If the client doesn't 'believe' in the reconfigured experience – not in a literal way, of course – the intervention won't work: the unconscious has rejected it. Unless the reconfigured experience is credible to the person, she will literally be unable to do that element of the process – despite her efforts and intention.

**Enquirer** The new experience is configured in the imagination. It doesn't have to be possible; but it does have to be credible. What does that mean?

**Mentor** Credible doesn't mean possible. Very often the reconfiguration is something totally impossible – at least to the adult mind. It can involve superheroes, relatives who are now dead, fictional characters, figures from history, great statespeople, popstars, fairies, fairy godmothers.

**Enquirer** Credibility doesn't require verisimilitude.

**Mentor** It doesn't have to be possible in actuality; it has to be conceivable in imagination.

**Enquirer** Credible without being possible – sounds paradoxical.

**Mentor** Yes, it does. For example: the person who, through tracking back, has returned to the age of seven, may not be able to imagine any situation in which mum would hug her; but she has no problem imagining her favourite aunt – whom she only got to know properly when she was older – giving her love and affection as a child whenever she needs it. Or, if not her aunt, her favourite popstar. Or a person may not be able to imagine her father giving her encouragement; but she has no problem imagining being protected from her father's criticisms by the powers of a fairy godmother, or imagining her favourite teacher giving her lavish encouragement.

**Enquirer**  A fairy godmother is credible and being hugged by her mother is incredible!

**Mentor**  Yes. Or it could be a superhero who intervenes, for example, to prevent her mother from criticizing her or her father from verbally abusing her. I know it seems strange. But the test here isn't reality; it's what it's possible for the person to imagine. Being imaginable is the key. If it's imaginable, it's credible.

**Enquirer**  I'm trying to understand the idea that a person may not be able to imagine something that is physically possible and easily conceivable, while being able to imagine something – a fantasy, such as the intervention of a fairy godmother – that is completely impossible.

**Mentor**  It is interesting, isn't it? We are used to listening to stories and suspending disbelief. But when unconscious protective mechanisms kick in it's not possible to suspend disbelief – uncomfortable feelings intervene as a reminder of the reality.

If the person tries to imagine something but is unable to suspend her disbelief, she will simply tell the therapist that she can't imagine it. She may say, for example, that she can't imagine her mother giving her affection; or she can't imagine her father praising her achievements. However, she will easily be able to imagine someone else – such as a relative, a famous figure, a fantastical character, or herself in the present day – doing this.

It's imperative always to ask the person how it went after she imagines the new event. You don't have to guess whether the person can imagine something or not: just invite her to tell you. However reticent she is to say she can't imagine it (because she thinks it must be some fault in her that prevents her, or doesn't want to disappoint her therapist), she won't actually lie.

**Enquirer** All right. I just about understand the mechanisms, but I don't feel I've yet got a clear picture of the application of the relearning work.

## Key points

The resolution work reconfigures experience so that the person is able to respond in a way that is non-pathological and behave in a way consistent with achieving her practical goal.

Relearning transforms the person's feelings in relation to the problem experience and sets a new, healthy, precedent for behaviour.

The relearning has to be *credible* to the person; it does not have to be possible. Credibility, which requires conception in the imagination, guarantees unconscious assent.

# 38

## Loretta

**Mentor** Let me give you an example of the whole Relearning Experience Process I think you'll find useful. You'll see how the relearning work is applied. The woman's name is –

**Enquirer** Loretta.

**Mentor** Loretta, then. She's in her early fifties, divorced, with two children in their early twenties who have left home. She has a partner whom she met two or three years ago.

Her presenting problems:

> *I don't know how to deal with stress.*
> *I'm experiencing incredible pressure.*
> *I don't have boundaries in my personal life.*

Loretta explained that she prides herself on her personal and financial independence, which was fostered and encouraged by her proud father. She is involved in charity work and helps other people: 'I've always been there for everyone.'

She has clear boundaries in her work, but in her personal life, in her words, she's a 'complete walkover'. Maintaining boundaries in her personal life would be her practical goal.

Generally, she hasn't had successful relationships with men. This is because, she said, she wants her partner to be like her dad. This is unintentionally ironic. Her boyfriend is indeed like her dad in a crucial, but unrecognized, respect. She has had unsuccessful relationships with men, not because she is looking for someone like her dad, but because she has been choosing men who are too much like her dad. This is far from a unique tendency. People will often choose a partner who is like their parent in a particular, and usually troublesome, respect. With a partner, and perhaps with each new partner, they will replay the unresolved problem they had with their parent.

**Enquirer** I've noticed that; but I don't understand why it is so.

**Mentor** I see it as opportunity to heal the issue with the parent. A healthy relationship may not be possible until the primal relationship has healed, because the primal relationship is the blueprint for future relationships. The primal relationship may be all the person has in terms of a model.

**Enquirer** It sounds rather like Freud's compulsion to repeat.

**Mentor** If there is an unresolved problem in a primal relationship, the body wants it to heal, and so needs to repeat the scenario until a solution is found. Repetition in itself doesn't heal the situation, of course, but it does mean it's impossible to bury it, and opportunities for healing are usually generously provided.

**Enquirer** People try so hard to bury their problems; but the problems won't play dead: they must be resolved. We have no choice but to keep developing – or keep digging.

**Mentor** Loretta reported that she has 'bailed out' – rescued – her current boyfriend financially. Her therapeutic goal was to feel okay about saying no. This would allow her to delineate her boundaries (her practical goal), and so reduce personal stress and the pressure on, of or in her relationship.

We talked further about this. She explained that she is able to say no initially, but then gives in to the 'whining' of her boyfriend. What made whining a winning formula for her boyfriend? The whining would upset Loretta because she couldn't bear to disappoint or upset people. This is also why, in her estimation, she cares so much for others and gives so much. However, she wouldn't let others be supportive of her reciprocally – perhaps because she feared they would disappoint her. Loretta added that she tended to take on boyfriends as 'projects'; she would take on one that needed mending. After she'd built him up, the job was done and she was ready to move on.

The whining of her boyfriend – let's call him James – was successful in getting what he wanted from her; but it left Loretta feeling angry, frustrated and very upset. She believed that he should respect her wishes rather than whining and manipulating her.

**Enquirer** How did you activate the feelings in order to track back to the origins?

**Mentor** I asked Loretta to imagine saying no to James about something significant. This gave her a tightness in her stomach, and that was the feeling we used to go back in time – to age ten.

At the age of ten Loretta was in conflict with her mother. Her mum hadn't wanted a girl, Loretta reported, and favoured her older brothers. Loretta was close to her father and believed this to be a source of conflict with her mother. She said that she and her mother distanced themselves from each other because of her attention from dad. She reported that her mum once left home and didn't return for ten days because dad backed Loretta and mum couldn't cope with it.

Whether or not Loretta's apprehension of the family motivations was accurate, and her mother had really left home because of dad's support for his daughter, it is clear that the conflict with her mother and closeness to her father was a significant issue for her and in the family. She described her mother as a social butterfly and thought of her as her father's wife rather than as her own mother.

When her mother tried to enforce discipline, her father stuck up for Loretta. 'My father never had rules for me,' she said; adding that she respected him greatly and never wanted to disappoint him. Her father never actively disciplined her, she said, but would punish her by ignoring her. Loretta agreed that this was an unhealthy way for her father to manage her behaviour.

**Enquirer** Yes, sulking is not a good method of guidance.

**Mentor** Her parents' relationship with each other was very good in later years, said Loretta; and her mother had been a wonderful grandmother to Loretta's children. Shortly before she died, her mother had asked Loretta for forgiveness.

**Enquirer** How did her experiences at ten relate to her therapeutic problem?

**Mentor** Loretta had an emotionally unhealthy disciplinary environment. She rejected the authority of her mother, with the apparent collusion of her father. Her father occasionally disciplined her in an inappropriate way, through silence, but mostly didn't appear to discipline her at all – he didn't have rules for her; he sided with her against mum. In the present, Loretta can't say no. Or, rather, she tries to say no, but gives in to the whining of her boyfriend because of a fear of disappointing him.

Remember, though, that the effectiveness of the work does not depend on an accurate analysis of the problem. Making connections is interesting, and helps the work to make sense, but it does not make the therapy more effective. Analysis is generally much easier retrospectively, and you may not understand what is going on at the time – even where, after the event, the analysis looks as though it should have been fairly obvious.

How does Loretta's past situation, the problem material, relate to her present situation, the present manifestation of her therapeutic problem? Let's analyse unnecessarily, for a moment.

**Enquirer** She didn't hear *no* as a child. Or, if she did, from her mother, she simply ignored it. Her father, whom she would have listened to, had he provided boundaries and discipline, seemed incapable of saying no and went into a sulk rather than telling her off. No wonder she had a problem with boundaries.

**Mentor** Yes. Her boyfriend is responding in a very similar way to her father. She didn't want to disappoint her father, as she doesn't want to disappoint her boyfriend: one sulked; the other whines.

**Enquirer** Whining or sulking are good strategies to manipulate Loretta, who doesn't want to disappoint.

**Mentor** Yes, they both worked well. She didn't have a clear no to respond to as a child, and is unable to give a clear no in the present. Wanting to please (her dad) was her motivation for self-discipline; it was an aspect of her adapted behaviour she developed in the absence of effective parental discipline. It might have been a successful strategy in her situation as a child, but needing to please to stay in favour is a very unhelpful way for a grown-up to interact.

**Enquirer** She wants to help and please people and has trouble saying no. That is why she has trouble managing and was feeling stressed and pressured. But why ten? What was particular about the age of ten?

**Mentor** She said that this was when her conflict with her mum was particularly bad.

**Enquirer** At ten years old she's learning that boundaries are not clearly delineated or straightforward; that she is under no obligation to do what she's told.

**Mentor** Yes. To reduce the emotional distress caused by the conflict with her mum, she courted the approval of her father. She did this by doing her best not to disappoint him. As long as she kept him onside she would be supported. Mum didn't understand her and wasn't sympathetic to her. Best to disinvest in mum's authority and keep dad onside. That was another aspect of Loretta's adaptive behaviour.

**Enquirer** Making strategic alliances is not healthy. But she also learned to be independent; to make up her own mind about things.

**Mentor** That's true. That was an empowering learning that resulted from her experience.

It seemed that she didn't trust the motives of her mum, but she knew her dad was looking out for her. He didn't give her clear directions about what was okay or not, but she knew when he was very disappointed because he would give her the silent treatment. So she invested in not disappointing her father. Her adaptive behaviour also involved ignoring the disciplinary attempts of her mother, which she saw as contrary to her interests. This behaviour was buttressed by her dad's refusal to support the disciplinary measures of mum.

**Enquirer** Ignore mum's direct attempts at discipline. Accept dad's indirect methods. That's a confusing learning.

**Mentor** Loretta was distressed by the conflict with her mother and wanted to please dad to compensate for her conflict with mum. She doesn't want to disappoint her partner James, just as she didn't want to disappoint dad. She hasn't learned how to communicate boundaries, because she didn't have effective boundaries as a child. Mum's no she felt to be in opposition to her interests; and dad wouldn't say no – so she never learned how to say no.

**Enquirer** Okay. We have a clear apprehension of the problem experience and how it creates the problem in the present. What does the relearning work involve for Loretta?

**Mentor** The aim of the relearning work, you'll remember, is to change the person's behaviour paradigm by adjusting the scenario in the past in a way that's credible to her. What did Loretta need in her family situation? What situation at home was required?

**Enquirer** Loretta needed a proper relationship with her mum. She needed her mum to respect her and she needed to respect her mum. She also needed her dad to manage her behaviour like a responsible parent.

**Mentor** That's right. Loretta needed a relationship with her mother based on mutual respect, so that her mother is able to enforce boundaries that are respected by her daughter – who would know that the boundaries are there for her benefit. She also needed her dad to impose boundaries in a much more appropriate way. Then both mum and dad could work together, as parents, supporting each other in establishing appropriate boundaries for their daughter.

This is what Loretta needed, and it's what we'll give her, retrospectively, in imagination. An experience of having appropriate parenting, where both parents give her appropriate boundaries, would give Loretta a good model of discipline and enable her to maintain her own boundaries. This would mean she would be able to say no and properly mean it, without the need to please.

**Enquirer** You're going to help Loretta's parenting. How did you do this?

**Mentor** I wanted to know what Loretta needed from her mum when she was ten. What would have allowed her to respond differently to mum? What would have allowed mum and Loretta to have a better relationship? What was required for mum to be able to be a mother to Loretta and for Loretta to allow this?

**Enquirer** This will help Loretta to get what she needed at the origins of her problem.

**Mentor** What is it that will help the person respond positively to her situation; or, alternatively, how can we amend the situation so that she can respond positively?

**Enquirer**  We can help the person to change her response; or we can change the problem situation itself.

**Mentor**  Yes. Loretta's mum was the one who provided the discipline – or tried to. If Loretta could respect her mum in this role, Loretta's lessons about discipline would be relearned.

I asked Loretta what she needs here at age ten; what would enable her to have a good relationship with mum? Loretta said she needs her mum to appreciate her particular needs and her difference, and be respectful of her.

**Enquirer**  You will help Loretta, in imagination, to have this different experience – where mum is respectful and appreciates her.

**Mentor**  That's right. Loretta had earlier told me that her mum had been a devoted grandmother and had asked for forgiveness from her daughter before she died. This suggested that her mum, at least in her later years, would be amenable to change and would respond positively to Loretta's requests. So I asked Loretta, in her imagination, to go back in time to when her mum had asked her for forgiveness, and at this point to ask mum to visit mum's younger self at the time when Loretta was ten years old with a particular request. Are you with me?

**Enquirer**  Yes, I think so. Loretta asks her mum to talk to mum's younger self. But if Loretta's mother hadn't been amenable to doing this you wouldn't have asked her to do it.

**Mentor**  I might well still have asked, to check if it were possible; but any suggestion might get a negative response. If it does, we try something else. Often we have to identify someone other than the parent to make such a visit to the younger parent. It needs to be someone the parent will respond positively to, such as a priest, or an admired political or historical figure; or it could be the client herself as an adult. But the parent's older self is the ideal person to do the visitation because a person is almost certainly going to respond positively to a request from her older self.

**Enquirer** You'd be a fool not to listen to the older you! Loretta asks older mum to visit younger mum. What's the particular request? What does older mum say to younger mum?

**Mentor** I suggested to Loretta that she asks older mum to ask younger mum to treat her daughter with greater respect, and to acknowledge Loretta's needs and difference.

**Enquirer** Older mum is asking younger mum to behave in a way that Loretta needed at the time. If her mum does this, Loretta will be able to respond in a more appropriate way and be amenable to discipline and boundaries. Does Loretta need to act all this out and speak out loud?

**Mentor** People are generally more comfortable doing it all in their heads, silently. In the first part of the resolution work she is just an observer. After that, she will step into the body of her younger self and experience it from the inside.

I emphasize to the person that she should remain in an observer position and watch it happening from the sidelines. She isn't going to take part at this stage, but just watch. So Loretta will watch from a third-person or observer perspective.

After discussing the details, I remind the person of the task. Loretta will approach her mother not long before her mother died and ask her to go back in time and visit her younger self, at the time when Loretta was ten. Loretta will ask her older mum to talk to younger mum, and ask her to be respectful of Loretta and to acknowledge her child's particular needs and difference.

If mum agrees, Loretta should adopt the perspective of an observer, and watch mum talk to her younger self. She should continue to observe as the mother of her ten-year-old self goes on to interact with the young Loretta in the new way that has been advocated. The person should take all the time she needs to do this (which may be a minute or two) and let the therapist know when she's finished.

**Enquirer** So Loretta watches her mother being respectful to the young Loretta and mindful of her needs and difference.

**Mentor** When Loretta indicated that she was finished, I asked her how ten-year-old Loretta responded and how she seems now. I want to check that it has worked: that her mother behaved as intended and that the younger Loretta has responded positively.

Note that I ask how the ten-year-old Loretta seems now; I don't ask how the young Loretta feels, because to know what she feels involves associating into the young Loretta, and I've asked her to remain in observer position for the moment.

**Enquirer** How does she know how the young Loretta 'seems'?

**Mentor** Just by observing. I'd rather not ask directly how ten-year-old Loretta *looks*, in case that isn't how Loretta is perceiving her younger herself in imagination. Most people do visualize, but not everyone; and I don't want to limit the response in any way.

**Enquirer** What was the response of the ten-year-old Loretta?

**Mentor** Loretta reported that her young self responded positively. She appeared happy. A positive response means we can continue the process.

She will imagine the scenario again, but this time from an associated position. I ask Loretta to step into the body of her ten-year-old self and experience what she has just observed but this time from the inside: from within her child body, looking out of her child eyes. From this perspective she will be able to feel what the child feels. This is no longer a witnessing, it's an encountering, a re-experiencing – a process essential to relearning.

The client does what is essentially the same thing twice: the first time as a dissociated observer; and the second time associated in the body of the younger person. The first time, when the client remains as a dissociated observer, is essentially a test. I'm checking that the outcome is as intended. I want to be sure that this re-learning work is credible, comfortable and is going to be effective. I also want the client to have all her adult resources available to formulate the scenario before she engages fully in the experience as the younger person.

At the end of the first phase of the process, when the person is in observer role, I ask the observer how the younger self responded. If she hasn't responded very positively, a problem is indicated and we'd have to find out what was going on and how to remedy it. It's also a check on the credibility of the relearning scenario. Can the person 'visualize' (that is, imagine) what has been asked? If she can't, it's an indication that the proposed relearning work was not credible to the client.

**Enquirer** If the relearning work isn't credible you won't get a positive response.

**Mentor** If it's not credible, she won't be able to do it. Occasionally, when the person is imagining the scenario, the dissociated version seems to work fine – or at least the client raises no objections – but when the person steps into her body to encounter it from the inside, she finds she can't do it.

**Enquirer** And this is again because it isn't credible to her.

**Mentor** That's right. It's not credible. We just have to work out a different way of doing what we want to achieve.

**Enquirer** Explain to me the second part of the resolution process, where Loretta steps into her child self and experiences it from an associated perspective.

**Mentor** While Loretta was observer, witnessing the past events, she was standing just outside of her life path. Now, if she reports that her younger self responded positively as she watched from observer position, I ask her to step back into her life path and into her ten-year-old body, and to see, hear and experience the relearning work as her child self.

She should now experience her mother behaving to her in this new and different way from inside her ten-year-old body. She lets me know when she's done that, and I ask her (using the present tense) to tell me what that was like for the ten year old: *How do you feel now as the ten-year-old girl?*

Running this again associated is vital for the effectiveness of the resolution work. As the observer, she only observes it; she doesn't experience it. She needs to be inside the experience for it to change how she feels and thinks. Now it's as if she's experiencing it voluntarily, through her own volition, which is totally different to conceiving it or imagining it as an observer.

**Enquirer** What did Loretta report after her new 'experience' as a ten year old?

**Mentor** She said that she felt she could now communicate with her mum. And that her relationship with her dad was stronger because she was no longer in conflict with her mum. She realized, she said, that she's a lot like her mum.

The resolution work wasn't finished yet, though. We also needed to work with dad. Dad in her imagination, that is. I asked Loretta to ask the more mature dad to go back in time and talk to his younger self – to the dad whose daughter, Loretta, was ten years old. He should ask his younger self not to 'punish' or 'discipline' his daughter by going silent and ignoring her but, instead, to talk to her, be cross if necessary, set boundaries explicitly, and so on. He should verbalize and make explicit his communications to her.

**Enquirer** That will give her a proper experience of discipline and boundaries.

**Mentor** That's right. From a dissociated position, she should watch her father interact in this new way with his ten-year-old daughter. Loretta reported that her child self responded well to this, and so I asked her to step into her ten-year-old body and repeat it from an associated perspective: to experience from the inside her dad asserting boundaries and imposing discipline in this new, direct way. As a result, Loretta reported, the ten year old felt much better. She was able to converse with her parents in a normal way. If the child Loretta wanted to say no about something, to a friend for example, she could talk to her parents and they could advise her. There were no more games involving dad supporting Loretta against her mother.

**Enquirer** That was what Loretta actually reported as her imaginary experience?

**Mentor** Yes. That's what she told me.

**Enquirer** That's surprising to me. It must seem very real to the person, for her to be able to respond in such a specific way. Can everyone do that – have such a meaningful encounter purely in imagination?

**Mentor** Yes. It may seem surprising. But everyone does seem to be able to do this – even the minority of people who can't seem to visualize very well (and prefer to use their auditory sense). Remember that the person has a problem in the present because a part of her is stuck at this time in the past. She may have not thought about the experience on a conscious level for years, but the experience is directing her behaviour in the present – so it's very close and very real.

**Enquirer** And now she has a different, or parallel, experience.

**Mentor** The old experience is still remembered. The new 'experience' obviously has no historical truth, except possibly as what should have been. But the old experience anyway has 'reality' only as memory and, more significantly, as cause of an emotional issue that has now been healed. The events themselves don't exist any more. They are real still only to the extent that they are carried in the mind and body of the person. The new 'experience', the relearning, provides an alternative reference. It's how it would have been if things had been closer to how they should have been.

The point of learning from experience is for the person to know how to maintain and re-establish personal dignity and guard against degradations. Loretta now has an 'experience' that provides a superior learning for her in this respect.

Loretta is newly able to respond to demands she doesn't like in a healthy way. She's learned how to say no. She has finally learned to accept discipline with grace and without manipulation. She no longer needs to operate by subterfuge, according to the old way. The old way was helpful to her all those years ago, because it was the only or best way she knew to handle the difficult circumstances at the time. The old behaviour helped to some extent to preserve her personal dignity; but its effectiveness was limited. In the new situation provided by the relearning work, Loretta's parents uphold her personal dignity through providing clear boundaries, and Loretta has no further need for the remedial strategies.

The two ways of responding, the original and relearned, aren't in competition. It's as if the new way is inserted into the life of the person where the original memory is, not as history but as reference.

**Enquirer** Why couldn't she have just been taught that? Why couldn't the therapist have said: *Loretta, you're having trouble with your boundaries. You need to learn how to say no and mean it. This is how to do it* . . . Why can't that work?

**Mentor** Teaching Loretta how to be assertive could only have very limited effectiveness, because the problematic learning in response to the original experience would still be in tact and operating exactly as it had before. Second-hand information, such as advice, works only on a conscious level, and doesn't provide the transformational learning that is gained from experience.

Loretta would still find herself manipulated by her boyfriend's whining behaviour, and have trouble asserting boundaries, despite her conscious efforts to behave differently. Her feelings, which direct her behaviour, won't have changed at all.

Not until we find the problem material do we truly know exactly what underlies the present manifestation of the problem, and therefore what intervention is required. The relearning is applied specifically to rectify the problem experience. The relearning isn't advice, it's an 'experience', albeit in imagination, inserted exactly at the site of the problem learning.

Effective intervention involves changing the unconscious response. No amount of conscious effort and intent can achieve a change in unconscious response. Relearning Experience achieves transformation on an unconscious level because it is able to identify and then modify the experience that created the problem behaviour in the first place. Without identifying when and why the problem behaviour was created, and providing an effective alternative response to those difficult circumstances, the conscious mind engages in a laborious and unwinnable struggle to overcome behaviour that the body learned in difficult times and invested in so decisively.

The relearning intervention of Relearning Experience does not try to impose, or superimpose, a belief on the person, as the anti-drugs advertisement tried to do. It doesn't proffer an alternative experience that would result in two competing experiences. This new 'experience' supplants the old experience – not as truth, but as an attractive, credible, hugely preferable and desirable alternative account, which was created and experienced (in imagination) entirely voluntarily by the person herself – making the old learning null and void.

**Enquirer**  Did it work? Did Loretta develop the ability to say no convincingly?

**Mentor**  Yes. When we returned to the present – by walking along the life path to the present – Loretta was unable to get back the bad feelings that she'd had earlier when she thought about saying no to James. Without the bad feelings, there's nothing stopping her from saying no and feeling fine about it.

**Enquirer** Was she literally not able to get the bad feelings back?

**Mentor** Yes. She could remember the bad feelings, obviously; she knew that she used to have them. But she wasn't able to feel them again.

It's a good test, because feelings are involuntary. Before, when she thought of saying no to James, she felt bad. She couldn't help the feeling; it was just there. Now, when she imagined saying no, she couldn't get the bad feelings back – even when she tried. She said she was sure that she would be able to say no in other circumstances more easily too.

A week later we had a follow-up appointment. There was no further therapeutic work to do. The work was complete. I asked Loretta what her experience now was about saying no and asserting her boundaries. She said, 'Very good. I've been able to put my foot down.' She described examples from her personal life – with her children, her boyfriend, the manager at a car-repair garage, and a charity organization. All had made demands of her and in each case she had comfortably asserted her wishes or said no. She had also – serendipitously – been offered a gift, and had been able to accept it, which was something she had found very difficult to do previously.

**Enquirer** Lucky to have had all those tests.

**Mentor** Loretta said that she was managing well and was seeing things in perspective, despite exacting demands, and that she was taking control of her life rather than letting others have control.

Remember that you don't need to analyse the process in the way that we have done here. You should just find out what the person needs and help her to get it. You can analyse it later – if you must.

**Enquirer** It certainly makes a lot of sense to me now. I feel I have an understanding – for the first time – of how therapeutic problems are created and why they manifest at a later time.

**Mentor** And do you understand how the problem material is identified; and how the problem is resolved at the source?

**Enquirer** Yes, I think I follow it all. But I need a bit more of an explanation about the resolution work. I'm not clear how you would approach resolving the problem material after it's been identified. I know you want to give the person an alternative experience, and this experience needs to be credible to the person. But I'm not sure how you determine what that alternative experience should be. Another example would be helpful.

## Key points

Problematic childhood scenarios are repeated in adulthood, providing opportunities for healing.

Applying REP effectively does not require interpretation and analysis.

Relearning involves giving the person what she needed at the time, enabling her to handle the problem experience in such a way that her behaviour and view of the world do not become distorted.

The relearning scene is neutrally observed and then 'experienced', or 'encountered', in imagination. The encounter effects the healing.

# 39
## Tana

**Mentor** Tana was separating from her husband and under a lot of stress. She felt responsible for the welfare of her husband. She expressed dissatisfaction about herself. She said she hates her beliefs, and stifles her beliefs because of a strong need for approval; and she accommodates the will of others at the expense of herself. She said she didn't believe she was really lovable and hated much of herself. She'd had quite a lot of therapy previously.

**Enquirer** Quite a few problems. Where do you start?

**Mentor** All the problems the person puts on the table are likely to be related to each other, even if this isn't readily apparent. Usually, you don't need to choose where to start, you'll gravitate to it as you talk. It's better if the starting point emerges rather than is chosen. Or you can ask directly one of the following.

> *Of all these different issues, which seems most significant right now?*
>
> *Which one would make the most difference to your life?*
>
> *Where would you like to start?*

The person's response would provide a focus for exploration.

Tana volunteered that she felt the need to be 'good', and somehow her self-esteem was dependent on her being good. But being good meant being approved of by others, and being compliant.

**Enquirer** Impossible project, then.

**Mentor** She went on to tell me about her difficult younger brother, whom she had always felt it was her responsibility to protect. She still felt she needed to protect him. The significance of this in her life I assumed related to her need to be good and approved of.

The feelings, through tracking back, took her back to three or four years old – which was when she first began to try to take on this responsibility for her younger brother. Little Tana needed to be assured that she was not responsible for her brother. Who is the best person to tell her?

**Enquirer** Her mother – ideally.

**Mentor** I suggested she ask her mother in the present (in imagination) to go back in time to explain this to little Tana. But Tana said she couldn't imagine this.

**Enquirer** It wasn't credible to her. Her mum still believed that Tana was responsible for her younger brother.

**Mentor** Yes, exactly. Tana explained that her mother was still, in the present, behaving in the same way: taking responsibility for her long grown up but still difficult son. In fact, she saw her mother's attitude as contributing to the perpetuation of her brother's issues. Mum still had the same problem – so Tana couldn't possibly imagine mum telling the young Tana that she wasn't responsible for her brother's welfare.

**Enquirer** Who did Tana employ for that role?

**Mentor** Herself. She went back in time and talked to her three- or four-year-old self and explained that she wasn't responsible for looking after her brother. But this advice was not sufficient to make Tana relinquish responsibility for her brother.

Tana realized that she had taken on this responsibility to make mum happy. Relinquishing this responsibility would make mum unhappy, and so couldn't be done immediately. The need to make mum happy needed to be addressed first.

Why did Tana feel she needed to make mum happy? It was of course to earn her love.

**Enquirer** If she felt she needed to earn mum's love, she didn't feel entitled to it or deserving of it.

**Mentor** That's right. She wasn't getting it; or felt that she wasn't. Why not, do you think?

**Enquirer** Difficult brother was getting all the attention.

**Mentor** Yes. Since children feel that their suffering must be their own fault, if she wasn't getting the love she needed, it was because she wasn't lovable. She therefore needed to earn her mother's love by doing what she knew mum would approve of: looking after her brother.

**Enquirer** Pleasing mum by taking responsibility for her brother (an impossible task for a child) will not bring her the attention she craves, because her brother will still demand all the attention. The belief that she must earn love will persist, despite all her efforts. This belief explains why she feels she has to be good, and compliant, in the present. To please others, she probably feels she has to compromise her own beliefs in order to gain approval; and this is why she says she 'hates' her beliefs: they're not even hers. It's also clear why she felt responsible for her husband's welfare – it's equivalent to being responsible for her brother's welfare. This responsibility means she is a good person, or a good wife. But she hates it. She's in an untenable position.

**Mentor** Yes, that's right. It is only by assuming this unwanted and inappropriate responsibility that she can deserve love. We now have a good explanation for her presenting problems. They come from this desire to please her mother so she can earn love.

She wasn't aware of these connections, but only of the idea that she had a responsibility for her brother.

The relearning work would involve helping the young Tana (1) to know that she is not responsible for her mum's happiness or for her brother's welfare; and (2) to experience love and attention from her parent or substitute.

Tana, as her present adult self, explained to little Tana that she is not responsible for mum's happiness. (She'd already explained to little Tana that she isn't responsible for her brother's welfare, you remember.) Tana also wanted her teacher to explain all this to the little Tana, and for her teacher to explain this to her mother. It seemed credible to Tana that mum would respond positively to the authority of the teacher. Tana also asked her dad to spend more time with little Tana, and to give her his love and attention. Dad was happy to do this. First she observed all this; then she experienced it as the young Tana.

After this, the uncomfortable feelings were no longer there in the past. Tana walked back along her life path to the present, where she was unable to get back any of the uncomfortable feelings.

**Enquirer** What was the result?

**Mentor** She said that she no longer felt responsible for her husband's welfare, and later confirmed that it was much easier to behave in accordance with her true beliefs, without fear of disapproval.

**Enquirer** And you achieved all that in just one consultation?

**Mentor** That's right. The unhealthy need to serve others was the present manifestation of Tana's assumption of responsibility for her brother. This unhelpful feeling of responsibility was itself underpinned by Tana's desire to earn her mother's love, which she tried to achieve through being a good girl and doing (what she hoped others thought was) the right thing, even where this conflicted with her own beliefs.

**Enquirer** Because she wasn't getting the love she needed, Tana thought she needed to earn her mum's love. The 'solution', or remedial behaviour, was to make mum happy by taking on responsibility for her younger brother. Mum will then think she is a good girl and give her love. In this way, Tana learned she should try to be good and seek the approval of others.

**Mentor** Once this had been relearned and Tana's child self no longer needed to be responsible for her brother, her therapeutic problem was resolved: she no longer needed to look after others or please them, and she was able to behave in ways consistent with her own principles. Tana didn't separate from her husband in the end and the couple are still together.

**Enquirer** A final example.

## Key points

All the problems a person reports are likely to be aspects of the same problem experience.

Children believe that their suffering must be their own fault because they are bad.

A child therefore feels that he is not deserving of and needs to earn love, respect or attention, for example, by being good (that is, by behaving in a certain way and, possibly, banishing wicked thoughts).

# 40
## Brooke

**Mentor** Brooke, a woman in her early thirties, was reluctantly coming to a realization that her relationship with a man, whom she really cared for, wasn't right for her. Brooke arranged a telephone consultation. She wasn't clear about what she wanted help with, but she knew that trying to let go of her boyfriend was bringing up some difficult issues.

Presenting her problem, Brooke said that: (1) she doesn't trust her own decisions and seeks affirmation from others; (2) she doesn't have confidence in what she thinks and needs reassurance; and (3) when things go wrong with her boyfriend she looks for comfort from her friends, but feels uncomfortable about doing this.

She recognized that she should confront her boyfriend with her concerns about aspects of his behaviour which upset her, but she felt unable to do this because, she said, she was worried that he would think she was being clingy, or overreacting; and, instead, went to her friends for advice and solace.

Different friends, she said, would give different advice. But she didn't know which advice to take, and didn't want people to think badly of her. At the same time, she didn't want to burden her

friends with more stories of her troubled relationships. She became (in her words) locked in mental arguments. She couldn't
make sense of her behaviour. 'Instead of doing what's right for
me, because I need reassurance, I seek advice and get into conflict
with myself.'

Brooke identified herself as clingy and overly concerned about
what others think; she seeks affirmation from others; and she
doesn't trust her own judgement. These were the issues coming
up in relation to separating from her boyfriend.

**Enquirer** Where did you start?

**Mentor** I wasn't clear what the main issue was and tried different tacks. Was it that she was needy? Did she have a fear of being
thought a nagging girl? Did she fear the negative judgements of
others? These were her attempts on a conscious level to articulate
the problem. Each had some validity – they were symptoms of the
problem – but none seemed to be the nub of it.

The thought occurred to me that she wasn't behaving according
to her values and principles. I asked her to say: *How I behave is okay
as long as it's according to my values and principles.* This gave her a
feeling in her chest, indicating that there was a significant issue in
relation to behaving according to her values and principles.

Her therapeutic goal was: *I choose to behave according to my values
and principles.* The feeling took her back to age 18, her first year at
university. This is what Brooke related.

She was with a number of friends in the student bar. An acquaintance entered the bar and greeted several of her friends. Then he
greeted Brooke, using a nickname which related, unflatteringly,
to her physical characteristics of being tall and slim – a nickname
to which she took great offence. She felt flustered and angry. She
couldn't remember if she said anything but she fled from the bar
and ran to her room. Her female friends followed her and gave
her support and sympathy. Even her male friends, she said, had
been understanding and sympathetic.

She explained that in those days she had felt sensitive about her appearance and hadn't considered herself attractive. She wasn't an outgoing person and could easily feel intimidated and humiliated.

**Enquirer** She encountered bad behaviour from a man who embarrassed and humiliated her. She responded by running away, and received solace from her friends. In future, this would be her paradigm at any time that someone (a man, specifically) overstepped her boundaries.

**Mentor** That's right. The sympathetic response she received had been very pleasing. It had worked well as a response to the perceived threat at the time. Advice was given, soothing words, affection, support. So in the present, when her boyfriend behaved in a way that overstepped her boundaries, or did something she didn't like, rather than confront him, she ran away and sought comfort from friends.

**Enquirer** Asking her friends for advice was an admission that she couldn't decide what to do for herself; she couldn't trust her own judgement, especially with regard to relationships with men. She gets different advice from different people. Because she can't trust her own judgement, she can't decide what action to take and keeps changing her mind. She knows that this isn't the right way to behave and feels uncomfortable doing it. She's worried about looking like a needy girl. Her actions are certainly not leading to an improved relationship with her boyfriend.

**Mentor** On a rational level she knows that she should confront her boyfriend when he overstepped her boundaries, but her feelings overwhelm her and lead her to behave in the way she learned at age 18.

**Enquirer** What made that particular therapeutic goal statement effective when it had been difficult to fix on a therapeutic goal?

**Mentor** Brooke was contravening her values and principles in several different ways.

First, though she was upset by her boyfriend's behaviour she did not challenge it. His behaviour contradicted what she wanted and expected from a partnership. By not challenging his behaviour (and by thereby permitting it) she was compromising values and principles that were very important to her. Second, her need to seek reassurance and advice from friends violated her principle of not wanting to burden her friends with her emotional baggage. Third, she tried to follow the contradictory advice of friends and couldn't rely on her own judgement. As long as she was not using her own judgement she was subject to the values and principles of others and couldn't behave according to her own.

**Enquirer** Her experience at the age of 18 taught her not to confront but rather to escape and seek the advice and reassurance of others – her friends. That's what she's doing in the present time. But she doesn't like it. If she acted according to her own values and principles she wouldn't have a problem.

**Mentor** Her practical goal, even if she couldn't articulate it at the time, was principally to have a healthy relationship based on clear communication. She couldn't achieve this as long as she wasn't being true to her principles.

**Enquirer** You've established the problem material. How do you go about resolving the problem?

**Mentor** I asked her what alternatives she had. Instead of running away and getting the reassurance of friends, what could she have done that would have been empowering?

She said that she could have told the person that she found his words insulting. I asked what stopped her from saying something like this at the time. She told me she had been worried that others – especially the males – would think she was overreacting.

I asked Brooke whether confronting the man could be considered more of an overreaction than running away. She replied that running away was more an overreaction.

We explored three responses available to her: (1) run away (the action she had taken); (2) keep quiet and pretend nothing had happened; or (3) explain that this way of speaking to her was unacceptable to her. We know the result of the first response: she received reassurance and sympathy, but was adopting a victim position that assumed powerlessness and led directly to her relationship problems in the present. The second response, she appreciated, could lead people to think it was all right to treat her in such a way, and that she would put up with such treatment passively. This response would make it more likely to happen in the future, and give the signal that she was an easy target. The third response would indicate clearly her willingness to take a stand against being spoken to in a disrespectful way. But there was also the possibility that she might be thought to be overreacting. Brooke knew immediately that she preferred to stand up for herself.

In imagination, Brooke (the adult in the present) went back in time to talk to her 18-year-old self shortly before the incident took place. She explained what was going to happen and suggested to her that, rather than run away, she should confront the man who insulted her and tell him that his behaviour was not acceptable to her. She reassured her younger self that the adult Brooke would support her in doing this.

She watched her 18-year-old self confronting the man. And then stepped back into her life path and into the body of her younger self and confronted him in an associated state. The effect of this behaviour was positive, Brooke confirmed, and she returned to the present.

I asked Brooke to imagine confronting her boyfriend when he overstepped her boundaries. That now felt comfortable to her.

She no longer had to run away and seek comfort and advice from others in response to a provocation. As a result, she would no longer be at the mercy of someone else's behaviour. She could determine her own response and choose action that was in line with her own values and principles, whether or not others approved.

**Enquirer** Thank you very much for your explanation. Can we conclude our discussion there? I feel I now have a good understanding of your work.

**Mentor** Thank you very much for giving me the opportunity to explain and explore this method. I really appreciate your attention and your interest.

**Enquirer** I'm ready to work with you on my issue . . .

**Mentor** That's wonderful. Let's do that.

**Enquirer** But I need to confess something. I'm actually a psychotherapist – who's dabbled in a number of different modalities. But I became disillusioned when I couldn't get effective help with my own issues, and haven't been in practice for a few years.

**Mentor** That explains a lot! Tell me, have you got a satisfactory answer to your quest?

# Glossary

*Adaptive behaviour* see *remedial behaviour*.

*Amelioration* (or *attenuation*) of emotional discomfort or distress (due to a degradation of personal dignity) relates to the motivation for the development of remedial behaviour: the purpose of the remedial behaviour is to reduce the dignity degradation.

*Antecedent age* is an age in the past accommodating the problem material or problem experience, which can be discovered through the process tracking (or tracking back).

*Antecedent event* is an experience in the past that contributed to the therapeutic problem.

*Attenuation* see *amelioration*.

*Dignity degradation*, or personal dignity degradation, refers to perceived attacks on personal dignity. When a person's dignity is attacked or frustrated, the person changes her behaviour to reduce the emotional impact of the attack and restore her personal dignity. To reduce the discomfort, personal dignity needs to be restored, as far as possible, and this requires a change in behaviour. The behaviour modification is termed remedial (or adaptive) behaviour.

*Emotional needs* are individual to a person, though many are shared in common, and may include, for example, love, comfort, safety, recognition, respect, admiration. When emotional needs are denied or frustrated, personal dignity is degraded.

*Manifest* (or *problem*) *behaviour* is undesired behaviour manifesting in the present.

*Manifest problem* is how the person experiences the therapeutic problem in the present. It will be what has prompted the person to seek therapy. The problem has its origins in the past and will have further manifestations in the future (unless and until it is resolved at origin through the relearning work).

*Personal dignity degradation* see dignity degradation.

*Practical goal* is an appealing and appropriate formulation of what the client wants to achieve in the world but is unable to achieve because of something in herself.

*Present manifestation* see manifest problem.

*Presenting problem* is the client's initial description of the therapeutic problem. Interrogation of the presenting problem leads to delineation of the practical goal.

*Problem* (or *manifest*) *behaviour* is how the remedial behaviour manifests as a therapeutic problem in the present.

*Problem complex* see therapy complex.

*Problem experience* see problem material.

*Problem feelings* are the uncomfortable feelings that drive a person to behave in ways contrary to what she wants or stop her from behaving in ways consistent with what she wants.

*Problem material* (or *experience*) refers to the description of past experiences identified by the person at the origins of the problem which directly led to the remedial behaviour.

*Relearning* (or *resolution*) *work* is REP's transformative intervention. It involves rewriting the problem material to give rise to a new learning, in place of the original learning. The intervention reconfigures the difficult experience. The effect is to bring to realization the therapeutic goal. As a result of the relearning work, the problem feeling is eliminated, the manifest behaviour loses its motivation, and the therapeutic problem is resolved. The problem complex dissolves permanently.

*Remedial* (or *adaptive*) *behaviour* is the behaviour that the person develops in response to a personal dignity degradation to attenuate the emotional distress of that degradation. This behaviour is therefore of a pathological nature and is experienced in the present as manifest (or problem) behaviour.

*REP* is Relearning Experience Process (or Psychotherapy).

*Resolution work* see *relearning work*.

*Therapeutic goal* is the quality or capacity that, when realized, will make it possible for the person to achieve her practical goal (or, at least, remove an obstacle to its achievement which is internal to the person). The therapeutic goal is not anything exterior to the person; it is latent within the person and is potentially realizable right now, in the present moment. Achievement of the therapeutic goal is the task and outcome of the REP consultation and is the result of the resolution work.

*Therapy* (or *problem*) *complex* encompasses all aspects of the psychological (or psychotherapeutic) problem: practical goal, therapeutic goal, manifest problem, remedial (or adaptive) behaviour, problem behaviour, problem feelings, and problem material.

*Tracking* or *tracking back* is the process that transports the person in imagination from the present to the origins of the therapeutic problem in the person's past.

# Index

# RELEARNING EXPERIENCE PROCESS
## Therapy and Training

*Experience REP therapy*

to overcome problems and achieve goals

jonathan@therapycoaching.co

www.therapycoaching.co

*Train as an REP practitioner*

jonathan@relearning.co.uk

www.relearning.co.uk